AN OCCULT GUIDE TO SOUTH AMERICA

Strange Tales of Witchcraft, Spiritualism, Lost Races and Religious Miracles

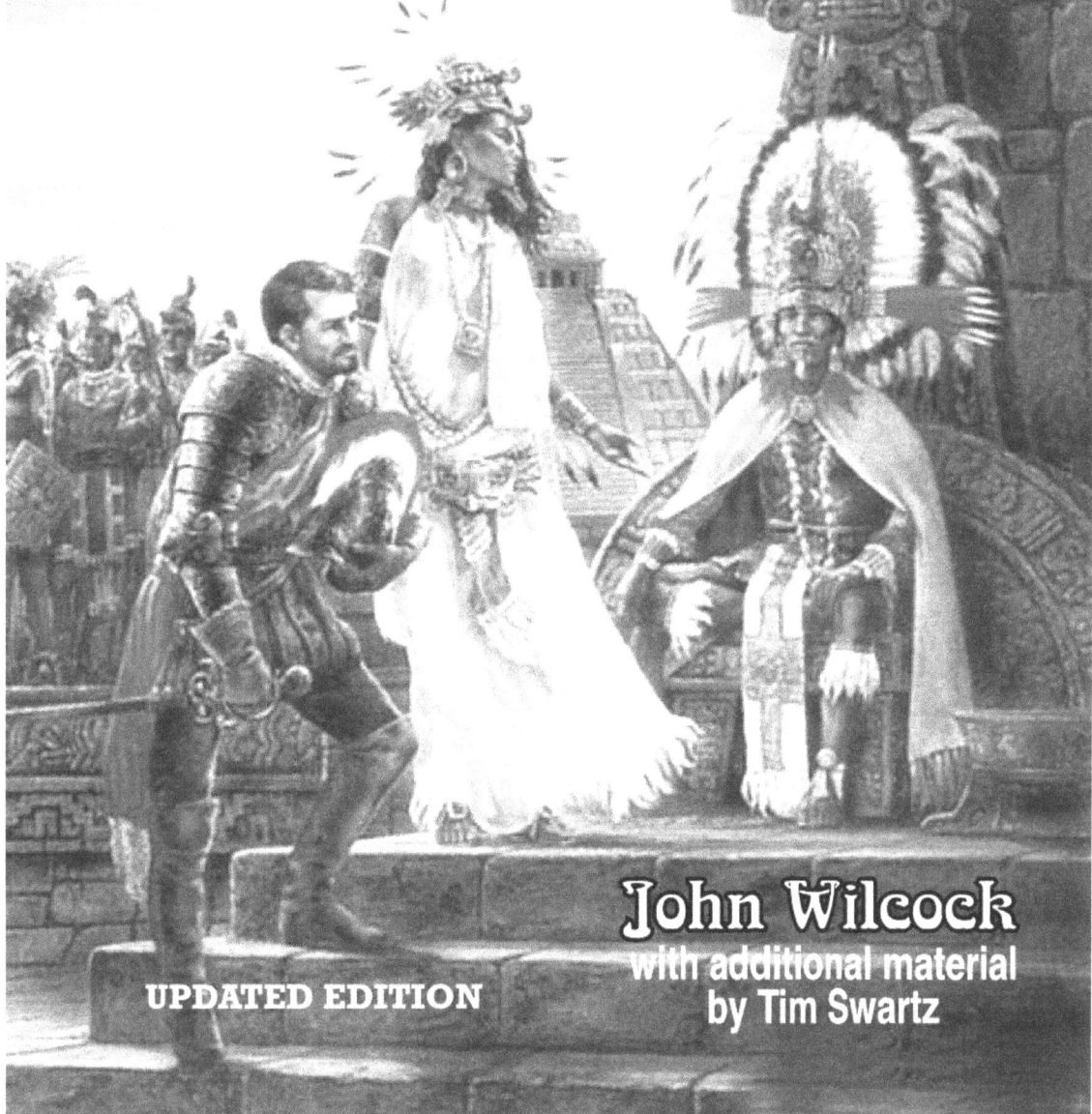

John Wilcock

with additional material
by Tim Swartz

UPDATED EDITION

An Occult Guide To South America

Strange Tales of Witchcraft, Spiritualism, Lost Races and Religious Miracles

Nonfiction · Updated Edition

Timothy Green Beckley: Editorial Director

Carol Rodriguez: Publishers Assistant

Sean Casteel: Associate Editor

Cover Art: William Kern

For free catalog write: Global Communications

P.O. Box 753

New Brunswick, NJ 08903

Free Subscription to Conspiracy Journal E-Mail Newsletter

An Occult Guide To South America

Strange Tales of Witchcraft, Spiritualism, Lost Races and Religious Miracles

Contents

Foreword

ON THE EDGE OF REALITY
by
Tim R. Swartz

John Wilcock, the author of Occult South America, was once described by Bob Colacello as an "aging hippie publisher." However, taking even a brief look at Wilcock's accomplishments over the years demonstrates that this is a man who has never feared to skirt the conventional in favor of the unorthodox.

In a 2006 interview for the Ventura County Reporter, Wilcock looked at himself as "probably the oldest person in the underground press." This referring to his extensive involvement with the early alternative press when he was in his mid-thirties; quite a feat considering the *"don't trust anybody over thirty"* maxim that was so popular at that time.

As well as being the co-founder of the Village Voice and Andy Warhol's Interview, Wilcock has been very successful as a travel writer. He has also authored a number of books including 1974's **Magical & Mystical Sites**, and 1977's **A Guide to Occult Britain**.

In North America, mystical and occult beliefs can be chiefly traced back to Old World influences. South of the border, however, the occult traditions of South America are an interesting mix that ranges from Old World Catholicism, Pre-Columbian Indian beliefs and more modern influences such as Spiritism.

When we look beyond the influence of recent invaders to South America, the religious, magical and philosophical beliefs of the aboriginal Native American cultures that evolved in South America are both unique and strangely similar to magical practices from Europe, Africa and Asia. Even though these Old World mystical traditions supposedly arose under isolation from the other side of the world, it is obvious that when it comes to human spirituality in any form, they all seem to radiate out from one universal source.

Foreword

South American folklore has its share of unique and fantastic myths and legends. There are incredible tales of magicians and their weird magical arts, strange creatures, ghosts, and other unexplained mysteries. The first explorers that entered Latin America were dazzled by the endless tropical rainforests, the strange and diverse wildlife, and the indigenous peoples and their mysterious ways. Even today, South America offers unique perspectives and influences on the paranormal that can not found anywhere else on the planet.

I have had the pleasure to travel quite extensively and have been to many of the most sacred sites on the planet, including those in Mexico, Central and South America. Considering the unusual things that have been told to me, as well as certain unexplained phenomena that I have personally experienced, I am convinced that South America is a land where the shadows from the darkest corners of our minds have the opportunity to occasionally make themselves real. And for those skeptics who insist that such things simply cannot be, I challenge them to get out of their comfy chairs and do as John Wilcock and I have done, travel to these mystical places and experience for yourselves the magic and mystery of Latin America.

The Dead Are Alive

The people of South America live in a world steeped in ancient traditions that enhance their lives with a rich tapestry of mystical beliefs. In modern Latin America, Catholicism is the predominate religion. However, especially in Brazil, Espiritismo (Spiritism), has become extremely prevalent since its beginnings in the mid 19th century. Spiritism, like Spiritualism, believes in the survival of the human personality after death and that mediums are able to communicate with the spirits. Followers of Spiritism believe in an afterlife. But, unlike Spiritualism, Spiritists believe that the soul will reincarnate after a period of time.

Spiritism originated in France with the publication in 1857 of *Le Livre des Esprits* or The Spirits Book. The book was written by a French educator named Hippolyte Léon Dénizard Rivail under the pen name Allan Kardec.

Rivail was a resident of Paris and a pro-

Foreword

fessor of mathematics, science, and grammar. In 1854 he was introduced to the "table turning" phenomena of the spiritualist seances then popular in Europe. His inquisitive mind was intrigued by a message given to him through two young girls who were mediums, and signed, *"Spirit of Truth."* In essence, the message informed him that spirits of a very high rank would continue to communicate with him through the two mediums, since he had been selected for a mission of the highest order.

A methodical man by nature, Rivail—who was not himself a medium—proceeded to "try the spirits." The spirit communications had been made at first through a code of taps of the séance table. A scientistic pedant, Rivail assumed that such patterned "effects" must have an intelligent "cause," the most plausible one being that which was claimed in the messages, the activity of spirits. He hit upon a system of "planchette-writing," whereby the spirits guided a pencil attached to a small basket, upon which the mediums' fingers were lightly laid. Rivail then began an extensive interrogation, in which the revelatory spirits guided, answered, and commented on a systematized series of questions concerning life and the universe.

On April 30 of 1856, the *"Spirit of Truth"* announced to Rivail that his mission on earth was to publish and promulgate, under the pen name "Allan Kardec," the teachings which he had received from the spirits. One year later he brought out *"Le Livre des Espirits,"* first in an abbreviated form, and, in a few months, in a second and fuller edition which has remained definitive for his followers to this day.

The book is said to be a collection of answers from highly intelligent spirit beings based on several questions painstakingly prepared by Kardec, and deals about spirits, the spiritual world, existence of God, relation between the spirit and material world, man's destiny, morality and spiritual laws.

Spiritism In Brazil

The publication of the Spirits Book became an instant success in Europe and attracted many followers. Two years after its publication, Kardec formed the Parisian Society for Spiritist Studies which became a center for the study and practice of the Spiritist doctrine.

Spiritism is not considered a religion, but a philosophy or a way of life by which its followers live by. Its followers have no priests or ministers and do not follow any religious rituals in their meetings.

Foreword

They also do not call their places of meetings as churches, and instead call them by various names such as centers, society or association. Their activities consist mainly of studying the Spiritist doctrine, applying spiritual healing to the sick and organizing charitable missions.

The teachings of Kardec were brought to Brazil sometime around 1860. However, newspaper archives show that as early as 1853, séances and the table-turning phenomenon, had reached the city of Rio de Janeiro. As well, Mesmer's "animal magnetism," together with homeopathic medicine, was already in use by a few Brazilian physicians during the 1840's.

The spirit of Sister Josefa materialized in 1965 in the city of Andradas, through medium Otilia Diogo.

The beginning of Spiritism in Brazil, however, is officially identified with a séance held in Salvador, Bahia on September 17, 1865, under the direction of Doctor Luis Olympio Telles de Menezes.

Brazil has always been a vast melting-pot of various Spiritist and psychic traditions, from the shamanistic magic of the original Tupi Indians, to the mixture of the beliefs of many different African tribes brought to Brazil as slaves by Portuguese settlers. Through the twentieth century, there have been two main strands of occult religion in Brazil: the magical Afro-Brazilian groups, Umbanda and Macumba, both analogous to Haitian voudou, and Kardec-style Spiritism. Both have possession by spirits as central to their practice.

Brazil is officially a Roman Catholic country. Still it is estimated that there are nearly four million people following these various alternative religions, many continuing to regard themselves as nominal Catholics. The complex interchange of religious and cultural traditions over the centuries makes precise distinctions difficult, since many nominally non-Christian blacks incorporate the figure of Jesus into tribal magic, while many Christians have fused tribal magic with Catholicism.

Foreword

The idea of the "fluidic" action of spiritual forces is important for the directions taken by Spiritism in Brazil, in view of the emphasis on magical and spiritual healing in that country. Allan Kardec adopted Mesmer's concept of "animal magnetism" as the operative force in spiritistic phenomena. It is through the mutual action of their perispiritic fluids that the medium and the incorporating spirits are thought to communicate and to channel efficacious forces to those in need.

One of the few references to healing made by Kardec in his major works concerns the basis for it in the action of a spirit upon the magnetic fluids. He gives further attention to the subject, in *A Ginese*, a large part of which is devoted to the "demythologizing" of the miracles of the Bible.

F. C. Xavier, through his influential books, has popularized the application of a scientific argot to the mediumistic processes, especially those of healing. In one of these books, the author purports to accompany Superior Spirits as they heal the sick through the instrumentality of devoted mediums. There is due association of the work with the names of William Crookes, the Curies, Roentgen, Einstein, et al., and the Spirits observe the inner states and actions of the mediums with the use of a sort of spiritual X-ray machine called a "psychoscope."

The authors speak of men as being "generators of electromagnetic force," who also emit ultraviolet radiations. The selfless devotion of the mediums, say the Spirits, puts them in "appreciable vibratory conditions—able, therefore, to project mental rays, assimilating superior currents, and enriching the vital rays of which they are dynamos in common." Despite the general admission among Kardecists that certain cases demand "doctor's medicines" and surgery, the ultimate causes of all illnesses are considered to be spiritual.

One of the most striking developments of the last few decades has been the emergence of a form of psychic surgery in which it is claimed that psychic healers without medical training perform surgical operations, sometimes with their bare hands, or with such primitive instruments as old penknives. The wounds, it is claimed, are paranormally closed and healed.

Two of the most famous Brazilian psychic surgeons are Edivaldo Oliveira Silva and Jose Arigo, who performed thousands of operations. Although psychic surgery remains a controversial subject and there have been accusations of fraud, there is also strong evidence of genuine operations, endorsed

Foreword

by competent American and European investigators.

Psychic healing has flourished in Brazil, in spite of the fact that both the Roman Catholic Church and the medical society have brought lawsuits for witchcraft or for illegal practice of medicine. Many high officials believe in the efficacy of such healing, a fact illustrated by former Brazilian president Juscelino Kubitschek's bringing his daughter to Arigo for psychic healing. Arigo has also successfully treated statesmen, lawyers, scientists, and doctors from many countries.

In the early 20th century, one of the more controversial aspects of Spiritism was spirit materializations. But unlike the Spiritualist mediums of North America and Europe, physical appearances in Brazilian séance rooms did not often occur.

Carmine Mirabelli

Historically, for Brazilian Spiritism, Carmine Mirabelli was one of the first spirit mediums to demonstrate actual physical materializations of spirits in controlled settings. Born in Botucatu, Sao Paulo, Brazil on January 2, 1889, Mirabelli lived a fairly normal life until the death of his father in 1914. Mirabelli's grief for his deceased father left him both physically and financially impoverished. It was during this time that his extraordinary paranormal activity developed.

In the shoe shop where Mirabelli worked, the shoe boxes suddenly took to leaving their shelves and flying around the shop, sometimes even accompanying him out into the street. He also started seeing the spirits of his dead family which included his parents, an uncle, his mother-in-law and his daughter.

Unfortunately, his fellow co-workers and neighbors became convinced that demons were responsible for the ghostly activity that occurred around Mirabelli. Consequently, he was forcibly taken out into the street and stoned.

Mirabelli was sent to an asylum, but local newspapers had gotten a hold of his story and pressed for a formal investigation of his strange abilities. His doctors soon determined that there was an excessive nervous activity in Mirabelli that prompted his ghostly experiences, and while this in itself was abnormal, he was not found to be insane and was duly released.

In 1919 the *Academia de Estudos Psychicos* "Cesar Lombroso" was founded. Mirabelli submitted himself for experiments in trance speaking,

Foreword

automatic writing and physical phenomena. During the experiments all the doors and windows were locked and the investigators were divided into three groups. One group that dealt with spoken mediumship had 189 sittings. A second group investigated automatic writing. The third group investigated psychic phenomenon. All sessions were held in daylight or in bright artificial light, (none in darkness) in rooms that were searched before and after each sitting. A report published in 1926 states: "The committee carried out with the first group (medical speaking) 189 positive experiments; with the second group (automatic writing) 85 positive and 8 negative; with the third group (physical phenomena) 63 positive and 47 negative experiments. The medium spoke 26 languages including 7 dialects, wrote in 28 languages, among them 3 dead languages, namely Latin, Chaldaic and Hieroglyphics. Of the 63 physical experiments 40 were made in daylight, 23 in bright artificial light."

During one séance, the complete form of a little girl materialized by the side of the medium. This incredible demonstration took place in full daylight in the laboratory of the investigating committee. As well, it occurred in full view of many people, (including 10 men who held degrees in doctorates of science). The Mirabelli experiments produced some of the most well documented full-bodied materializations of spirits that were witnessed and photographed under the most stringent, scientifically controlled circumstances.

Dr. Ganymede de Sauza was present and confirmed that the child was his daughter who had died a few months earlier, and that she was wearing the dress in which she was buried.

Another observer, Colonel Octavia Viana, took the spirit child in his arms, took her pulse and asked her several questions, all of which she answered with understanding of what was asked. Photographs of the apparition with her father and other guests were also taken and attached to the investigating committee's report.

After this, the child floated around the room and disappeared after having been visible in daylight for 36 minutes. At another séance under controlled conditions, Mirabelli himself dematerialized to be found later in another room. Yet the seals on the doors and windows of the séance room were intact, as were the seals and bonds that held Mirabelli to his chair.

Despite his obvious abilities, Mirabelli was shunned by the Brazilian Spiritism community, and because of pressure from the Catholic Church, he had to appear in court on fifteen occasions to answer charges that were raised against the work that he was doing. Notwithstanding these problems, he successfully demonstrated that his abilities were real and convinced many who witnessed his extraordinary feats on the reality of communication with spirits.

In view of the number of witnesses involved, the phenomena observed, and the mode in which these occurred, there can be little doubt that Carlos Mirabelli was a spirit medium of considerable ability.

The Two Ways

The people of Brazil are always conducive to different aspects of the process of mixing of ethnicities and customs. Spiritism is divided in two conceptions of the astral worlds: the popular and scholarly. These two ways can be distinguished considering their culture, their aesthetic, folklore, and even their ethical aspects. There's the Orthodox Spiritism, a classical conception, with the base, essentially, in the teachings of Allan Kardec. The other is a syncretic conception. It is a point of view that mixes elements: the Africans, the European, the indigenous and ideas more exotic, of most recent origin.

It is a typical conception of Brazil but has its similarities among religions of Mexico and the Caribbean. This last configuration, regarded as a syncretic solution, instructs the religious thinking of the Afro-Brazilian cults. They are: the Candomblé, the Umbanda and the Quimbanda. In this spiritual universe there is a pantheon of entities, saints, angels, spirits and Africans gods. Just as there is the human geography, there also exists a Spiritist geography. The spiritual world also has its archetypes. These archetypes are configured, according to its cultural environment. They represent human types which are inspired in the real world.

In this way, locals are visited by popular astral entities as they are defined by their respective personalities. The "Terreiros" are the places where rituals are conducted. These places are, generally, large sheds or warehouses. These sacred places are frequented by the spirits of mestizos known as "The Caboclo."

In the sheds of the Umbanda and the Kimbanda, there also appear the traditional spirits of old: "Blacks old" and "Black Moms." These are thought to be spirits of former slaves who return to Earth to assist their descendants in times of need.

Foreword

Demons And Sinister Spirits

Other countries in Latin America take a much dimmer view of communication with the spirits. Reporter to the paranormal Scott Corrales (http://inexplicata.blogspot.com) uncovered a fascinating story from Argentina about allegations of demonic possession in Villa Lanus. In January 2006, the Catholic Church was evaluating cases where the owner of the statue of the "Bleeding Virgin" and a young woman experienced strange signs of aggression and violence.

The time was noon at district A.3-2 of Villa Lanus and no one was sleeping the siesta or listening to dance music. All of the residents of city block #3 were focused and alarmed over what was taking place at House 22. In front of the house, a group of women sang and prayed the Our Father and the Rosary almost shouting.

The young men who usually wonder what to do during their vacation time were reading the Bible. The women's prayers ceased for a moment and their silence appeared to be a signal. Almost at the same time, cries of pain and horror emerged from within House 22, almost beyond the limit of what a normal person could scream, given its intensity and duration. The scene turned blood-curdling when the prayers and evocations of the women were added to the terrifying screams, pleading to God and Jesus to make evil depart from the body of La Polaca, a 15 year-old girl who has kept the entire neighborhood of relocated individuals on the edge since before Christmas.

Some 40 minutes earlier, Father Bronislaw Lagocki had entered the home to read prayers of deliverance from evil and, like everyone else in the neighborhood, was amazed. He hoped for a happy outcome.

"We are evaluating the case. It is likely that it involves what one would term possession, but all of this must be researched and weighed by the Bishop (Ruben Martinez) and he will be responsible for authorizing a priest or someone with special authority to carry out the exorcism," Father Lagocki told the newspaper El Territorio, much as he had explained only minutes earlier to the girl's terrified parents. For the time being, she must remain within her home and wait for the arrival of the Catholic Church's representatives.

No one wants to say how or what triggered the mystery. All agree that two days before Christmas, La Polaca was at home and decisively stepped out to the street and headed strangely toward the house where one year ago, an image of the Virgin of Caracupa began bleeding from her eyes, a phenomenon that attracted people from all over the province. A distance of 50 meters separates La Polaca's home from that of her neighbor: she arrived and confronted Rafael Mendez, the man whose daughter had given him the image of the Virgin, and in a heavy voice asked if he needed help.

"It wasn't her. It was the evil within her. She asked me several times if I wanted His help and I always said no," says Rafael, who still has the trances of another strange phenomenon that has ensnared him.

According to the accounts given by his children and witnesses to the incredible event, Rafael, after refusing La Polaca's strange offer, fell to the floor and began experiencing convulsions. Without any logical explanation, his body began to experience wounds on the abdomen, arms and his right nipple. The marks appear to be bullwhip-marks or tremendous scratches.

"It was stronger than me. It got into my mind - I recall nothing. All I know is what I've been told," said Rafael, who has suffered blackouts since that restless December afternoon.

"Last night it came in again. It was inside my home and was so strong that it toppled me again and the marks burned me greatly."

Rafael went to Fatima yesterday morning to chase away "the evil spirits, who avenged themselves on me for refusing to submit to their will," he said while resting, or at least trying to. His home has once again become a place of pilgrimage for many people.

"It's astonishing. All of this is incredible. I think that the truth of the matter must be investigated. I have no idea how it all began, but they say that the kids were apparently trying to summon spirits—something very Umbanda-like—until the pact was made and evil seized the girl," said district leader Cesar Melgarejo in an interview with El Territorio.

"I was very frightened, because the man bled profusely and shook on the floor," he added with hesitation.

On January 28, 2005, when the phenomenon of the Virgin of Caracupa gripped the home of the Mendez family, many neighbors told El Territorio that this was a bad omen and said that since the Virgin cannot speak, she weeps, and if she weeps blood, it is because she is greatly troubled. Basilia Silvero had said as much on an equally warm afternoon before breaking

Foreword

into tears.

"In all my 64 years this is the first time I've ever seen this. It's very bad."

Creatures From Out Of This World

In the 1890's an Argentinean explorer, geographer and adventurer, Ramon Lista, was hunting in Patagonia (located in both Chile and Argentina), when a large, unknown creature covered with long hair, ran past the party. To Lista, the creature looked like a gigantic armadillo. The party shot at the beast, but the bullets seemed to have no effect. Professor Florentino Ameghino, a paleontologist in Argentina, heard the Lista story and began to wonder if the strange beast was a giant sloth that had survived from the Pleistocene. He might not have put much stock in the Lista story if it had not been for legends he'd collected from Indians in the Patagonia region about hunting such a large creature in ancient times. The animal in the Indian stories was nocturnal, and slept during the day in burrows it dug with it's claws. The Indians found it difficult to get their arrows to penetrate the animal's skin.

Ameghino also had a piece of physical evidence. A small section of apparently fresh hide found by a rancher named Eberhardt on his property in a cave in 1895. The hide was studded with small, hard, calcium nodules and would have been impervious to the teeth of Pleistocene predators. It seemed likely that it would have also resisted Indian arrows and Lista's bullets.

So sure was Ameghino this was the creature Lista had seen he named the creature after Lista: *Nemoylodon listai,* or "Lista's new Mylodon".

Expeditions to Eberhardt's and other caves, recovered additional pieces of hide along with evidence the Eberhardt's cave had been home to both men and Mylodon. With the development of the Carbon-14 dating method in the twentieth century the age of Mylodon remains in the Eberhardt's cave was settled. Dung found in the cave was more than 10,000 years old. The skin was estimated to be 5,000 years old. Because of this evidence, it could be likely that the giant sloth survived into modern times.

The giant ground sloth thrived during the ice age where it probably fed on leaves found on the lower branches of trees or bushes. The largest of these ground sloths was Megatherium, which grew to the size of a modern elephant with a weight over five tons.

Foreword

Giant Sloths had very large, dangerous-looking claws. Despite their size they were probably only used to strip leaves or bark from plants. Their teeth were small and blunt in keeping with their herbivore diet. Examinations of their hip bones suggest that they could stand on their hind legs to extend their grazing as high as twenty feet.

Like other giant creatures that disappeared at the end of the Pleistocene period (about 10,000 years ago), the giant ground sloth died out. Or so scientists believe.

South America allegedly is also home to a number of different types of giant reptiles that look suspiciously like long extinct prehistoric dinosaurs.

The earliest report of an "out-of-place" dinosaur was an 1883 account of "an extraordinary saurian" killed along the Rio Beni in what is now Bolivia can be safely discounted as farcical despite its appearance in such a prestigious publication as *Scientific American*. The account describes a three-headed monster nearly 40 feet in length - obviously the creature is too fabulous as to be taken seriously as a cryptid.

The Lost World

Another account was published in the January 11, 1911, issue of the New York Herald. Its author, a German named Franz Herrmann Schmidt, claimed that one day in October 1907 he and a companion, Capt. Rudolph Pfleng, along with Indian guides, entered a valley composed of swamps and lakes in a remote region of the Peruvian interior. There they discovered some strange, huge tracks, indicating the presence of more than one unknown animal in the waters, and crushed trees and vegetation. They also noticed

the "queer" absence of alligators, iguanas, and water snakes.

Despite the guides' visible
fear the party camped in the valley that night. The next morning
expedition members got back
into their boat and resumed
their search for the animals. Just
before noon they found fresh
tracks along the shore. Pfleng
declared that he was going to
follow them inland, however
dangerous the quest. Just then they heard the screams of a troop of monkeys which had been gathering berries from some trees nearby. According
to Schmidt's account:

A large dark something half hidden among the branches shot up among
the monkeys and there was a great commotion. One of the excited Indians
began to paddle the boat away from the shore, and before we could stop
him we were 100 feet from the waterline. Now we could see nothing and the
Indians absolutely refused to put in again, while neither Pfleng nor myself
[sic] cared to lay down our rifles to paddle. There was a great moving of
plants and a sound like heavy slaps of a great paddle, mingled with the cries
of some of the monkeys moving rapidly away from the lake.... for a full 10
minutes there was silence, then the green growth began to stir again, and
coming back to the lake we beheld the frightful monster that I shall now
describe.

The head appeared over bushes 10 feet tall. It was about the size of a
beer keg and was shaped like that of a tapir, as if the snout was used for
pulling things or taking hold of them. The eyes were small and dull and set
in like those of an alligator. Despite the half dried mud we could see that the
neck, which was very snakelike, only thicker in proportion, was rough knotted like an alligator's side rather than his back.

Evidently the animal saw nothing odd in us, if he noticed us, and advanced till he was no more than 150 feet away. We could see part of the
body, which I should judge to have been eight or nine feet thick at the shoul-
ders, if that word may be used, since there were no fore legs, only some

great heavy clawed flippers. The surface was like that of the neck....

As far as I was concerned, I would have waited a little longer, but Pfleng threw up his rifle and let drive at the head. I am sure that he struck between the eyes and that the bullet must have struck something bony, horny or very tough, for it cut twigs from a tree higher up and further on after it glanced. I shot as Pfleng shot again and aimed for the base of the neck.

The animal had remained perfectly still till now. It dropped its nose to the spot at which I had aimed and seemed to bite at it, but there was not blood or any sign of real hurt. As quickly as we could fire we pumped seven shots into it, and I believe all struck. They seemed to annoy the creature but not to work any injury. Suddenly it plunged forward in a silly clumsy fashion. The Indians nearly upset the dugout getting away, and both Pfleng and I missed the sight as it entered the water. I was very anxious to see its hind legs, if it had any. I looked again only in time to see the last of it leave the land—a heavy blunt tail with rough horny lumps. The head was visible still, though the body was hidden by the splash. From the instant's opportunity I should say that the creature was 35 feet long, with at least 12 of this devoted to head and neck.

In three seconds there was nothing to be seen except the waves of the muddy water, the movements of the waterside growth and a monkey with its hind parts useless hauling himself up a tree top. As the Indians paddled frantically away I put a bullet through the poor thing to let it out of its misery. We had not gone a hundred yards before Pfleng called to me and pointed to the right. Above the water an eighth of a mile away appeared the head and neck of the monster. It must have dived and gone right under us. After a few seconds' gaze it began to swim toward us, and as our bullets seemed to have no effect we took flight in earnest. Losing sight of it behind an island, we did not pick it up again and were just as well pleased.

This story appears in the course of an otherwise credible sounding narrative about an expedition along the Solimes River. Schmidt writes that a few months later, on March 4, 1908, his companion Pfleng died of fever. Thus the story cannot be checked. Of the tale Mackal remarks, "The details ... seem to ring true and probably reflect the experiences of an actual expedition. It does not necessarily follow that the encounter with the alleged creature also occurred and may be nothing more than a clever addition to an otherwise authentic expedition."

Foreword

Still, Schmidt's is not the only reference to a huge swamp dwelling beast in the South American backwaters. In the early twentieth century Lt. Col. Percy H. Fawcett surveyed jungles for the Britain's Royal Geographical Society. A careful, accurate reporter, Fawcett wrote that native informants had told him of "tracks of some gigantic animal" seen in the swamps along the Acre River, near where the borders of Peru, Bolivia, and Brazil intersect (and 500 to 600 miles from the site of Schmidt and Pfleng's alleged encounter). The natives said they had never actually seen the creature responsible for the tracks.

Farther south, according to Fawcett, along the Peru-Bolivian border "some mysterious and enormous beast has frequently been disturbed in the swamps—possibly a primeval monster like those reported in other parts of the continent. Certainly tracks have been found belonging to no known animals—huge tracks, far greater than could have been made by any species we know."

Living Dinosaurs

Since then few reports or rumors of South American dinosaurs have found their way into print. In two articles published in Pursuit between 1977 and 1980 Silvano Lorenzoni suggested that the flat-topped, steep mountains of the Guavana Massif, which have remained geologically and ecologically stable for tens of millions of years, may harbor surviving dinosaurs. For his intriguing idea, however, Lorenzoni had only the thinnest supporting evidence: a trader's report of three "plesiosaur like things" in a lake on one such plateau, Auyantepuy, in southeastern Venezuela where Angel Falls originates. He also noted reports of exceptionally large, lizard-like reptiles in mountain valleys near the Venezuelan coast. Karl Shuker mentions an account of an Iguanodon encountered along the Magdalena River in Colombia, but no

details are available. In 1931, Harald Westin saw a creature comparable to the African nguma-monene along Brazil's Rio Marmore—a 20-foot long creature which resembled a legged boa constrictor.

Researcher Leonard Clark reported that he had heard tales when traveling up the Rio Perene in Brazil. He was told by the natives of herbivorous creatures which sounded very much like prehistoric sauropods. Finally, in 1975, a Swiss businessman was told by an elderly guide, Simon Bastos, of a creature like that reported by Pfleng and Clark. The long-necked creature had destroyed Bastos' canoe after he had landed along a riverbank. Bastos was later told that such longnecked creatures frequented deep waterholes, and rarely came out on land.

No discussion of South America's supposed "dinosaurs," though, would be complete without discussion of the Argentine lake monster Nahuelito, reputed to dwell in and around Lake Nahuel Huapi. Several reports originate from zoologist Clementi Onelli. In 1897, a Chilean farmer in Patagonia reported hearing the sounds of something heavy being dragged along the pebble beach near White Lake. Sometimes, at night, he said, he could see a long-necked form in the water. A man named Vaag discovered animal remains and spoor along the banks of the Rio Tamanga. Onelli was convinced that the traces Vaag found were those of a plesiosaur. Onelli revealed a third sighting in 1913, when he said that a similar report surfaced from the Santa Cruz area.

In 1922, a fourth report was brought to Onelli's attention. A prospector named Martin Sheffield encountered a similar monster in the hilly Chubut Province of Patagonia. Sheffield's creature had a swanlike neck and moved like a crocodile. Onelli mounted an expedition to find Sheffield's monster, but it failed.

Here There Be Giants

Many early explorers reported encountering natives of extraordinary height in the Americas in the 15th and 16th centuries. Later, early settlers in South, Central and North America would report finding huge skeletons in mounds and other burial grounds. These reports were memorialized in the voyage accounts and in scientific literature of the day. Here we reproduce briefly some of those reports.

During explorer Sebald de Weert's time in the Magellan Straits there were some anthropologically noteworthy events that are associated with him. One instance of which is that De Weert and several crew claimed to have seen members of a "race of giants" while there.

De Weert described a particular incident when he was with his men in boats rowing to an island in the Magellan Strait. The Dutch claimed to have seen seven odd-looking boats approaching which were full of naked giants.

These giants supposedly had long hair and reddish-brown skin. The Dutch claim to have shot three of the giants dead with their muskets before the giants finally retreated to the shore.

On the shore the giants were apparently able to uproot trees from the ground to protect themselves from the musket fire and they waited with spears and stones so they could attack the Dutch intruders should they make a beach head. In fear of the giants, the Dutch dared not land.

De Weert's claims to sightings of giants were not totally unusual for this region as Magellan also first recorded sighting in 1520 in the straits at San Julian.

It was also claimed that Magellan captured two male giants as specimens to return to Europe, but the giants died en route. These creatures were supposedly over three meters (10 feet) tall.

Many others including Francis Drake, Pedro Sarmiento, Tome Hernandez, and Anthony Knyvet claimed to have seen giants in the Straits of Magellan with the last sighting having been at Cabo Virgines in 1764 by Commodore John "Foul Weather Jack" Byron.

De Weert's expedition is the only one to have claimed to have witnessed aggressive behavior on behalf of the giants.

Also according to Theodore de Bry (1528-98) in Part IX of his landmark *Historia Americae Sive Novi Orbis* (History of American Grand Voyages), Sebald de Weert reported how his crew had captured and imprisoned a Tierra del Fuegan mother with two children on the south side of the Magellan route heading eastward. While they released the mother and the younger child, they carried the older daughter forward to Europe, where she soon died.

De Weert noted that the mother had fed the children on raw birds, which was an oddity well noted in de Bry's work.

Amerigo Vespucci was an Italian merchant, explorer and cartographer.

Foreword

He played a senior role in two voyages which explored the east coast of South America between 1499 and 1502. On the second of these voyages he discovered that South America extended much further south than before known by the Europeans. This convinced him that this land he was part of a new continent, a bold contention at a time when other European explorers crossing the Atlantic thought they were reaching Asia (the "Indies").

After we were cured we recommenced our navigation; and through the same cause we were often obliged to fight with a great many people, and always had the victory over them.

Thus continuing our voyage, we came to an island fifteen leagues distant from the mainland. As at our arrival we saw no collection of people, eleven of us landed. Finding a path inland, we walked nearly two leagues and came to a village of about twelve houses, in which were seven women who were so large that there was not one among them who was not a span and a half taller than myself.

When they saw us they were very much frightened, and the principal one among them, who seemed certainly a discreet woman, led us by signs into a house and had refreshments prepared for us.

They were such large women that we were about determining to carry off two of the younger ones as a present to our king; but while we were debating this subject, thirty-six men entered the hut where we were drinking. They were of such great stature that each one was taller when upon his knees than I when standing erect. In fact, they were giants; each of the women appeared a Penthesilia, and the men Antei.

When they came in, some of our number were so frightened that they did not consider themselves safe, for they were armed with very large bows and arrows, besides immense clubs made in the form of swords. Seeing that we were small of stature they began to converse with us, in order to learn who we were and from what parts we came. We gave them fair words, and answered them, by signs, that we were men of peace and intent only upon seeing the world.

Finally, we held it our wisest course to part from them without questioning in our turn; so we returned by the same path in which we had come, they accompanying us quite to the seashore, till we went aboard the ships.

An excerpt from Charles Debrosses '*Historie des navigations aux terres*

Foreword

australes', published in 1756, contributed to the giant saga:

The coast of Port Desire is inhabited by giants fifteen to sixteen palms high. I have myself measured the footprint of one of them on the riverbank, which was four times longer than one of ours.

I have also measured the corpses of two men recently buried by the river, which were fourteen spans long. Three of our men, who were later taken by the Spanish on the coast of Brazil, assured me that one day on the other side of the coast they had to sail out to sea because the giants started throwing great blocks of stone of astonishing size from the beach right at their boat.

In Brazil I saw one of these giants which Alonso Diaz had captured at Port Saint Julien: he was just a boy but was already thirteen spans tall.

These people go about naked and have long hair; the one I saw in Brazil was healthy-looking and well proportioned for his height.

I can say nothing about his habits, not having spent any time with him, but the Portuguese tell me that he is no better than the other cannibals along the coast of La Plata.

Captain Cooke also wrote in his ship's logs of a race of giants that inhabited Patagonia. He even claimed to have captured one of the giants. Unfortunately, the giant escaped by breaking the ropes that bound him to the mast and jumped off the ship, overboard into the sea.

In an additional excerpt, Capt. Cooke wrote in his log that he himself was 6 feet 3 inches tall, which was unusual for a time when a mans average height was about 5 feet 4 inches, and that he could easily stand under the arm of one of these giants.

In 1767 Captain John Byron and the H.M.S. Dolphin returned to port and published ***Voyage Round the World in His Majesty's Ship the Dolphin***. In his book he hailed the voyage as "...putting an end to the dispute, which for two centuries and a half has subsisted between geographers, in relation to the reality of there being a nation of people of such an amazing stature, of which the concurrent testimony of all on board the Dolphin and Tamer can now leave no room for doubt."

A subsequent publication under his name ***Voyage*** includes the following tale. Captain Byron is credited with having had the precaution to take ashore with him a number of trinkets, such as beads and ribbons in order to convince the Patagonians of their peaceful and amicable disposition.

"...giving to each of them some, as far as they went. The method he made use of to facilitate the distribution of them, was by making the Indians sit down on the ground, that he might put the strings of beads around their necks; and such was their extraordinary size, that in this situation they were almost as high as the Commodore when standing."

Giants From Beyond

Tales of lost lands filled with giants seem to be a thing of the past. However, it seems that the giants have not just given up and disappeared forever. Once again paranormal researcher Scott Corrales (http://inexplicata.blogspot.com/), has uncovered some fascinating cases where it seems that the giants have moved up in the world and are now flying around the skies of South America in UFOs.

One such case was reported in January 2002, by Argentinean researcher Pablo Omastott. The event, involved a motorcyclist and a giant entity, had appeared in the January 15 issue of the Cordoba newspaper.

Enrique Moreno, 19, is a clerical employee with the Ika-Renault Corporation, whose nocturnal job involves acting as a courier for business documents from one company office to another. Arriving at one of Ika-Renault's offices in the dark of the night to lay some paperwork in the middle of a table, he realized that the facility's lights flickered on and off inexplicably. Moreno paid no mind to the power fluctuation and hopped on his motorcycle, heading for his next destination.

Upon reaching a site where vehicles were parked before being sent out across the Andes to Chile, Moreno was amazed to see a giant green figure some 150 meters away. Thinking at first that it might be a welder carrying out his duties at that time of the night, the courier got on his motorcycle and drove toward the figure. When he came within thirty meters, his otherwise dependable bike backfired and hesitated, shuddering and becoming almost unmanageable. Moreno had to perform extraordinary efforts to remain in control of his two-wheeler, but he was much more distressed by the glowing figure than by his vehicle's unaccustomed reaction.

"I froze after seeing it," said Moreno. "It was like a robot standing more than two meters tall. Its angled head was hairless; it had shining, luminous eyes, and was dressed like a frogman, wearing a belt with a wide oval buckle around its waist."

The ungovernable motorcycle shot like an arrow out of control crossing an open gate and going straight across the road without its driver being able do a single thing about it.

"My arms still ache; it robbed me of my strength," he told the interviewer from Cordoba. "I felt as though I was in the middle of a magnetic field. It was cold that night, but the area surrounding me was very hot."

After the experience, Moreno stumbled through the factory's gates feeling a terrible buzzing in his head, as though it were about to explode. Factory personnel immediately drove him to a clinic where he was given sedatives. Although the newspaper considers that the young courier may have hallucinated the experience, it adds that there were other witnesses to the entity that very same evening: a nurse at the same medical facility Moreno had been driven to had administered a sedative to a woman who claimed having seen the same colossal figure levitate through the air and enter an unidentified flying object, an event which was confirmed, in turn, by residents of Villa de El Libertador, who had seen the alleged spacecraft that same evening.

As if these corroborating accounts were not enough, there is also the case involving trucker Luftolde Rodriguez, 52, who was slowly turning his tractor-trailer around and was terrified to find the green giant standing in front of his rig. The giant's presence appeared to drain not only the vehicle's power source, but the trucker's wristwatch and portable radio as well.

Given his proximity to the unknown figure, Rodriguez was better able to describe it. The giant, he said, was looking at him inquisitively; it had a flattened head, was completely bald and lacked eyebrows and eyelashes. Its ears were long, and it wore a glowing light blue outfit with a broad black belt and white boots. An interesting detail is that Rodriguez reports that the giant had a ball "similar to a billiard ball" in its left hand.

The article in Cordoba offers the following conclusion: "The giant's attitude was entirely harmless and could be said to be one of observation. The entity was completely made of energy, perhaps belonging to a form of life in which protoplasm no longer plays any part."

Foreword

The Pombero

If you don't believe that strange creatures seen in Latin America could all come from landed flying saucers, then consider the Pombero, an allegedly mythical monster from Paraguay. The Pombero is known not only throughout Paraguay, but also in Argentina and Brazil. It is usually described as a short, ugly man with hairy hands and feet that give him the ability to walk virtually silently. Sometimes it is clothed with a large hat and knapsack.

He is considered by locals to be a wandering vagabond character. It is often referred to as *"Cuarahy jara,"* which means "Owner of the Sun." In Argentina, it is sometimes known by the Spanish translation *"Dueno del Sol."*

Pombero is nocturnal, living in the forests or rural areas. It roams about at night in search of mischief. It is famous for performing pranks like opening gates, stealing eggs, or scaring horses. Since it is a forest spirit, it can imitate the sounds of animals, especially birds and is sometimes considered a protector of them.

It is also known for impregnating young girls, either by mere touch or by raping them. Many unwanted pregnancies are conveniently attributed to Pombero. In this way it is like another mythological figure, Curupi. It is a kind of Boogyman and his stories are used to frighten unruly children.

Pombero often whistles, so if you see a strange vagabond at night whistling, you can be sure it's Pombero. People will try to avoid being the victim of its pranks and leave offerings for it like cigarettes and alcohol.

Belief in Pombero is still widespread even today. A Paraguayan man recently claimed to have seen Pombero. The eyewitness was gathering firewood one night with an American friend, when they saw a strange creature about 10 feet away. He said it reminded him of the maned wolf, but it had a human face. After a few seconds it disappeared into the woods.

The next day, after hearing the story, the local farmers confirmed it was Pombero. One of them even said he had missed a chance to make a deal with Pombero. If he had offered it alcohol, cigarettes, or *yerba mate*, (a kind of South American tea) in exchange it would protect him. The same farmer claimed to have been doing the same thing since he was 15 and never has had any problems with his enemies.

Argentina recently has had a series of sightings of what appears to be gnomes, or at least some sort of small, humanoid type of creature. These sightings started in General Guemes, Salta, Argentina in 2007. Some reports claim that a survey showed that 90% of locals believed in the creature with over a hundred claiming to have actually seen one of the creatures; however contrasting reports claim that very few locals actually believe in it.

In March 2008, a "creepy gnome" who wore a pointy hat was caught on video by local teenagers on their cell phone. According to Jose Alvarez, the video was taken when he and a group of friends were out one night basically just hanging around.

"We were chatting about our last fishing trip. It was one in the morning. I began to film a bit with my mobile phone while the others were chatting and joking. Suddenly we heard something—a weird noise as if someone was throwing stones... We looked to one side and saw that the grass was moving. To begin with we thought it was a dog but when we saw this gnomelike figure begin to emerge we were really afraid... This is no joke. We are still afraid to go out—just like everyone else in the neighborhood now... One of my friends was so scared after seeing that thing that we had to take him to the hospital."

Locals had reported seeing gnomes (or duendes) for several decades, however reports increased in 2007 after railway workers reported seeing one run around the tracks. They reported seeing a short humanoid creature that ran sideways and wore a pointy hood.

So come along and take a journey to a place that is not so different from our own; a place of mystery, adventure, and surprises. A place where the dead speak to the living, a place where creatures of the past still roam, a place where reality and unreality mix and mingle.

So put down your video games, hang up your cell phones and join us for a trip of a lifetime, or several lifetimes, and use this book as your guide for occult South America.

an occult guide to South America

AN OCCULT GUIDE TO SOUTH AMERICA

an occult guide
to south america

john wilcock

AN OCCULT GUIDE TO SOUTH AMERICA

Acknowledgments

Apart from the scores of authorities I have cited, I would particularly like to thank Richard Rubinstein, George Romero, and Resource Investments, Inc., for making this book a reality.

In addition, thanks are also due to the following: Lucy Allen, Pat Bernesser, Candace Cornell, Betty DaCosta, Rona Edmunds, Evelyn Callando, Lee Goldberg, Mike Gornick, Susan Hofmann, Katherine Kolbert. Tuli Kupferberg, Marvin Lieber, Ike and Sylvia Lisenberg, Jose Luis de Luna, Djadja McCleod, Stephanie Miller, William Rubinstein, Donna Siegel, Stuart Snodgrass, Sara Sprague, Barbara Stacy, Sol Stein, Ira Wolfman, and Martha Zenfell.

AN OCCULT GUIDE TO SOUTH AMERICA

Contents

AN OCCULT GUIDE TO SOUTH AMERICA

Preface

Once upon a time, as every book about magic might appropriately begin, people believed in the gods of nature to whom they appealed for help and, as a matter of course, propitiated and appeased with sacrifices. These pagan gods—the Sun, the Moon, the Stars, the Sea, the Wind, and a host of other divinities—are still around us and are all worshipped. To believe in magic is to accept that the pagan gods have more relevance to our lives than those of any other religion and that faith itself can move mountains.

This nature-worship, magic, has gone into hiding or disappeared altogether in many parts of the world and when we go in search of it we find only traces of its memory, preserved in the metaphorical amber of legend and folklore. But in South America (as opposed to say North America or Europe where the memories are pretty much all that can be found), magic is still today a living, breathing thing.

The Polish-born anthropologist Bronislaw Malinowski (1884-1942) described how myth "as it exists in a savage community" is not merely a story told but a reality lived" and he went on to suggest that magic is related to anxiety. In ordinary, everyday pursuits there is no need for it but that, when the outcome of some enterprise is uncertain or when there is danger involved, the native has recourse to magic, just as the Christian might go to church and pray to his gods.

The International Encyclopedia of the Social Sciences puts it more succinctly: In nonliterate societies," it declares, "folklore is virtually identical with culture, but in literate societies it is only a fragment of culture."

This book, although cast in the mold of a contemporary travel guide, is largely a tour of nonliterate societies, and examination of cultures past and present that are rooted in magic. Briefly, its underlying themes are Indians, Incas, archaeology, and Easter Island because we must, of necessity, concentrate more upon ancient times than modem.

After the sixteenth-century Spanish conquest of South America, many able commentators recorded their impressions of the pagan societies through which they traveled and, as a result, we have a pretty clear picture of conditions at that time. Some of the writers most frequently quoted in the text of this book include: Cristobal de Acufia, a Jesuit priest who traversed the Amazon river in 1639 on the orders of the Spanish Crown, publishing his writings in two minutely detailed volumes; Father Casper de Carvajal who accompanied the expedition of Antonio de Orellana down the Amazon in 1542 and whose account of the journey was published (in translation and with a commentary by Jose Medina) in 1934; Cristobal de Molina, a Spanish priest who lived in the Incan capital of Cuzco, mastered the Quecha language and wrote (about 1575) what is probably the most comprehensive work on the Incan religion, Pedro de Cieza de Leon, a much traveled Spanish soldier whose *Cronica del Peru* (written in 1551, the second part remaining unpublished until 1880) was appraised by John Howland Rowe as "honest, conscientious and thorough"; and Garcilaso de la Vega (sometimes known as "El Inca"), the son of an Incan princess and a conquistador, whose *Comentarios Reales* were a compilation of legends, customs, and memories of historical events gleaned from his family.

Coming to the present day, the absolute, basic, bedrock authority for information about the civilization and culture of the natives of the subcontinent is the formidable *Handbook of South American Indians,* a seven-volume (including index) set of works collated and published by the Smithsonian Institution's Bureau of American Ethnology between 1944 and 1957. This is an invaluable and endlessly fascinating work and it is difficult to see how anybody could write knowledgeably about the subject without consulting it. Most of the major names in anthropology, archaeology, ethnology, and all branches of the social sciences contributed their talents and analyses to this series and, as a result, it is possible to read up on the culture, habits, religion, tribal structure, language, beliefs, and history of virtually any tribe on the subcontinent of which there are any traces.

As a general rule, wherever any of these authorities have been cited in this book I have used only the authority's name, it being a simple matter to check the handbook itself in any library for the author's qualifications, affiliation, etc.

Extensive as this volume is, it cannot do more than touch upon huge areas of terrain, both geographical and occult, and despite the fact that I have now visited and written about the " occult sites" of nineteen countries, I have tried to maintain an objective attitude towards the subject. This is a reportorial book in the sense that, except on rate occasions, I have confined myself to other people's comments on the subject of magic and refrained from expressing theories of my own—not because I have none but rather because I placed a higher priority on answering three basic questions: Why is this place magical? Who says so? and What are their credentials?

If I have reached any single conclusion at this point in my quest it is that natural energy can be tapped, stored, and redirected in a variety of ways that we have come to describe as "magic." The places at which this has been done and the manner of doing it form the substance of this book.

New York, August 1976

John Wilcock

AN OCCULT GUIDE TO SOUTH AMERICA

Chapter 1

Manaus

The Indians of Amazonas

To the romantically inclined armchair traveler, Brazil conjures up images not so much of wild nights in Rio but of the exotic Amazon whose majestic course bisects the upper portion of the country. The Amazon is not the world's longest river (the Nile is slightly longer) but it is the biggest, containing almost one-fifty of all the earth's fresh water. From its origin, 17,000 feet above sea level in the Andean mountains of Peru, to its outlet on the Atlantic where its mouth is 20 miles wide, it flows almost 3,550 miles and at least two-thirds of this is navigable by oceangoing liners.

It is fed by more than 1,000 smaller rivers or tributaries from both sides of the equator—which the Amazon roughly parallels—and, for parts of its course, reaches a depth of 300 feet and a width of eight miles. Truly, it dominates the area through which it runs, a region estimated to be about 2.5 million square miles, comprised of the states of Amazonas and Para and in one way or another almost all life in this region relies upon it. Most of the area, indeed, has no roads to speak of and, apart from aircraft, is dependent on the water's course for transport.

Almost five centuries ago, when the Amazon was first discovered by the Spanish captain Vicente Yanez Pinzon, its fertile basin sheltered two million Indians divided between hundreds of tribes. Their relationship with nature was harmonious. The pagan gods they worshipped had been good to them and their customs and practices in many cases had remained intact since the Stone Age.

But then came "civilization" with its formalized religions, its superior attitudes, and its multitudinous diseases. Enslavement, massacre, and Christian teachings have managed to decimate the tribes until it is doubtful if more than 100,000 pure Indians remain in northern Brazil today. They are widely scattered, most of them, isolated in the inaccessible regions of the upper Rio Negro in Brazil's mountainous northwest. Rapids and submerged rocks prevent all but the most persistent visitors from reaching them, and their rights are protected by the government's National Indian Foundation, known as FUNAI.

What became the first cities of Brazil—Sao Paulo, Rio, and its neighboring suburb of Niteroi across the bay—were originally Indian settlements and, when the white man came, it was the Indians who acted as guides, hunters, and laborers.

But the "taming" of the Indians, if such a phrase can be used for a process that has never been completed, really began under the guidance of a celebrated explorer, himself of Indian descent, Candido Mariano de Silva Rondon. It was Rondon, much admired in present-day Brazil, who developed the policies of acculturating the Indians through a series of "approach posts" or temporary shelters from which initial contact could be made. Great patience was needed, as well as gifts and trinkets, before the mistrust of the elusive natives could be overcome. But eventually a tenuous contact was established.

It has not, however, been able to halt the process under which more than 80 of the 230 surviving jungle tribes have become extinct since the turn of the century, and the huge new tunneling projects now under construction in the Andes—which will hopefully irrigate Peru's coastal deserts—are liable to create even more disturbances in the lives of the remaining tribes.

At the time when it was first discovered by the Portuguese, Brazil was inhabited by tribes related to each other both in Manaus language and culture, as Claude Levi-Strauss wrote in **A World on the Wane** (Criterion, New York, 1961). "We grouped them under the collective name of Ge. They would seem to have been pushed back, not many centuries before, by Tupi-speaking invaders who were already in occupation of the entire coastal strip; the struggle against them was still going on. The Ge of southern Brazil had fallen back into regions difficult of access and whereas the coastal Tupi had quickly been mopped up by the colonists, the Ge had survived for several centuries."

AN OCCULT GUIDE TO SOUTH AMERICA

In general, FUNAI does a good job, endeavoring to maintain a fine balance between preserving and protecting the Indian way of life and, as government policy expresses it, "promoting the imperative of national integration and the ambitions of the Brazilian community anxious to expand and develop." Today, the largest percentage of Indians are in touch, at least occasionally, with one or another of the 250 Indian posts that FUNAI has established since 1967. Most of these remaining Indians live somewhere within reach of the Amazon, and the more remote tribes, though slightly influenced by Christian ideas, stilt practice shamanism with the attendant use of a mask to personify supernatural spirits. They believe that sicknesses can be cured by magical touch or by the blowing of smoke on the affected area, and they gather for ancestral rites next to the sacred *juazeiro* tree.

Masks, used in many ritual ceremonies, are often made of straw to represent birds and animals. Some cover the dancer from head to foot and are colored with dyes from the annatto or *seripap* trees. Falcon down covers the body, applied with a mixture of tree resin and coconut oil, and women of one tribe, the Kayapo, specialize in painting dresses on their bodies—complete with sleeves and plunging neckline, though this is usually saved for ceremonial occasions.

Henry Bates (***Naturalist on the River Amazons***) said that on religious holidays some Tupi tribes celebrated by dressing as animals, especially the *caypor*, a sort of sylvan deity resembling the Curupira who is generally regarded as the protector of game animals. "He is not at all an object of worship," Bates wrote, "nor of fear, except to children, being considered merely as a kind of hobgoblin."

The Mundurucus, most of whom are located in the southern sections of Para and Amazonas states, about 500 miles South of the Central Amazon port of Manaus, are considered to be among the most expert workers of feathers, but the garments they produce are tied so closely to their religious ceremonies that they are reluctant to part with any of them. Robert Murphy in his ***Mundurucu Religion*** (University of California, 1958) concluded that it had been only in recent years that the relationship between the world of men and the world of hunted animals had ceased to be the central element in the Mundurucus' religion. "The disappearance of this belief," he wrote, "brought momentous culture changes," for the Indians were dependent on animals for their subsistence and to some extent it was a mutual dependency, promoted by the celebration of rituals.

AN OCCULT GUIDE TO SOUTH AMERICA

Mundurucu trophy heads are famous, says Alfred Metraux; because of the skill with which they were prepared. "After the brain and soft parts had been removed, they were plunged in oil and then exposed to the sun and to smoke. The empty sockets were filled with artificial eyes made of wax and cutia teeth. A carrying cord was laced through the lips."

Another explorer, Charles Domville-Fife visited a Mundurucu settlement about half a century ago when he observed the puberty ceremony of a teenage boy being tattooed by the medicine man with a bunch of palm needles dipped in red dye made from achiote seeds. It was obviously painful, the onlooker wrote, but the boy made no sound until it was over at which time he was ceremoniously handed a bow, some arrows and a spear, before being presented with a young girl. He then led his new "wife" by her hair to a newly built hut.

The dye with which he was tattooed is one of several forest-made dyes commonly believed to have magical properties. More than a century ago, an American naval officer, William Herndon, explained in detail the elaborate way in which the plant known as *bixa ovellona* was nurtured to produce a crop of seeds which were then dried and crushed to produce the red powder. It has been conjectured that *urucu*, and a similar colored dye extracted from the pulp surrounding the seeds of the annatto tree, were so widely used for body decoration that they gave rise to the tag "redskin" to describe Indians.

Although "pure" Indians are in short supply, Brazil, in common with most Latin American countries, has a large proportion of mestizos (half-Indian, half-white) brought about by Indian blood mingling with that of other settlers in the three or four centuries since the country was opened up by Europeans.

The first white man to traverse the Amazon from end to end was the Spanish captain Francisco de Orellana in 1531. Just over a century later, in 1637, the Portuguese soldier Pedro Teixera led an ambitious expedition of 2,000 men aboard 47 boats from Para (now Belem) on the Atlantic coast, to Quito in Ecuador, and back again. On his return Teixera took along a Jesuit priest, Cristobal de Acufta, who meticulously documented details of the tribes he encountered.

Nearer to our times we have the record of Charles W. Domville-Fife (*Among Wild Tribes of the Amazons*, J. P. Lippincott Co., 1925). who, in the grand tradition of legendary explorers, set off with camera, gun, trinkets, and native bearers for the remotest regions he could reach. He visited the Apiaca, once the mortal enemies of the Mundurucu, whose fierce reputation was confirmed for him when he saw them drinking from cups made out of human skulls, the eye and nose sockets plugged by dirty red clay. The Apiecas, he reported, believed that the spirits of the dead were reborn in the form of birds and animals, and that the moon was an evil spirit whose satellites in the river would drag down to a murky depth any Indian who bathed under its pale light.

Domville-Fife reluctantly came to accept such hitherto untested items as monkey, tortoise, and lizard as part of his diet, was bitten in turn by mosquitoes and a vampire bat, and observed, but didn't share, the anthropophagous habits of a tribe of Itogapuks who believed that by drinking a cupful of the blood of certain animals "they gain the strength, cunning or intelligence of their victim."

On a later visit to the Cashibo Indians he was shocked to discover that "the aged are killed and eaten because it is considered better to be devoured by a friend then by birds or beasts of prey.... I tried to differentiate between the body and the soul, and although no definite results were obtained, it seems that these natives believe that having eaten the heart, brain, eyes, ears and hands, they absorb the good qualities, cunning and spirit of the departed. So far as I could make out they do not kill and eat captives of other tribes because they look upon neighbors as inferior in all respects to themselves and therefore unworthy to be absorbed,"

Domville-Fife's most ambitious expedition began at the tiny settlement of Boa Vista, about 450 miles north of Manaus, from which he set off up the Uraricoera and Parime rivers. He sought, and found, what he felt must be the world's largest stone, the immense **Rock of Inscriptions**, which rises "like a huge balloon" from the level prairie. There exists no record of the Rock's origin or purpose. High up on the outer surface can be seen a narrow platform from which there is no visible means of descent and from which human sacrifices were said to have been hurled to a terrace a hundred feet below. On one side of the rock an enormous dark cavern may have been a sacred temple in which more bloody sacrifices took place. Carved, undecipherable inscriptions cover much of the rock's face.

The intrepid explorer's next stop was among the Uaupe Indians to the west, a tribe whose designation comes from the small vulturelike bird of the same name which devours the bodies of the Indians when they die. "The bones are then powdered and mixed with an intoxicating drink which is imbibed by all the relatives, the idea underlying this repugnant custom being that it is better to be inside a friend than inside an insect or reptile."

The Uaupés, who live in enormous communal huts 160 feet long and 40 feet high, center their religious rites around a devil-god called Juripari and the sect's ceremonies are so secretive that any unmarried woman of the tribe who beholds them is immediately put to death. "The ritual of Juripari is still, in large measure, one of the unsolved mysteries of the great forests," he comments.

The Uaupés River along the banks of which these tribes live is more usually known as the Uaupés and the first sketchy references to it come in the accounts of the sixteenth-century Spanish explorers Hernan Perez de Quesada (1538) and Philipp von Hutten (1541). Various missions were established in the region during the centuries that followed but few survived until late in the nineteenth century. The Uaupé Indians appear to have been little influenced by European contact.

Probably the most thorough exploration of the Amazon in the last century was that made by the American naval lieutenant William Herndon who, while at Valparaiso, was ordered by the U.S. Navy to traverse the Amazon from beginning to end.

He started the journey into unfamiliar terrain somewhat fussily (I had occasion afterwards to laugh at our fastidiousness in objecting to a mutton chop broiled upon a coal of cow dung," but by the time he reached the sea, was a confirmed Amazonophile-as all its long-term visitors seem to be.

Herndon's journey began in August 1853 and in his **Exploration of the Valley of the Amazon** (Washington D.C., 1853) he frequently came into contact with the Indians and their superstitions. Encountering a tribe of Cholomes at Tingo Maria, 335 miles east of Lima, he had his first sight of blowguns (*pucuna*), eight feet long and topped with a squirrel's tooth for a sight. Its owner, he learned, would not fire the weapon at a carrion bird because that would magically destroy the efficacy of all the poison in his gourd. Nor would he fire it at a snake because that would bend the blowgun into the snake's sinuous shape. Similarly, the Cholomes believed, a rifle fired at a crocodile would twist the weapon.

AN OCCULT GUIDE TO SOUTH AMERICA

The lieutenant was distressed by what had happened to the Indian in the three centuries of "progress" since the white man came. "It is sad to see (their) condition. . . . They make no progress in civilization and are taught nothing. The generally good, hardworking and well-meaning padres who also attempt anything like improvement seem contented to teach them the doctrines of the church, observance of its ceremonies and to repeat the doctrine like a parrot without having the least idea of what is meant to be conveyed. The priests say it is the fault of the Indian—that he cannot understand."

But, on one occasion, when he was taken to some ceremonies where Indians were singing to cure the sick, Herndon was enchanted by their incantations. "I had heard nothing like this before. The tones were so low, so faint, so guttural and at the same time so sweet and clear that I could scarcely believe they came from human throats; they seemed fitting sounds in which to address spirits from another world."

Several early visitors to the Amazon, notably Father Carvajal and Captain Orellana, made mention of the robust female Indian warriors, the Amazons, from whom the region got its name. Whether or not these women were mythical, the Jesuit Acufia commented, "there is nothing more common than the report of these women who dwell here." He was told by the Tupinamba Indians that "they are women of great valor who have always kept themselves from ordinary intercourse with men."

In the mid-eighteenth century, a French visitor, Carlos de la Condamine, was told the women had retired to the mountains of Guiana or the upper Rio Negro. "But old Indians remembered hearing their fathers speak of them; and the curious ornaments of green stone worn as amulets were ascribed to them." The stones were said to have been given to the men who visited them annually to propagate their race, an encounter that produced female children only. All others were destroyed. The men, of course, went home, returning for stud duties the following year.

In a narrative about his first voyage to the New World, Christopher Columbus mentioned hearing of the women and Sir Walter Raleigh in 1595 affirmed that they lived in Guiana and had sexual relations with men only in April. "At that time all the Kings of the borders assemble and the Queenes of the Amazons, and after the Queenes have chosen, the rest cast lots for their Valentines. This one monthe they feast, daunce and drinke of their wines in abundance, and the moone being done they all depart to their owne provinces. . ."

The green stones, *muira-kitans*, that are usually connected with these stories are of a hard crystalline rock, generally jade, feldspar or quartz. They are highly prized even today, and are reputed to cure certain diseases.

Although the heady days of exploring the Amazon in the fashion of Herndon and other pioneers are long past, and tribes of nomadic Indians are hardly likely to be encountered by today's casual visitor, just to visit this majestic river still has its rewards. In actual fact, Brazilians refer to its upper stretches as the river Solimaes, and it is only where this fast flowing reddish current merges with the inky black Rio Negro just east of the city of Manaus that it actually becomes the Amazon. The "meeting of the water," as it is termed, is a famous spot, not only symbolically but because the currents remain apart-flowing side by side without blending for many miles—and are easily distinguished by their separate colors.

Manaus (pop. 300,000,) though a bit shabby, with its downtown cathedral surrounded by cheap clothing stores and bargain marts, is a surprisingly big city. This is mainly because of its former glory as the center of a rubber trade which made many local fortunes. The trade began to decline around the turn of the century after Asian plantations began to undercut rubber prices, but such local landmarks as the floating dock (built by the British to cope with fast changing river levels), the Amazonas Theatre (still in use) where Caruso sang on opening night in 1899, and a wrought-iron market designed by Eiffel (of Paris tower fame) remain in sleepy splendor.

The seven hundred-seat theater, restored in 1974, is replete with chandeliers, marble columns, parquet floors, elegant seats made from jacaranda wood and plush velvet, sculpted busts of literary and musical figures, allegorical paintings and elaborately decorated ceilings. The original stage backdrop depicts a rather romanticized version of "The Meeting of the Waters" complete with nymphs and dolphins.

Actually, dolphins may be seen in the Amazon beyond the famous meeting place (12 miles east of Manaus) and an Indian legend explains that the two species, like the currents themselves, were actually warring tribes, transformed by the gods to avoid the bloodshed of their inevitable squabbles. It is still possible for these botos to assume human form, the legend says, and occasionally they do so, appearing at riverbank parties to attract maidens who can only confirm their real identity by looking for the hole in the top of their heads.

The most colorful section of Manaus, as might be expected, is the waterfront mercado. Apart from predictable wares you'll see candies, incense, herbs, and other artifacts for the practice of macumba, the Brazilian voodoo which is centered mostly in the state of Bahia to the southeast (see chapter 11).

The market itself does not cater to tourists, but in adjoining streets some Manaus stores offer for sale "toy" blowguns described by the distributor as "a very simple yet precise hunting instrument." They are constructed by the Macu Indians of the upper Rio Negro who make them from two palm tubes, one inserted inside the other and glued with tree resin. The darts are palmwood slivers which, in the bush, are tipped with curare poison.

When the riverside market closes around 1:00 P.M., the stallholders sit around and have lunch, often feasting on such specialties as the hard-shelled bodo; the basslike tambaqui and other local fish, pirarucu and pacu.

In one especially rich fishing area of the Amazon known as Manaquiri, more than one thousand varieties of fish abound, among them both the tambaqui (which is attracted by the seeds of the rubber tree) and the popular pirarucu—often sought on the Madeira River by Indians beating the water with the toxic timbo plant which stuns the fish.

The market is watched over by an ominous flock of big black birds with the appearance of vultures who leave their habitat on nearby corrugated iron roofs and descend to the space between the stalls to compete with mangy dogs for whatever fish heads, chunks of moldy meat, or other debris might have escaped the sweepers' hoses or brooms.

Here and there steps lead to the river where small boats dock. At the eastern end, known as La Rampa, a flotilla of boats await passengers for the interior. For hundreds of miles around, practically the only method of transport up into the jungle is by boat. The passengers, usually residents of these far-flung villages or traders carrying wares to therm, live in hammocks on deck for days at a time. For tourists, such trips may seem romantic but are not recommended.

It is easier to get a taste of the jungle by taking one of the tours which traverse the tangle of *igarapes* ('canoe paths") south of the main river, paths which the Indians claim are tracks of the enormous water serpent Mai d' Agua ("Mother of the water"). These extend for miles, sometimes barely wide enough for a boat to pass between the submerged trees, occasionally wandering into waterways wide enough for a flotilla. Such a trip is a delight, yielding glimpses of beautifully colored birds: the jarpim with yellow striped wings; *jarcas* or white herons; a flock of green parrots. The olive green *uirapuru* With its red tail has a voice so enchanting that primitive tribes believe that a potion made from the ashes of its burned body is a cure for unrequited love.

Unless you make the trip at night it is unlikely you will see any crocodiles, and the swarms of deadly *piranha* (which can strip a body of its flesh in seconds) and the immense *anaconda*, said to grow to a length of 30 feet, are hardly ubiquitous. Nor are there many reports of the Mapinguari—the Amazon equivalent of the Abominable Snowman—a fearsome creature with claws, thick red body hair, and a reputed immunity to bullets unless shot through its navel.

Practically speaking, of course, if you habitually bathed in Amazon waters you would have to watch out for such real life predators as the *piranha* (which grow to more than a foot long and whose sharp teeth are often used as cutting instruments) and the even more insidious *candiru*—which are attracted by the odor of urine and have a nasty habit of swimming up human orifices and lodging there until surgically removed, unless a fatal hemorrhage occurs first.

The piranha, though as edible as other fish, is hard to catch; its razor-sharp teeth bite through nets, lines, and occasionally the fisherman's fingers. The biggest variety are the black piranha of the Rio Negro which attain a length of 18 inches and weigh five pounds. Caught, stuffed, and lacquered, they are sometimes sold as souvenirs in Manaus stores.

Despite these natural dangers, quite a few natives live in palm-thatched shanties on the banks of the flooded forests—the trees survive presumably because of their respite from January to July when the river drops as much as 30 feet, leaving them high and dry—in ramshackle houses on wooden stilts.

The traditional Indian forest dwelling is a single-roomed hut of branches roofed with leaves, straw, or sape grass. Some tribes, the Xingu of Brazil's central Mato Grosso, for example, prefer communal huts that house up to fifty or more people, usually of the same family.

As you continue along the *igarapes* you'll frequently see strips of jute, from which coffee sacks are woven, and household washing hang out to dry side by side; occasionally a woman will be seen laundering clothes in the murky river, or a shallow canoe will pass carrying some householder with his load of firewood.

A call might be made at a small house beside a clump of rubber trees whose crop is tapped annually (such trees usually produce for fifty years or more) and with this and a flock of hens, a vegetable garden in hollow logs above the water, and regular fishing, its inhabitants manage to eke out a living.

For the visitor to Manaus, the next best thing to encountering the Indians in person is to take a look at the Ethnological Museum or, better still, the Museo do Indio, adjoining the Santa Terezina church on the Rue Duq de Caxias (a fifty-cent taxi ride from downtown). It is open from 8:30 to 11:00 A. M. and 2.00 to 5:00 P.M. every day but Sunday. Several rooms on the second floor contain tableaux, photographs, and artifacts including life-size paintings of typical riverbank clearings and cutaway models of huts containing hammocks and utensils. One room is devoted to funeral ceremonies and includes a macabre "corpse" covered with straw in a wooden coffin; others display necklaces of feathers, beads and teeth as well as pottery, arrows, pieces of amber and bone, drums and plaited mats, sandals and reed bags decorated with radiant butterflies made from feathers. There are window cases of brightly colored flowers among which dwell—almost imperceptibly—equally brilliantly plumaged birds.

Living so close to nature, the Indians naturally had identities for all the living things around them. Dr. Couto de Magalhaes wrote in 1876 that they believed in three superior deities—the sun, Guaracy, creator of all animals; the moon, Jacy, creator of plants; and Peruda, god of love who promotes the reproduction of humans. Beneath these were a whole pantheon of lesser gods such as Guarapuru, protector of the birds; Anhanga (field game); Uauyaro (fishes); and so on ... ..each in turn has as many inferior gods as the Indians admit classes. . . until every lake and river and kind of animal or plant has its protective genius or mother."

When Herbert J. Smith arrived late in the last century he was also warned of many dangerous spirits about which to be cautious. In **Brazil, the**

AN OCCULT GUIDE TO SOUTH AMERICA

Amazons and the Coast (Sampson Low, London, 1879) Smith told of the *anhanga*, a white deer with fiery eyes whose vision produced fever and sometimes madness, the *curupira*, a fearsome little brown man with green teeth whose feet pointed backwards so that running away from his tracks led one into his grasp; and a dwarf with one foot so big that when the sun was hot he lay down and held it above his head for shade. But most feared of all was the Tucano-via, a bird with the evil eye that killed everything it looked at, even after a hunter cuts off its head.

The Amazon has always been renowned for its flora and fauna, at least since the middle of the last century when the English naturalist Henry Bates spent eleven years collecting 15,000 specimens of insects, birds, reptiles, and mammals, of which more than half were totally new to scientific records of the time. In his 1863 classic work, ***The Naturalist on the River Amazons*** (Dover Books reprint), Bates mentions the universal belief in the "monster water serpent... many score fathoms in length" and identifies the Mundurucus, inhabiting the right bank of the Tapajos, as perhaps the most numerous and formidable surviving tribe.

Knowledge about the Amazon was hard won over the centuries by a series of courageous explorers and scientists who braved vicious stinging insects, spiders, centipedes, jaguars, anacondas, boa constrictors, and alligators, to name but a few of the discouragements. The twenty nine-year-old Frenchman Carlos de la Condamine not only charted unknown rivers but was the first to bring back quinine, rubber samples, and curare. Notorious as a deadly poison, curare has applications in modem medicine as a muscle relaxant, though it is still used by some jungle tribes for killing small animals. On larger animals the effects take too long; in humans the simple antidote is to rub salt immediately into the wound. The Pebas, who live north of the Amazon near the Nape River, make an antidote to curare by mixing urine, honey, and ripe bananas.

Hunting in the jungle is not entirely an economic matter, Nunes Pereira has written, but helps also to increase the hunter's control and self-esteem. Monkey meat is much appreciated, being regarded as an aphrodisiac, but the big prize Is the *anta*, or Amazonian bull, one of the few animals that can stand its ground against the dreaded *sucuri*, or boa constrictor.

Despite increasingly lengthy and often hazardous journeys, occasional explorers still go in search of the Indians. One such was Tom Sterling who traveled way up the Catrimari River in search of the estimated one thousand remaining aborigines of the Yanoama tribe. Their magical beliefs, it seems, have changed little throughout the centuries. Yanoamas still put magic stones in rivers to bring fish within range; sniff a hallucinogenic powder called opera to induce visions and call up spirits; and don't believe in burial, preferring to powder the bones of their dead relatives and swallow them.

In his **The Amazon** (Time-Life Books, 1974) Sterling reports a conversation with a local priest, Father Giovanni Suffirio, who single-handedly operates a mission at Cujubim Falls on the Serra do Pimento. The padre told him that Yanoama beliefs resembled the "evil eye" fears of his native Piedmont Region and that none of the Indians would admit their real names believing, in common with many native peoples, that to learn somebody's true name gives power over him.

To the Indian, the universe is thronged with the souls of the dead, with spirits of water and jungle, and all must be appeased if life is to run smoothly. Today, a century after Henry Bates's report, the pajé, that blend of sorcerer and medicine man, is still regarded as an essential member of the community. It is he who remembers the sacred history of the tribe, initiates the ceremonies, and takes charge of the masks and sacred objects. He still foretells the weather and is the one to whom the sick turn for intercession with the spirits.

But the isolation of the past is being eliminated, and it is possible to believe that eventually there will be nowhere left in the world that is out of reach. At present the only roads leading from Manaus, to anywhere at all, are but two: to Itacoatiara, 180 miles east through farmlands and virgin forest; and to Manacapuru, 54 miles to the west. (There are two daily buses to Manacapuru, a trip that takes four hours.)

Nearing completion, however, is the ambitious Trans-Amazonica Highway, a 3,400-mile link from the Peruvian border to Recife on Brazil's east coast. At its nearest point, this new highway passes about 120 miles south of Manaus.

Not far from Manaus near the Tapajoz River, a tribe called the Maué have a near-monopoly on the production of guarana, a substance with a high caffeine content. It is made from the pounded seeds of a plant called *paullinia sorbilis* which is grated and mixed with water to be used as a medicine (called *capo*) against diarrhea and fever.

AN OCCULT GUIDE TO SOUTH AMERICA

Guarana, kept in hard sticks, is always grated with the bony tongue of the pirarucu fish which is kept in a buckskin purse, for the Indians believe that to use a metallic grater would cause the substance to lose its magical power.

A Portuguese ethnologist who visited the Maué in 1939 reported that they believed guarana to be a lucky charm which brings rain, protects the farms, cures diseases, and brings success in love and war.

Some of these beliefs have been confirmed by the French pharmacologist Paul le Cointe who describes guarana as a refreshment, tonic, heart relaxant, and curative for various ills. Its use is widespread in northern Brazil and it is even the base of a popular carbonated drink.

In Maué legend, the moon god sent the guarana berry as "burning stones of fire" into the eyes of a dead child who had been killed by a rattlesnake due to black magic. The stones grew into saplings which later bore a fruit with the appearance of human eyes. Guara-na, in the local language, means "living eyes."

So vast are the distances in northern Brazil that the new Trans-Amazonica Highway won't even come close to the world's largest ranch, a 6,000-square-mile chunk of Amazon jungle under development by United States millionaire Daniel Keith Ludwig, sometimes tagged as the world's richest man. The ranch, one-third the size of Israel and containing four cities, already has rice fields and livestock. It will eventually be planted with 70 million trees of a fast-growing African variety known as *gmelina arborea* which are expected to produce one thousand tons of paper pulp per day by 1980.

At present, Manaus is accessible only by air (a new jetport was opened in 1975) and by boat from Belém to the east. This trip takes four or five days and runs weekly on a casual schedule. Passenger ships also run between Manaus and Rio, an eleven- or twelve-day trip costing anywhere from $150 and up.

Varig's weekly flight from Miami (Wednesday nights) takes about six hours and heads onwards to Brasilia. If, as sometimes happens, the airport at Manaus is fogged in you may find yourself diverted to Belém on your northern entrance to Brazil, and as there's nowhere at the Belém airport to change money it's advisable to have a few loose dollars with you. In fact that's good advice wherever you go.

AN OCCULT GUIDE TO SOUTH AMERICA

Once at Manaus, your best bet is the luxurious Tropical hotel, relatively new to the airport but about 15 miles from downtown to which it is connected by free hourly bus service. The Tropical, one of a chain, is expensive but lavish, with solid oak doors, spacious lobbies, halls stretching to infinity, a swimming pool, and offering memorable cuisine. Rates are about $30 for a single, $45 for a double.

Downtown are the first-class Amazonas and the lpanema (around $20 for a single, $28 for a double) with cheaper hotels to be found around the cathedral. If you need more specific information take a taxi to the downtown Hotel Amazonas where the Salvatur Tourist Agency in the lobby displays a full list of local accommodations with prices. You might want to try spending a night at the Agency's own Floating Lodge on Lake January from which you'll find it convenient to take jungle tours both by day and night.

Because Manaus is a free port, everybody's bag is carefully checked at the airport on leaving. There are forms to be filled out and long delays, so allow yourself plenty of time to clear customs.

If you have ample time for your traveling you might decide to wait for the right boat to come along and cruise leisurely down to the Amazon's mouth, almost 1,000 miles to the east at Belém. Founded in 1616, this city (pop. 800,000) quickly became the major port of northern Brazil, one which offered access to the entire northern part of the continent.

The most colorful part of Belém is the famous Ver-O-Peso (Meaning "check the weight") market—one of the largest on the continent—which is jam-packed with leopard tails, dried boa constrictor heads, crocodile teeth, and sparrowhawk skeletons to frighten ghosts away, as well as more conventional food, fish, and flowers.

It is one of the places where the thriving Bataque sect organizes colorful, mystic ceremonies which are a mélange of singing, dancing, praying, and mysticism of the type we shall examine more closely in Bahia, our next destination.

Be sure to sample some of the characteristic local foods while in Belém: the sauce-covered roast duck dish known as pato no tucupi; tocaca (manioc, cherry pepper, dried prawns); the various fish dishes made with the popular pirarucu; and the more exotic tortoise (casqinho de nucua) or baked alligator tail (cauda de jacara ao forno).

AN OCCULT GUIDE TO SOUTH AMERICA

You might also like to take a trip down river to the island of Marajo, where you can stay on a buffalo ranch in the dry season (in the rainy season the island, only three feet above river level, is mostly flooded) and explore some of the one hundred or more burial mounds. When these were first discovered in 1870 they were found to contain distinctive, richly decorated pottery in which the ancient Arua Indians had buried the ashes of their cremated dead. The German archaeologist L. Netto, uncovering two mounds in the shape of a tortoise in 1890, found beautifully decorated urns containing large-sized women's bones which suggested an origin for the legend of the Amazons.

The star attraction of Belém, however, is a natural phenomenon—a thunderous boom tide known as the Pororoca, caused by unusually high (12-foot) waves crashing into the 30-mile-wide mouth of the river with a roar that can be heard for miles. It is, however, a relatively rare event.

Moving eastward from Belém in the state of Pari we encounter the Tenetehara, a tribe which overlaps into the neighboring state of Maranhao and who, despite sporadic contact with missionaries for more than three centuries, retain many of their original beliefs. Among these tenets are faith in the power of the pajé to control the spirits of the dead—*ekwe* for those who die naturally; *azang* for those who die an ugly death, having broken the incest laws or been bewitched. Dead animals also have spirits (*piwara*) and these, too, can be controlled by the pajé or shaman who has acquired the power to -call" (i.e., be possessed by) them. Three of the strongest spirits—the forest demon (Maranauwa), the jaguar (Zawara), and the toad (kurura), who must be summoned by swallowing live coals re so powerful, says Columbia University anthropologist Charles Wagley, that no modern shamans dare to "call" them.

The toad, incidentally, plays an important part in what Gilberto Freyre refers to as Afro-Brazilian sexual magic, becoming "the protector of the faithless wife who, in order to deceive her husband, has but to take a needle threaded with green silk, make with it a cross on the face of the individual to be affected, and afterwards sew up the eyes of the toad. On the other hand, in order to hold a lover, a woman must keep a toad constantly in a pot beneath her bed. In this case, the toad is a live one, fed on cow's milk."

Anyway, as we continue our magical journey, southward and east toward the coast of Bahia, it will become increasingly evident that the fetishism of the imported African slaves, the belief in spirits of the native Indians, and the totenism of both fused with the already slightly tainted Catholicism of the colonizing Portuguese to produce a set of Brazilian religious beliefs that are entirely unique.

AN OCCULT GUIDE TO SOUTH AMERICA

Chapter 2

Salvador

City of the Spirits

The city of Salvador (pop. 1 million) is the capital of Brazil's coastal state of Bahia and is itself often referred to as "Bahia." For two hundred years, after its founding in 1549, it was Brazil's first capital, and it has never ceased to be the country's most magical and exciting city. It positively throbs with life and color, its energy bubbling over several times a year into uninhibited carnivals and fiestas that fill the streets with music and dancing.

Renowned for Colonial architecture, baroque churches, and marvelous islands and beaches, Salvador is a favorite haven for artists and writers. It is built on two levels: the waterfront Cidade Baixia which sprawls along the coast in two directions and the more modern Cidade Alta on the cliffs above to which it is connected by giant elevators.

One of the city's best-known diversions— if such an integral part of its life could be described so lightly—is the *candomblé* ritual, a fusing of ancient and modern religions into something at least as pagan as it is Christian. Almost two-thirds of Bahia's population is of African descent and the original settlers brought their rituals and religion along with them.

Since most of Brazil's early records and files of the slave traffic were destroyed in the 1890s, after the birth of the Brazilian republic, the candomblé rituals remained as one of the few links with the past.

Salvador's airport is almost 20 miles from town with the route skirting the ocean most of the way. It costs 75 cruzeiros by taxi but an air-conditioned bus makes the trip for only 10 cr. The tourist desk in the airport lobby is helpful and offers a map. The bus starts and ends its journey at the Praca de Sé, adjoining the Cathedral de Sé and as this is close to the elevator which leads to the lower town you might find it convenient to stay fairly close. The

AN OCCULT GUIDE TO SOUTH AMERICA

Praca de Sé and its neighboring plaza usually shelter circles of men watching an instant lottery or resisting the wiles of some local con man. The headquarters of the local spiritism movement is just down the block so that, too, creates plenty of pedestrian traffic.

The more lavish, more expensive hotels tend to be located at the far end of the Ave. 7 de Septembre, near the Victoria section of town, but two short blocks north of de Sé is the Palace hotel which is not particularly palatial nor cheap (about $15 for a single with breakfast, $22 for a double) but is certainly clean and comfortable enough. An even better suggestion at around the same price might be the stylish 45-room Hotel Pelhourhino (Rua Alfredo Brito, 22, tel: 24517) which is reminiscent of New Orleans. It has a terrace restaurant overlooking the old town below and oodles of captivating charm.

The Pelhourhino area is one of the oldest parts of Salvador, being the place where slaves were once beaten (pelhourhino means "stick') and is said by some to harbor the uneasy energy of those fearsome days. After 353 years, slavery ended here in 1883, one year later than the rest of Brazil, but there's still a certain morbid fascination with its consequences (not the least of which is candomblé) and one of the local sights pointed out to tourists is "Laziness Street," a harborside lane where slaves were allowed a 10-minute rest stop each day to take a drink of water. One tour stop always seems to be at one of the sugar cane stands where sticks of cane are fed into a crushing machine ("Just like the slaves used to do," the guide whispers), the resulting dark green juice being poured over ice and proffered in a tall glass

The slaves were first brought here in the early sixteenth century to work on the sugar, cocoa, and coffee plantations, products for which Brazil is still famous today.

Coffee plays its part in Afro-Brazilian sexual magic according to Gilberto Freyre who quotes Basilio de Magalhaes as saying it is taken with much sugar and "a few clots of the menstrual fluid of the sorceress herself."

Brazil's original influx of slaves came from the former Portuguese African colonies of Angola, the Mina Coast, and Guinea. The Bantu-speaking Angolans went mainly into agriculture whereas the others and, in particular, the nagos, an elitist cult who succeeded in setting down roots for their native religion in the new country, took up domestic tasks as servants in the homes.

Under slavery it was hard for the cults to make much headway, and police repression (always wary of the political implications of black gatherings) further restricted their growth. But late in the eighteenth century, the influx of slaves to work in the gold mines slowed down and this aided the concentration of nagos in Bahia. Gradually the mines closed down and the former slaves moved onwards.

The cults range all the way from Bahia's candomblé, which prides itself on the purity of its Yoruban or Dahomey (West African states closely associated with the slave trade) derivations to the macumba of Rio whose roots are mainly in the Bantu-speaking peoples of Angola and the Congo region. The different cult centers (sietas) tend to be snobbish about their respective beliefs with candomblé *aficionados* sneering at macumba practitioners and almost everybody feeling superior to the sects whose native American influences have led them to practice what the others term caboclo. In truth, of course, almost all the cults are a mixture and have been additionally influenced by Indian rituals. Some caboclo practitioners wear elaborate Red Indian feathered headdresses and feather anklets.

The Portuguese began their conquest of Amazonia in the seventeenth century, prompted by their search for spices, but in this area their work force was Indian rather than Salvador Negro and the inevitable religious cults developed in a different manner.

At Cearn and Paraiba in the northeast, the Indian influence triumphed, resulting in *catimbo* which has little connection with the African cults. The latter manifest themselves in dancing to drum rhythms, but *catimbo*—which seems to have its origin in the native cult of *jurema* (a potion extracted from the bark of the mimosa which offers hallucinogenic visions to those who drink it—is a closed religion with no dancing.

Pelhourhino, Bahia's original slave quarter, still packs plenty of punch today: pedestrians and taxis compete furiously for space in its narrow cobbled streets, and everybody seems to be hustling something. An easy target for locals are the visitors to the Museo do Ciudad, but you should certainly be one of them for it is there that most people get their first introduction to candomblé, that special Bahian brand of magic.

It has been remarked that Brazilians are officially Catholic but in reality pagans, and that unique blend of spiritual faith that makes the country so susceptible to its numerous faith healers appears to have its roots here in Salvador. If Brazil has a mystical center, then Bahia is the place.

AN OCCULT GUIDE TO SOUTH AMERICA

The Portuguese were always different from the average colonialist. Possessing neither the white Anglo-Saxon Protestant traits of the British, nor the Inquisitorial uprightness of the Catholic French, Italian, or Spanish, the Portuguese bloodline was "mongrelized" early by its African contacts. As colonial masters in Brazil, the Portuguese were already tolerantly inclined towards the pagan beliefs, not only of the native Indians but also of the black slaves they imported to handle the back-breaking labor essential to empire building. The consequence was a curious acceptance of customs, beliefs, and gods that would have been an anathema to the "one true faith" anywhere else.

Numerous writers have pointed out that sexual mores had a great deal to do with this; it was hard for a master to sleep with his superstitious slaves and not become at least partly prey to their beliefs. In any case it was, as always, easier to bend with the prevailing wind and accept things than to make an issue of them. And so a tolerance of "heathen" customs grew up alongside the official rejection of them.

Half a century ago there were still complaints about the manner in which the candomblé rituals and practices were encroaching upon Salvador's day-to-day life. A letter in the Salvador newspaper *A Tarde* for December 9, 1935, said: "Now the African cult is to be seen even in the best residential areas." But formal acceptance came long ago, and candomblé sessions are now touted as tourist attractions. Local politicians serve as sponsors (*ogans*) and, despite allegations that some of the sessions turn into "religious orgies," in actual fact the spectators are segregated by sex at different sides of the room, no smoking or drinking is permitted, and the "services" are as respectable as those in any Catholic church, which, in fact, they closely resemble.

The most bizarre application of this can be noted in world-renowned Bonfim Cathedral (to which we'll return in a moment) where the statues of the saints would certainly prove unfamiliar to those reared in orthodox religious households; here the gods of the slave-exporting Yoruba nation have been totally fused with those of the Christian faith.

Naturally they are all black, and at first glance most appear, too, to be women; the explanation for this lies less in a premature feminism that in the fact that most gods are presumed to be bisexual, embracing neither sex exclusively.

AN OCCULT GUIDE TO SOUTH AMERICA

The saints, then, all have two names: the familiar one of the Catholic faith and his/her equivalent in the Yoruba tongue. The candomblé gods are known as *orishas*. Candomblé itself is sometimes used to refer to the *tereiro* or place where the ceremonies are conducted: at least 920 are registered with the police in Salvador itself) and several books list their characteristics and equivalents.

Oshala (sometimes known as *Oshalufan*), for example, represents Christ himself. His special day is Friday, his necklace milky white beads, his sacrifice a guinea fowl, white hen, pigeon, or she goat.

Some other *orishas* with their syncretic equivalents are Shango (St. Jerome), Oba)Joan of Arc), Omolu (St. Lazarus), Oshossi (St. George), and the popular war god Ogoun (St. Anthony). And mention must be made of Eshu, sometimes erroneously identified with the devil but more correctly regarded as a messenger, a mediator between gods and humans who must himself be a propitiated first at candomblé feasts unless the participants are literally asking for trouble. Eshu (or Exu in the native spelling) often carries a trident and a mallet with its handle shaped like a human head, and is especially propitiated at crossroads (usually with offerings of popcorn and flour mixed with palm oil) where he is presumed to rule.

Often an *ebo*, or a small box or vase containing a dead chicken, a silver coin, piece of cloth, fruit and popcorn, all covered with palm oil, will be left at a crossroads to ward off the malevolent Exu, but the *ebo* also has other functions. For example, it can be left in somebody's doorway, or along the route they are expected to pass either to bring them misfortune or to transfer an illness.

The gods of candomblé carry both African and Catholic names, but, Roger Bastide writes, "Catholicism is only a white mask over a black face. There is a touching faithfulness to the African culture—music and myths are the same as in Africa, necklaces and bracelets with the symbolic colors of gods are identical on both sides of the Atlantic. Ships from Africa carry to Brazil all the ingredients necessary for the performance of the cult and often black Brazilians go to Nigeria to be initiated,"

In Africa, Roger Bastide says in **Brasil, Terre des Contrastes** (Hachette, 1957), priestly functions are mostly carried out by men; in Brazil, women, more conservative, replace the men.

There are numerous *orishas* of the waters, the most famous being

AN OCCULT GUIDE TO SOUTH AMERICA

Yémanja, the *Mai d'Agua* whose long green tresses and misty eyes have lured many an innocent to their doom.

Like Lorelei, Y'manja sings temptingly as she floats along the surface of the river, lake, or sea; she is celebrated both in Bahia and Rio on February 2 with annual processions of supplicants dressed in white and carrying on their heads all kinds of toilet articles that the goddess might find useful. One of the Bahia processions is to a small lake called the Diquéé on the outskirts of town, but Yémanja is to be found wherever there is water and she is celebrated at many points around the bay including the beaches of Rio Vermelho, and Itapua.

Devotees of candomblé take it so seriously that some of them virtually hand over the direction of their lives to their particular *orisha*, accepting the guidance that comes to them much as people in other societies tend to be influenced by astrology.

In addition to the leader (a *mai de santo* or *pai de santo*) and the drummers, each cult center also has from six to twenty initiates who have become *filhas de santo* (daughters of saints) and whose part in the candomblé ceremonies is something like that of a Greek chorus. They dance ecstatically and with complete abandon until at some point the appropriate *orisha* takes possession of them and thereby communicates indirectly with all present. Occasionally, but rarely, there will be a male initiate, a *filio de santo*.

Not everybody cares to be initiated, for it entails responsibilities. First comes complete seclusion during which the initiate's head is shaved and stripes painted on the face (a modem substitute for ancient tribal scars). Then an African fruit, the *obi*, is placed in the initiates's hand and musical invocations by the male a*tabuques* (drummers) call for the appropriate *orisha* to come and take possession of the novice's body. (This, of course, is a not uncommon event at candomblé where people are often seen to writhe about, contort themselves, fall on the floor, and afterwards to remember nothing of it.)

To verify her acceptance by the *orisha*, one observer wrote, an initiate may be required to undergo rigorous physical tests without showing any evidence of being harmed. This could be having to place her hands in boiling palm oil, or to chew on thistle leaves or even to swallow the flaming wicks of candies. The initiation ritual of ducking the candidate in water is meant to signify a symbolic transference from the profane to the divine world.

AN OCCULT GUIDE TO SOUTH AMERICA

Once having given evidence of her possession by a god, the neophyte retires to seclusion for seventeen days with a *xaoro* (anklet of bells) around her. A public ceremony called Orunko is the special occasion when the new initiate, by then known as a *filho de santo*, makes her debut and the name of her particular *orisha* is revealed. After this she remains for long enough to learn the candomblé rituals and songs before returning to her day-to-day life.

When a filha dies her ceremonial costume and accompanying paraphernalia are dropped into the sea so that the waves will take them back to the shores of Africa.

Originally the candomblé was always a temple with clay walls and an earth floor, on which devotees had to walk with bare feet. But these days candomblé are held in all manner of places (the Salvador tourist office steers tourists in a hurry to one near the airport called *Alto da Itinga*—it's signposted) and the initiation rites which used to last seven years have been trimmed to just three months.

Once initiated as *filha* ("daughter of saint') or *filho* ("son of saint"), the devotee has an enhanced standing in the religious community and many years of candomblé observance and practice might lead to a *mai de santo* ("mother of saint') classification which generates a degree of respect, even awe.

The City Museum (where this brief lecture began) is a good place to start an acquaintance with candomblé, for it is there you can see full-size representations of many of the *orishas* in complete costume and carrying the ritual implements (staff, crown, brazen fan, spears, double axes, etc.) with which they are associated. The museum is open 8:30 A.M. to noon, 1:30 to 5:00 P.M. daily except Sundays.

Most tourists, of course, rarely get to see really dramatic candomblé sessions. It is not that the nightly candomblé are not authentic, but rather that, being open to all, they are less revealing than some of the more private ceremonies. As one of these latter reaches its climax, participants in a state of self-induced ecstasy are seen whirling around, beating their heads against walls, writing on the ground, or possibly strangling a chicken and tearing its flesh as the hot blood splatters their face and clothes. Drinking the still-warm blood from a glass, the devotee is quite likely to chew fragments of glass, apparently without noticing. Later, exhausted, bruised, and bloody she will lie helpless on the floor, tired and aching, but possibly considering the price well worth paying for a few moments of transcendent bliss which she could identify with possession by the spirits.

A skeptical observer might note that the mothers-of-saints and, even more, the fathers-of-saints, appear prosperous and well dressed in sharp contrast to the poverty of their worshippers. "They don't work," a French visitor muttered darkly. "We have a word for such people back home."

Candomblé is found in other parts of Brazil but its stronghold has always been on the coast of Bahia, undoubtedly because that area was the one in which most of the original slaves were concentrated.

In general, the cult's appeal is to the poorer and less sophisticated members of the black community. "All this low stuff ought to be done away with. It's a sign of a very backward people. It has even disappeared in Africa.... Only in Bahia do these old customs hang on," the nephew of a prominent *babalao* (cult leader) told Donald Pierson.

Indeed, the author of **Negroes in Brazil** continued, in his experience it was the whites who were more tolerant of the ceremonies than either the blacks or those of mixed blood, who were seeking to establish themselves socially and usually disassociated themselves from what they felt were lower class elements.

"The primary social function which the candomblé appears to serve," Pierson observed, "is that of reinforcing by way of the collective experiences of ritual and ceremony those attitudes and sentiments which distinguish the Africanos and their descendants from the European population and from the major portion of the mixed-bloods. By promoting a measure of solidarity and group consciousness it tends to slow up the process of acculturation . . ."

But a highly respected candomblé leader was more explicit: "The *Nago* (Yoruba) worships nature because he is realistic and wants to see what he worships. He can't see the Catholics' God."

Even a good folklore performance often embodies some of the candomblé rituals, performed by genuine devotees, albeit decked out in "showbiz finery." Most of Salvador's better nightclubs are out of town on the road to the airport (one such is the Marie Chela on Ave. Amanalina) and for convenience it's probably best to spend the $20 for a tour. This will include transport, dinner, show, and dancing. Turismo Xango (Ave. 7 de Septembre 1420) is reliable. Ask for the amiable and articulate Alex, who speaks English; not all guides do.

In addition to music on the one-stringed berimbaud and a taste of candomblé, the nightclub show is also likely to include a demonstration of *capoeira*, the distinctive foot fighting that the slaves originally brought with them from Africa and which faintly resembles Thai boxing except that the participants rarely seem to connect.

After the former slave quarter of Pelhourhino, the most interesting spot in Salvador is the Modelo market, across the plaza from the foot of the elevator in the old town. A distinctive statue standing nearby is by Mario Cravo and is called "Thoughts of the Mind." The Modelo market is located in a century-old building and is stuffed with the usual tourist wares plus some really nice examples of craftsmanship that are hard to inspect without the usual hard sell that accompanies all buying trips to places of this nature. But it is not so much the goods for sale that are interesting as the general ambience of the area around it. A pleasantly unpretentious upstairs restaurant has a sunny balcony overlooking the boat dock and, between that and the downstairs entrance to the market dozens of entrepreneurs cook and sell their own specialties. Special magical herbs and incenses are available, some of which can be smelled from a block away. On one corner is a well-frequented tourist office whose occupants are used to odd questions from Americans.

It is from this dock, beside the row of fruit stalls, that boats go to Itaparica which has been described as the most magical place in Brazil. Its pyramid-shaped temple at Mar Grande is the third point of an "esoteric triangle" which includes Sao Laurenco in Brasilia and Guaruya in Rjo. Mar Grande's sacred waters have been the site of many sacrifices to Urnania. The boat for Itaparica (7 cr.) leaves at 9:00, 10:30, and noon each day with additional boats every afternoon but Sunday. The sea can be rough for the 45-minute journey which sometimes entails transferring to a smaller boat once in the shallow waters of the island. You'll disembark at Mar Grande and can see the pyramid shaped temple, built by Brazil's Theosophical Society in 1967, atop a slight hill behind the harbor.

Mar Grande is a tiny community with little to offer but atmosphere. A 10-minute taxi ride will bring you to a bigger harbor (where the car ferry docks) and from which you can hop a VW bus for the half-hour ride to the island's northwestern tip where the community of Itaparica itself is located. Note the times of the buses and boats back unless you plan to stay on the island overnight. Itaparica is said to be where the most fervent candomblé in Brazil is practiced and it is in rural island communities like this that the worship tends to be most occult. The Grande Hotel de Itaparica (tel: 54555 in Salvador for reservations) is the island's best hotel, but accommodations in cheaper pensions are available.

There are also beaches at the charming fishing village of Arembepe, about 30 miles away, but getting there is a chore: first a 20 cr. taxi to the outlying Rodovaria bus station, and then a lengthy bus ride to Arembepe itself. A much easier route is along the coast via an Itapoan bus from the depot in the Praca da Sé, getting off at the last stop before it turns inland from the coast. This takes 35 minutes and costs less than two cruzeiros. You'll find yourself outside a noisy open air restaurant, jammed with happy drinkers and musicians (sometimes the musicians invade the buses in Salvador but instead of collecting from the passengers seem content to get their rides free).

A word of warning: in the rainy season storms arrive very suddenly in Bahia. One minute you'll be enjoying the sun, the next the roads seem lined with blood as the water washes the red soil from the hillsides.

Possibly the best-known landmark in Salvador are the twin yellow towers of Bonfim Cathedral which stands on a slight hill called Monte Serrat in the northern section of the city. The cobbled square in front of the church is invariably thronged with hawkers and gawkers, among whom are usually a handful of tourists buying, if nothing else, the brightly colored ribbons stamped *Lembranca Do Senhor O Bonfim da Bahia*. Sold by dozens of small boys, they are most often bought by young girls in search of a husband. The works of art on sale at nearby stalls are in a primitive style, reminiscent of Haiti, and more often than not consist of carvings made on flat wooden boards and then painted.

Bonfim is the scene of a ten-day religious festival in January when, to the accompaniment of constant drum-beating, the ceremonious "washing of the church" takes place.

It is traditional to make three wishes before entering the church, as Bonfim has some of the charisma of Lourdes. Many "miracles" have been recorded here and the evidences of these fill a small room off to one side. Here every inch of space on all four walls is covered with photographs of believers who came to be cured. Many accompany testimonials of gratitude for cures effected by the saints. Hanging grotesquely from the ceiling, are hundreds of wax reproductions of legs, arms, feet, heads, and other parts of the human anatomy, presumably representing cures. The room, always filled with people, is another impressive testimonial to the power of faith healing. Blend together a native Indian population, whose beliefs always included an assumption that the medicine man need only blow on or touch an affected limb to heal it, with the Yoruba descendants who had observed many miracles in their native African villages. Add to this mixture the true faith (and suggestibility) of Colonial Catholicism and what you have is an atmosphere where anything can happen.

In his book, ***The Moon and Two Mountains*** (Souvenir Press, London, 1966), Pedro McGregor describes the growth of Brazilian spiritualism which, beginning with the homeopathic ministrations of two doctors in 1840, blossomed into more than 3,000 societies and almost 2,000 homeopathic groups, all offering free spiritual healing via prescriptions dictated through mediums by spirit guides. Much of it stems from the popularity of a book, ***The Book of Spirits***, first written in 1856 by the Frenchman Allan Kardec, and containing 1,018 questions and answers about "the problem that has tortured the human mind since the dawn of history—"Is there a life after death? And what is the purpose of our life here?"

The Book of Spirits and subsequent works like ***The Mediums' Book*** and ***The Gospels According to Spiritism*** had a tremendous appeal to mystically minded Brazilians. They are still best sellers more than a century after Kardec's death and are largely responsible for an estimated total of four million practicing Kardecists in Brazil today.

The triumph of the movement is the establishment of a city, Palmelo, about 160 miles from Brasilia, where a spirit healer named Jeronimo Candido Comide cures the sick with the help of spiritual guides. "I am only an instrument," he says.

In his book documenting some of the better-known healers, Pedro McGregor tells the story of a remarkable man, José Arigo, who, despite a complete lack of medical training, cures people of tumors, cataracts, cysts, etc.—or did until he was jailed for "witch doctory"—with no other implements than a kitchen knife, nail scissors, and a scalpel. Nor is there any question of fraud, according to McGregor, who says that thousands have witnessed the operations and hundreds of others, including doctors, journalists and scientists, have signed testimonials to his skills.

Arigo, who never charges for his operations claims that he too is merely an instrument and is guided in his actions by a German surgeon, Dr. Fritz, who was killed in World War 1.

McGregor quotes the words of the judge who sentenced Arigo: "The man who, without being a doctor, determines the nature of a sickness or illness by their symptoms; who, without being a doctor, makes operations; who, claiming to be in 'control of a 'spirit,' in trance prescribes or operates or supplies herbs; who uses 'passes,' attitudes, postures, words, prayers, exorcisms or any other means to facilitate child births, cure a rebellious cough, snake bites, cancer, lower fever, tuberculosis, haemorrhage, cataracts, deafness, etc.—this citizen represents a tremendous danger to the health of an undetermined number of people whose custody unquestionably is entrusted upon the state."

But it is obvious where McGregor's sympathies be: "Surely," he asks, "the country's health problem would be better dealt with trying to find more Arigos, while encouraging more of the younger people to train for a medical career?"

Unstated but implied in the author's conclusions is the suggestion that must have occurred to many readers by now: that it is the very faith itself, manifested by thousands of followers, that is so effective in working the "miracles" so often reported by the faithful. In other words, believe strongly enough and it will come to pass.

The final triumph of Brazil's Kardecism, McGregor suggests, is that its appeal to the intellect gave the subject of spirit communication a new respectability. "Before its appearance in Brazil, all Negro cults, however often Brazilians resorted to them in secret, were dismissed as animistic, fetichistic mumbo jumbo. Kardecism was the bridge needed to span the gap between the black and white cults, and what attracted them mainly was that they practised magic which Kardec denied them."

One of the greatest results of Kardecism was the cult of umbanda. Rio de Janeiro was and is its stronghold, and it is there that our mystical tour takes us next.

Chapter 3

Rio

The Indians Come First

The combination of mountains, tropical forest, and sea which forms its backdrop makes Rio de Janeiro (pop. 5 million) one of the most spectacular cities in the world. Although no longer Brazil's capital (it followed Salvador in this role, and preceded Brasilia), it is one of the most popular tourist sites in South America, largely because of its fabulous beaches (year-round swimming), legendarily beautiful women, and reputation for nonstop *joie de vivre*. It's a delightful place to explore, and although too sprawling to check out fully on foot, is well worth investigating by car, taxi, bus, or cable railroad. From street level you can admire some of the oldest architecture on the continent and also some of the newest and most adventurous. And from the hills that surround, and even intrude upon the city, unforgettable panoramic views abound.

Claude Levi-Strauss, whose book **A World on the Wane** (Criterion, 1961) is one of the classic anthropological works on South America, is among the few writers who does not rave about the city's beauty. He confesses that its landscape is not constructed to his sense of proportion and adds: "Rio de Janeiro is not built like an ordinary city. Originally built on the flat and swampy area which borders the bay, it later pushed up into the gloomy escarpments which glower down on every side. Like fingers in a glove too small for them the city's tentacles, some of them 15 or 20 miles long, run up to the foot of granite formations so steep that nothing can take root in them."

If you arrive at Rio's Galaeo airport on a domestic flight, you'll be able to stop by the tourist desk while waiting for your luggage. The staff is very helpful and there is always someone who speaks English and will assist you in finding a hotel. They have a list of them, along with prices, and will readily make a reservation on your behalf. (An excellent, moderately priced choice is the Center Hotel at Ave., Rio Branco 33, tel: 223-8365. It's as central as the name implies, situated only a block or two from where Ave. Presidente Vargas, one of the major thoroughfares, terminates at the famous Candelaria church.)

One thing you might consider before making your hotel reservation is which airport you plan to fly out of when you resume your journey. Santos Dumont is practically downtown and most hotels in the central area are only a $1 cab ride away from it.

There is a hotel called the Aeropuerto Hotel though it isn't actually at the airport but rather on the road between Santos Dumont and city center. (Okay, so it's the nearest hotel to the airport, but still too far to walk.)

As for night spots and restaurants, I'm loathe to devote space to them here, because you can find them listed in any of the numerous city guides. Suffice it to say that there are excellent restaurants representing the world's cuisines but, as you're in Brazil, make a stab at the local specialties: *feijoada* (pork with black beans and rice); the *churrascos* (barbecues) which are a legacy of the gaucho; the chicken ragouts and various seafood dishes of shrimp and lobster.

Rio's equivalent of candomblé is *macumba* (which, incidentally, is the term for marijuana), although upper-class types lean more to be the sophisticated version known as *umbanda*, both cults being much less African in origin and more influenced, as indicated in the previous chapter, by Allan Kardec's spiritualism. Another ingredient of Rio's spiritism is the belief in the spirits of long dead black slaves (*prethos velhos*) who were thought to have died before their worldly mission was completed.

In his classic and much-quoted book, **The Masters and the Slaves** (Alfred A. Knopf, 1946), Gilberto Freyre commented that it was not unusual for the Brazilian cults to import items for use in sacred ceremonies from Africa and he mentions not only the herb *macumba* (which he said was now grown domestically) but also kola nuts, cauri shells, teceas (rosaries), heres (copper rattles shaken in Xango ceremonies), oil of the dende palm and a certain blue ink used for writing cabalistic signs on a board (the board was then washed and the ink-impregnated water used as a charm).

Freyre also discussed the significance of the color red both in everyday life and in magical rituals. He noted, "Among the Africans, the color red is associated with the chief ceremonies of life," and concluded that it was a classic example of the way the three influences, the Amerindian, the African, and the Portuguese, "would appear to have united into a whole without antagonism or attrition."

The purpose of red coloring among the Indians, who painted themselves with the juice of the urucu shrub, was both to protect themselves against insects, and as "a prophylactic against evil spirits," Freyre explained.

The greatly respected Brazilian sociologist Arthur Ramos described one of Rio's macumba temples in his famous book **O Negro Brasiliero**, in 1934. Situated on an isolated hill, it was irregularly rectangular in shape and constructed of mud walls that were open at the front and halfway down one side. Guests gathered in an anteroom of the larger chamber where the ceremonies took place. Other small rooms were kept for umbanda consultations and also for storing the articles of worship. A room running across the entire width of the building at the rear housed the altar of the patron saint, in this case Ogun, represented by St. George.

After an invocation to the patron saint, with the men lined up on the left and the women on the right, the worship began with invocations to other friendly deities including household gods and spirits of ancestors. Next, the officiating priest passed among the worshippers' inquiring after their health, giving advice, and settling differences. As the evening wore on, the elder retired to a private room where he continued with his consultations (for a small fee) and the macumba ceremony continued without his participation.

"In the Macumbas of Rio," Dr. Ramos observed, "possession by the spirits rarely attains that violent form which marks the candomblé of Bahia. There is move artificiality and considerably less spontaneity. . . The Rio de Janeiro macumbas of today are little more than seances of elemental spiritism, interspersed with a few elements derived from the African cults."

Incidentally, the much-misused word "voodoo," sometimes used to define macumba, is nothing more than a derivation of Vodun, the Dahomey word for "God," just as *orisha* is the Yoruba equivalent.

The number of adherents to macumba in Rio is further supplemented by the various candomblé sects which have opened "branches" in the city, probably, suggests Charles Wagley, because here their income is higher and the big city also offers more attractions.

In his book, **An Introduction to Brazil** (Columbia University Press,

1963), Wagley said that fanatical religious movements still pop up from time to time in Brazil. He recalled the horrifying events of but eight years before when, in the small town of Catule, in the state of Minas Cerais, "four children accused of being possessed by the devil were sacrificed by the leaders of the community . . . one of whom claimed to have seen the devil in the form of a cat issuing forth from the body of a small girl."

Wagley attributed this event (it ended with the state police killing the two leaders and arresting other adults in the community), and an even more horrifying event a century earlier in central Pernambuco, to the weak control of the Church over isolated rustics.

The Pernambuco affair, which happened in 1836, began with the announcement by a mestizo named Joao Santos that two 100-foot monoliths near the town of Pedra Bonita marked the exact location of an enchanted country in which were hidden immense stores of treasure, and which was destined to be the New Jerusalem. After having stirred up the locals to such an extent that he had to be removed from the area, Joao was followed a couple of years later by another Joao, his brother-in-law, who whipped up the populace to even greater frenzy, making fantastic promises to those who would make the necessary sacrifices.

Negroes and mestizans would become whites, aged persons would become rejuvenated and poor people would become millionaires, "all-powerful, immortal," is how T. Lynn Smith reports it in *Brazil* (Louisiana State University Press, 1972).

The preacher always added that blood would be necessary to bring about the transformation, blood which would be used to bathe the statues and irrigate the fields, and on May 14, 1838, when Joao announced that the time for sacrifice had arrived, a number of people offered themselves, among whom were Joao's father and an old man who carried his two grandchildren up one of the monoliths and threw them into space. The frenzy continued unabated for three days by which time "30 children, 12 men, 11 women and 14 dogs had been executed."

Eventually the police arrived, but rather than surrender, most of the fanatics "rushed to the combat singing religious songs. " A further twenty-two people were killed before the affair came to its conclusion. It was a frightening event but, as subsequent writers have confirmed, perfectly in character with a fanaticism that not so long ago lurked below the surface of Brazilian rural life.

It is estimated that there are more than one million spiritualists in Brazil with those at the top preoccupied with extrasensory perception; the ones in the middle devoted to "the gospel according to Kardec"; and the remainder patronizing mediums possessed by African gods or American Indian spirits.

The Indians were already in Rio when the Portuguese arrived in 1531 and, showing predictably good taste, had settled on the charming island of Paqueta in Guanabara Bay. There the Tarmoio "whose gods were the sun, the moon and the voice of thunder" (as the tourist office succinctly puts it) were fishing, hunting, and doing some primitive farming.

Of course, they are long gone from the area, but Paqueta is a popular island today with uncrowded white-sand beaches and no automobiles. You can rent a bicycle or ride in a buggy. Stay at the hotels Flamboyant or Lido or just go over for the day and have some fine Italian food at the Porto Fino restaurant.

Ferries for Paqueta leave at 7:10 and 10:15 A.M., and at 1:30, 3:00, 5:30, 7:00, and 10:30 P.M. from the pier at Praca 15 de Novembro, but you can also take a speedy hovercraft (25 min.) which gets there in one-third the time. An especially interesting jaunt to Paqueta is on one of the air-conditioned Bateaux Mouches which leave from the pier at Ave. Nestor Moreira, beside the Sol e Mar restaurant. The. 9:30 A.M. boat sails past the beaches of Rio, stopping at Niteroi to allow sea bathing. The 2:30 P.M. boat passes under the Rio-Niteroi bridge, the longest in the world, and stops at Paqueta for 50 minutes to allow visitors to look around. The Bateaux Mouches have a bar and restaurant and take three hours each way.

A tour is certainly the quickest way to orient yourself to Rio's vastness. Try to take one that will whisk you out past the Macarana Stadium and up into the coolness of the vast Tijuca Forest which still throbs, some nights, to the beat of macumba drums. One tour goes way up to the 2,300-foot Corcovado peak (topped by the tremendous statue of Christ with outstretched arms) and this is a perfect spot, by day or night, from which to get the whole city in perspective. The nicest way to climb Corcovado, by the way, is on the charming eighty-four-year-old Corcovado Railway which starts from Rua Cosme Velho 513 (tel: 225-0016 for schedule) and crosses the forty-two arches of the eighteenth-century Carioca Aqueduct before heading up into the hills.

Rio really is enormous and the view from Corcovado is panoramic. To your left is the international airport, Galaeo, at the northern end of Guanabara Bay, which is spanned by the bridge across to Niteroi in the east. Heading down the coast on the Rio side, comes the domestic airport, Santos Dumont, and then the seafront area of Flamengo with its skyscrapers and public buildings all erected on reclaimed land that earlier in this century still belonged to the sea.

Sugar Loaf Mountain, with its spectacular cable-car ride, dominates the southern end of the bay, and south and west of that come the famous beaches: Copacobana, lpanema, Arpoador, Castelhino. Behind them, bordering the Jockey Club and Botanical Garden is the inland lake whose real name, Iagoa Rodrigo de Freitas, hardly anyone can remember. (It's always referred to as *el lagoa*.)

In the downtown area you might start your walking tour at the Praca 15 de Novembre in front of the eighteenth century House of Viceroys, later the Royal Palace and the place where the law that finally abolished slavery was signed in 1888. Today it's the headquarters of the Post and Telegraph Department (although oddly enough you have to go elsewhere to buy a postage stamp) and is flanked on one side with dozens of bookstalls offering literature in many languages

Here it is still possible to pick up a tattered edition of **O Livro do Feiticeiro**, subtitled **"Secrets of the Notorious Witch Juca Rosa,"** who was said to have been arrested while searching for a stone that would make him invisible. This ancient book of suspect spells also gives details about divination by means of such diverse aids as mice, lamplight, smoke, mirrors, onions, salt, bones, and precious stones.

Only a block or two from the bookstalls of the Praca, the National Historical Museum (open noon to 5 P.M. weekdays, 1:00 to 5:00 P.M. on weekends; closed Mondays) is located almost on the waterfront in the Fortress Of Sao Tiago, once a prison for slaves and now housing relics of the reign of Emperors Dom Pedro I and II (1822-1889). As you might expect, it dwells lovingly on all the details that made Colonial life so graceful at the ruling level: jacaranda tables and chairs, portraits, silver plate, painted fans, four-poster beds, upholstered royal coaches with carpeted steps and decorative lanterns, and enormous paintings depicting bishops in full finery "converting" the Indians.

Rio is blessed with many fine museums, but apart from the National Historical Museum, we shall deal with only two others. Either will begin to give you a feeling for Brazil's real heritage, and they are within walking distance of each other: the National Museum (closed Mondays) is situated in lovely Quinta Boa Vista park at the northern edge of town near the 200,000-seat Macarana Stadium; and the Museu do Indio, Museum of the Indians (closed weekends) is on Rua Mata Machado, almost opposite gate 13 of the stadium.

At the National Museum we are almost immediately confronted with large displays demonstrating the rich mix of races that has formed the Brazil of today.

By far the greater proportion of one of the best collections of natural history in the world (all contained in a building that was the home of Brazil's early emperors) is devoted to the Indian. There are flutes, feathered head-dresses, necklaces, carved wooden fish from the Mato Grosso, baskets, arrows, nets, hammocks, wooden hammers with stone heads, and a sequence of photographs demonstrating the "slash and burn" techniques that nomadic tribes use for cultivating land in the forests and which we have made note of in the Amazon regions.

A display devoted to weapons highlights curare, that deadly poison derived from the strychnos vine, showing the location of the main tribes using it and with examples of the quivers, the six-foot long pipes through which the arrows are blown, the pots to hold the poison, and the arrows themselves, dressed with wads of fiber in place of the more conventional feathers.

Actually, curare has taken different forms, the more common variety being derived from strychnos (sometimes with extra ingredients added for magical effect) but another version (according to the Colombian etymologist Gregorio Hernandez de Alba) being cooked up by the Venezuelan Caberre Indians from a certain swamp plant. The root was mashed and cooked slowly under the supervision of old women "who usually died from the fumes." To test the poison, the chief put a small amount of it on a stick which he held near the open wound of another Indian without making contact. The poison was ready for use if the wound stopped bleeding.

Another use of poison is in fishing, when the waters of a specific area are beaten with timbo vines. The vines release a substance that paralyzes the fish, causing them to rise to the surface temporarily stunned and thus easy to spear or net.

The museum also displays wooden boats hollowed out from trees, ceremonial costumes in the shape of animals, coiled ropes looking just like suburban clotheslines, coats shaped from skins, and case after case of utensils ornaments, agricultural tools, musical instruments and hunting implements from spears to nets and fishhooks.

Among the best sculptors of the Amazon region are the Tucuna tribe whose main habitat is the region to the north of the Solimos/ Amazon river, and the museum has some fine examples of their elaborately carved sticks with animal heads. These are reminiscent of the ivory tusks which some of the aborigines of Africa's Ivory Coast sculpt into panoramic scenes of lines of elephants marching into crocodile jaws.

The Tucuna, incidentally, are also skilled at making masks and full-sized costumes (sometimes in the shape of animals) out of tree bark and these play a part in the puberty rites of the young girls in the tribe when they reach their first menstruation.

Obviously it would be impossible for any museum, even one as well stocked as the National Museum, to do more than hint at the elaborate practices behind all the artifacts on display. To do so would require ten times as many rooms and a much more comprehensive method of presentation embodying films, slides, and tape-recorded commentaries. But as the wide variety of items on display are so much more fascinating to those who know something about their background, it's suggested that a little preparatory study about the life-style and mannerism of Indian tribes would greatly enhance your visit.

The final section of the museum, once past the bust of Candido Mariano de Silva Rondon, the celebrated Indian explorer, is a display of natural history and entomology with the accent on mosquito eradication projects; the brightly colored parrots, toucans, owls, and larger fauna of the jungle; and the insects, crustaceans, scorpions, and other frightening specimens that inhabit the less developed areas. Even here, the lesson is drawn of how much the people are influenced by their surroundings. Side by side with the back-lighted spider webs and the explanations of how and why they are constructed in those particular ways, are examples of finely woven native lace, duplicating their intricate patterns.

Outstanding as the museum is, it is overshadowed in some ways by the third of our trio: the Museum of the Indians, tucked away in a decrepit building that seems ready to collapse at any moment. Appearances are deceiving: inside, the museum is attractive, substantial, and as imaginatively laid out as any in the world. There are life-size photos, bigger and better than can be seen elsewhere, and a major exhibit devoted to the relatively little-known Craho, a Gé tribe whose habitat is around the Tocantins River which runs south from the Amazon almost to the capital city of Brasilia.

The sophisticated mats and ceramics of the Craho (spelt Kraho in the display) who dwell near the Tocantins River seem a cut above the others, and the exhibit is dominated by an enormous photograph of one of their tiny villages, a photograph which demonstrates their organizational structure. About a score of huts line a circular pathway which, in turn, encloses a grassy plot across which well-worn paths run like the spokes of a bicycle wheel to the central cleared area. This is not, of course, a unique layout for a tribal village but the harmony and symmetry of this particular one is impressive. The Crahos abandon such villages about every twenty years or so and promptly duplicate the layout at a new site.

Apart from the exhibits themselves, the Indian Museum has a marvelous library, absolutely invaluable for any serious student of aborigine culture and habits, and it is there that the curious seeker can find what is probably the most comprehensive collection of literature in South America about the magical ways of medicine men.

As one of our major authorities we turn to the English Army officer Thomas Whiffen (**The Northwest Amazons**, Duffied & Co., 1915) who, reminding us that to the Indian mind pain, sickness, and death are all products of an evil spirit sent by an enemy, explains that magic must be countered by magic and that is where the tribe's shaman enters the picture. Just as in more conventional medicine, however, the cure lies less in the purges and narcotics than in the patient's faith in the healer. Much more effective than all the drugs and ointments is "the medicine man's virtue as represented by his breath. It is sufficient for him to breathe over food and drink to render it healthy; to breathe on some place to secure removal of pain; to breathe on the sick to promote recovery. . .The medicine man will breathe on his own hand and then massage the part of the patient that is affected.

AN OCCULT GUIDE TO SOUTH AMERICA

"And if stronger measures are required he will suck the place, or as near to the place as his mouth can be put, and possibly spit out a black liquid; the tobacco juice taken by him during the performance explains the color. The avowed object of the search is that it draws out the poison, the evil spirit."

Whiffen goes into detail about the thorn, fishbone, or similar object the shaman then produces with "some degree of charlatanism" indicating it is the manifestation of the evil spirit, and adds; this is the usual accompaniment of the shaman's rites and too universally indulged in by the wizard fraternity to need any particular comment."

We seem to have wandered quite a long way from Rio's best-known attributes, its carnival atmosphere and in particular its famous Mardi Gras celebration held in late February each year. Actually you can get a taste of what's in store far in advance of Mardi Gras when, starting in November, about a dozen or more samba schools open their doors to allow visitors to attend rehearsals. It's well worth stopping by one of them to see what this frenetic beat is all about and, if you can't find a casting in the local papers, check with that excellent bilingual guide, called *Quatro Rodas*.

Rio's neighboring city of Sao Paulo is the largest city in South America and supposedly growing faster than almost any other place in the world. Viewed from the air it seems to go on forever, and the planes coming in zoom so low over the city's skyscrapers you might have a momentary feeling that you're going to end up on the top floor of one of them. The major things to see are the huge Sunday morning Market in Parca da Republica; the poisonous snake farm at Butanta Institute (where venom is extracted for serum); the Botanical Garden and the Aviary and Orchidarium where orchids bloom from October to December.

Almost everybody takes a day trip to Santos, Brazil's impressive major port with its 15 miles of inner harbor offering fascinating glimpses of dockside activity.

Our next stop, however, takes us far away from the hustle and bustle of the cities to a place where, despite a constant decibel level comparable to that of a supersonic jet, we will be back with nature. This is Iguacu Falls, a series of gigantic waterfalls whose waterflow is double that of Niagara Falls. It is on the border between Brazil, Argentina, and Paraguay, and there are daily flights from Rio, stopping at Sao Paulo.

Chapter 4

Iguacu

Rainbows and Cannibals

The Iguacu river, which meanders across the southwest corner of Brazil before plunging hundreds of feet over cliffs to produce the spectacular Iguacu Falls, actually has its origin many hundred miles away in the coastal mountains of Curitiba. In its unhurried path it is joined by more than a score of other tributaries, so that by the time it reaches the falls, its volume is about double that of more-famous Niagara.

Planes en route to Iguacu circle the falls, giving what is probably the most impressive view except for the eight minute ($25) helicopter trips available at the hotel Cataratas. You will probably want to stay at the Cataratas as well; it's the only one in the National Park, overlooks the falls (and what else did you come for?) and its rates ($22 for a single, $30 for a double without meals) are reasonable considering what it offers. There's an old world charm to it, not to mention a swimming pool, bar, luxurious lounge, and a good restaurant. A bus from the hotel meets most flights and a local bus comes from the nearby town, Foz de Iguacu, every hour on the hour.

In Foz itself, 14 miles away down the Estrada das Cataratas, the Bogari Palace Hotel is better than most and boasts a large swimming pool. It is also near the international bridge, Ponte da Amizade, at the Paraguayan end of which is the Casino Acaray. Of course it's also possible to stay on the Argentina side of the falls, at the hotels Argentino or Iguacu, but the Brazilian side is traditionally supposed to have the better view.

Foz is a rather drab little place without much to offer the visitor except shops and movie theaters, but the one-hour bus ride (41 cruzeiros) from Cataratas calls at the airport on its way between Foz and the falls, and on the return trip also, so don't be panicked into taking an expensive taxi ride. Both hotel and town are 12 kilometers from the airport—in opposite directions.

There's a good view of the numerous falls from the Cataratas hotel grounds, but to see the biggest ones you must leave the pleasant swimming pool and the voracious, brightly colored macaws (which will bite towels, your legs, whatever comes within their range) and walk up the road about half a mile. Here an elevator descends almost to river level and you can walk across a narrow bridge (which dead-ends in the center of the river) and admire both falls and rainbows closeup.

One of the tours available at the hotel takes intrepid adventurers almost to the edge of the bridge and also makes a stop at the tiny village of Puerto Iguacu. Other optional tours are to the Gran Hotel, Casino Acaray with its gambling rooms (across the border in Paraguay), and a trip to the Three Border Mark (where Brazil, Paraguay, and Argentina meet) on the Parana River.

Torrents of water pouring over the falls provide a steady background of sound, although the visitor quickly becomes so accustomed to it that a stroll through the woods (along a paved but rustic path) seems a symphony of rushing water and melodious birdsongs. The walk is best taken either early in the morning to the accompaniment of blue skies and brightly colored butterflies, or after dark when the enveloping trees promote an air of mystery. Some of these lovely butterflies are mounted on satin and offered for sale framed at the airport.

The biggest of the more than two hundred separate falls (some very tiny) is called the Devil's Throat (330 feet high) at the foot of which, wrote José Vasconcelos (**The Green Continent**, Knopf, 1944), who visited it in 1944, is a "swirling, boiling mass which has never stopped moving throughout the ages. Nothing but rock and water in this magnificent chaos of forces, seemingly sterile yet mysteriously potent, for this friction can generate the power that life can utilize."

It wasn't until 1541 that the falls were discovered by one of the numerous Spanish explorers who were crisscrossing the terrain of South America. This was Alvar Nunez Cabeza de Vaca, a Spanish official, who named the falls Santo de Santa Maria. The name didn't stick and soon reverted to Iguacu, the name by which they were known to the Guarani tribes who lived nearby. In Guarani, iguacu, means "great waters."

There are dimly remembered stories of the long-dead Guarani chief who was swept over the edge of the falls while in hot pursuit of his enemies, but considering how many centuries the Guarani tribes have inhabited the terrain around the Parana river, it sounds unlikely.

According to the Smithsonian's famous anthropologist Alfred Métraux, cannibalism was an honored practice among the Guarani, as among the neighboring Tupinamba. The victim, usually taken captive in battle, was often kept for months or years, treated well and married to one of the woman of the tribe before being ceremonially sacrificed on the village plaza. "Children were urged to crush the victim's skull with small copper axes and to dip their hands in his blood, while they were reminded of their duties as future warriors," Métraux wrote.

The rituals of tribes practicing cannibalism were very similar, he explained. The prisoner, with only a symbolic cotton thread around his throat to remind him of his fate, usually feigned indifference, even though his execution date was well known in advance. Guests were invited to the impending feast from nearby communities and portions of his body were allotted (in his presence) to various people.

No attempt to escape was made because there was nowhere to escape to. The suffocating jungle stretched for miles around and the captive knew that to return to his own group after being captured meant certain death. It was better to die ceremonially, painted black, and covered in green eggshells and red feathers. On his final night, for example, he was the honored guest at lengthy festivities, invited to dance and even given fruits and missiles to throw at his enemies.

The following morning, while he was being dragged to the plaza for his execution, "old women painted black and red with necklaces of human teeth darted out of their huts carrying newly-painted vases to receive the victim's blood and entrails. A fire was lit and the ceremonial club was shown to the captive. Every man present handled the club for awhile, thus acquiring the power to catch a prisoner in the future. Then the executioner appeared in full array, painted and covered with a long feather cloak.

The executioner, incidentally, appeared to be the one most haunted by his task. After the killing he had to run quickly to his hut and keep running, as if escaping from his victim's ghost. His goods were looted, his name was changed and his wrists rubbed with the eye of his dead victim. "The lips of the dead man were sometimes given to him to wear as a bracelet," and before he could return to the community as a full-fledged member he was required to go into seclusion and slash his body with an animal's tooth.

But we are straying far from Iguacu Falls where obviously such barbarous practices are unknown today. Of more relevance, perhaps, are some of the numerous legends about gods of the water, which can hardly have been far from the minds of any people whose very existence depended on the giant rivers which characterize Brazil.

Writing about the Botocudo, a tribe whose normal habitat was neighboring Bahia, Alfred Métraux explained that one of their central beliefs was that a great snake was lord of the water and signaled to the rain to make it fall. The rainbow was called "urine of the great snake."

Other tribes regarded the rainbow as an evil omen but shared the image of it as being a giant anaconda in the air, the sight of which was particularly dangerous to young women, who were liable to become supernaturally pregnant.

The widespread belief in the magical powers of the greatly feared anaconda is demonstrated by Indians of the almost extinct Cashinawa tribe whose home territory is in southwest Amazonas state.

"When the Cashinawa see an anaconda," writes Walter Krucheberg in **Pre-Columbian American Religions** (Weidenfeld, London, 1968), "they gather around it and each man points in turn to a different golden patch on its skin and pronounces the name of the game animal he wants to kill. Then they kill the snake and from its skin they make headbands which will bring them success in the hunt.

In a similar manner, many tribes invoke the name of the water spirit and pray for success in catching plenty of fish before setting off on a fishing expedition.

From Foz de Iguacu's airport there are daily flights to Buenos Aires and to Rio de Janeiro and recently a new bus route was opened up linking Iguaqu and Rio. Buses leave both places at 200 P.M. each day for a 1,475-kilometer trip that takes twenty-five hours.

Adjoining Iguaqu, however, as we have seen, is Paraguay, and where the Paraguay River empties into the Rio de la Plata above Buenos Aires is Uruguay. So we shall deal briefly with these relatively small countries before heading into Argentina.

Chapter 5

Paraguay and Uruguay

Yerba Maté to Gauchos

Landlocked Paraguay gets its name from the Paraguay River which bisects the country, serves as a natural border adjoining Brazil on the northeast and between Paraguay and Argentina in the southwest, and runs into the Parana river which flows into the sea near Buenos Aires.

Geographically isolated from the outside world to a large extent, Paraguay has produced a self sufficient, nationalistic people who have fought bitterly for their independence.

There are currently estimated to be about 26,000 Guarani plus another 23,000 people who speak other Indian languages. This represents a relatively low 2 percent of the national population compared with other South American countries to the north and west. Most of these Indians have been absorbed into the Paraguayan mainstream, but isolated groups of Morotoco and Guayaki Indians still live in the jungle.

Paraguay's most famous folkcraft is lace making, centered around the town of Itaugua where delicate circles of lace are created known as *nanduti* from an old Guarani Indian word meaning "spider web."

Western Paraguay was, until recent years, a prairie or semi -wasteland called the Chaco, a sanctuary for birds and animals that offers little of value except the hardwood *quebracho* tree and yerba maté. The eastern half of the country consists of rolling, fertile plains, grasslands, and heavily wooded areas. The Chaco, which in ancient times may have been an inland sea, is now being opened up, especially with the development of cattle ranches, but two-thirds of the country's population live east of the river, most of them in the area around the capital, Asuncion.

Founded in 1537 as the seat of government of Spain's colony along the Rio de la Plata, Asuncion is a pleasant city with wide, tree-shaded avenues and spacious plazas. Visit the Ethnographic Museum for an introduction to aboriginal art and see the sun set from the hilltop Parque Carlos Antonio Lopez, overlooking the city. Also worth visiting is the Parque Caballero, with its many pools and waterfalls and an old house which now serves as a National Historical Museum.

Among the trees in the Parque Caballero are yerba maté, familiar in the Chaco to the west and south but not often seen in cities. Sometimes known as Paraguay tea, yerba maté is prepared from the leaves of the Ilex plant and acts as a mild stimulant. The leaves are dried overnight on a platform above a fire and then powdered and added to hot water as with most other teas. It is usually sipped through reeds or bone pipes with strainers built into the end.

When the area was first penetrated by white men, the Indians regarded yerba maté as a magical herb used by their shamans as a way of communicating with the spirits. The Jesuits, who for years operated missions in Paraguay, sent parties of Indians off into the bush to collect it in skin bags and then exported it to raise money for the missions. In the Chaco regions, a few handfuls of yerba maté are part of the regular monthly wage for Indians employed on the vast *estancias*.

The other major product of the Chaco region is the *quebracho* tree, the harvesting of which did so much to wreck the culture of the local Indians. The *quebracho* (its name means "axe-breaker") is cultivated for the red dye, or tannin, it yields and the medicinal properties of its bark. The tireless British traveler W. H. Koebel wrote in 1910 of seeing *quebracho* logs sailing down the river, so heavy that they had to be supported on a raft of lighter wood.

Until recently, he wrote, the wood had been used for posts and railway sleepers, but when the value of the dye that could be extracted was realized, the wood was almost entirely devoted to this purpose. The establishment of lumber camps to harvest the *quebracho* was followed, in the 1930s, by Bolivian incursions into the Chaco, which of course meant corresponding retaliation by the Paraguayans and, eventually, a war between the two countries which pushed the Indians back even further.

AN OCCULT GUIDE TO SOUTH AMERICA

The forests which cover more than half the country produce, in addition to yerba maté and *quebracho*, a bitter orange tree which yields *petitigrain* oil used as a perfume base and for flavorings; the *mangaba* tree which can be tapped for rubber, the *palo santo* tree, from which a medicinal oil called *guiacwood* oil is obtained; and the *caranday* palm, whose fiber can be woven into hats

Best known of the Chaco tribes are the Toba, who came into possession of horses in the seventeenth century which turned them into "a vagabond tribe of mounted warriors" and, although most of them have long ago been assimilated, Alfred Métraux says they are still regarded by their neighbors as "a proud people who refuse to yield to servitude and are always ready to avenge an insult."

Although the Chaco bush country seems forbidding, it actually yields many different kinds of food including the all purpose carob tree for the mostly nomadic Indians who roam its plains.

The pods of the carob tree provide both food and drink. Algarroba beer is brewed between November and February when the seeds are ripe. The pods are pounded in a mortar and mixed with hot water, the fermentation aided by the input of a small amount of the substance which, before being added, is prechewed by an old woman.

It is common practice to hasten the maturity of the pods by banging on drums, a practice also used to assist girls in their first menstruation. Chaco Indians believe strongly in the efficacy of drums and rattles and use them to keep evil spirits away. Unusual magic power is attributed to rattles Paraguay and Uruguay made from a special gourd filled with sacred beetles.

Other natural resources of the Chaco include beans, figs, palms, wild rice, ample fish in season, and at least sixteen different kinds of honey. Even the intermittent swarms of locusts are roasted or fried in fish oil by the Mocovi.

Some of the Chaco's Indian culture can be studied in Asuncion's museum which adjoins the zoo at the city's Botanical Garden, four miles from the center in the suburb of Trinidad. It is situated on a former estate along the banks of the river, and is well worth seeing. There is also an Indian reservation maintained by the ***Sociedad de Proteccion al Indio*** on the outskirts of the city.

Prices are reasonable in Paraguay. Asuncion's best hotel, the Guarani, costs about $18 for a double. It is in the center of the city and has a swimming pool and nightclub.

The 1,500 kilometers of river between Asuncion and Buenos Aires can be covered by steamer in four to five days but passenger service is suspended at the moment. This leaves access by rail (the train being ferried across the Parana river at Posadas), by bus, (23 hours), and by air. There are a score of flights to Asuncion each week from Buenos Aires, daily flights from Rio and Sao Paulo. The steamer trip, however, is charming and will hopefully be revived.

But before moving on to Argentina, we still have Uruguay to explore.

Uruguay, the smallest of South American nations, is a pastoral country with almost four-fifths of its land area given over to grazing livestock (of which it is one of the world's largest producers.

The herds of cattle and sheep, totaling about 30 million, outnumber the human population by ten to one, and in the summer the grass on which they live grows thick and the plains are covered with fragrant, blooming verbena.

At the time the territory was first explored by the Spanish, it was inhabited by the Charrua Indians, fierce warriors who were good bowmen and even better with the bola (a stone on a string). An early Spanish explorer, Juan Diaz de Sotis, who discovered the Alote river and landed in 1515, was killed by them, near what is now Montevideo.

The Charrua continued to resist the invaders but all were finally pushed out of their native territory, decimated, or assimilated. There are virtually no native Indians left in the country today.

Almost half of Uruguay's total population lives in Montevideo, a cosmopolitan city with a temperate climate that is bounded on two sides by a bay and the Atlantic waters of the Rio de la Plata.

That indefatigable Spanish traveler Femando Magellan is said to have given the city its name when in 1520 a lookout on his ship saw the hilltop of El Cerro and yelled out, "Montevideo" ("I see a mountain') The Spaniards and Portuguese fought for a long time for control of the north shore of the Rio de La Plata, and for a brief period it even fell into the possession of the British. After its successful fight for independence in 1828, the immigrants poured in from Europe, more than 650,000 of them in the century that followed, and the Argentinian cattle buyers arrived to establish formal *estansias* or protected ranches, setting a pattern that has continued to this day.

Montevideo's temperate climate (often better than Rio's between December and April) draws a big tourist crowd from other South American countries but is not as popular among North Americans. Prices are low, probably the lowest of any Latin American country, but advance reservations may be necessary at the height of the busy season. The luxurious twenty-one-story Victoria Plaza, on the Plaza Independencia, is the city's best. Doubles here cost about $25, without meals.

Even more so than Buenos Aires, Montevideo is patterned after Paris, with a pleasant ambience that is enhanced by the numerous flower stands and outdoor cafés

A magnificent landscaped boulevard called the Rambla skirts the bay and the river, running from one end of the city to the other; each section it runs through is named after a different foreign country.

Residents and visitors alike devote plenty of time to the city's largest park, El Prado, once the private estate of a European financier who sprinkled it lavishly with fountains and artificial lakes, statuary, exotic plants, and flowers and animals for a well-stocked zoo. There are more than eight hundred varieties of roses in the rose garden, all of which bloom gloriously in November. Also in the park are the Museum of Fine Arts and the History Museum.

Sunday morning in Montevideo is best spent visiting one of the street markets or *feria*s which are a combination of the flea market, street fair, London's Petticoat Lane and New York's Delancey Street.

Uruguay's entire Atlantic coast, all the way north to the Brazilian border, is lined with magnificent beaches of every kind, some lavish millionaire playgrounds, others relying on an unspoiled natural beauty. The white-sand beaches begin in the city itself, the most fashionable being Carrasco at the southern end of the Rambla, about nine miles from the city center.

Like Rio, Montevideo also has a pre-Lent carnival when most of the population turns out in masks and costumes to parade, perform, watch a procession of decorated floats, dance in the streets, and generally have a good time. Another annual festival takes place at Easter time when admirers of the gaucho life-style (a glorification of the great outdoors) converge on the city's Prado Park for a rodeo.

Despite its present status as one of Latin America's military dictatorships, Uruguay has a pioneer reputation for social reform, it being the first country on the subcontinent to grant suffrage to women, to legalize divorce, and to put into practice the eight-hour work day. In style it is somewhat European; English is widely spoken and the custom of afternoon tea is observed as in England.

Chapter 6

Argentina

Home of the "Serpent of Fire."

The largest part of Argentina is a vast plain, the pampas, which comprises more than half of the country's total area, is home to 44 million cattle, and produces an annual wheat crop of 7 million tons.

"So numerous are the cattle here," Jesuit missionary Carlos Gervasini wrote almost 250 years ago, "that any landowner may take from ten to twelve thousand to breed from, merely for the trouble of lassoing them and taking them home.

But relatively speaking, the pampas are deserted and more than two-thirds of the population of South America's second largest country lives in a handful of cities of which the biggest, of course, is Buenos Aires.

As long ago as the turn of the century, a thoughtful English traveler was reassuring his readers they had nothing to fear from the natives of Argentina, a country, he said, which was fortunate in its freedom from any internal racial question.

"An infusion of African blood, such as has occurred in tropical Brazil has never come into being here," he noted. The few cases where the blood of the native pampa warriors has entered into the composition of society afford a distinctly favorable result.

In Buenos Aires, in fact, no human feature exists that distinguishes the town in any way from London or Paris. I emphasize this for the benefit of those who may picture the Argentine as strolling about costumed in feathers and a dagger!"

Buenos Aires itself is not the kind of city whose sight-seeing landmarks leap out at you, their names on everybody's lips. In fact, apart from the impressively wide Ave. Nueve de Julio (once tagged as the world's widest street until Pekinophiles demurred) and the Plaza de Maio where Peron used to address adoring throngs, there isn't much that's memorable about the downtown area. Even the Metropolitan Cathedral, on Plaza de Maio, is a poor copy of the Madeleine church in Paris, just as the city, some skeptics aver, is a poor copy of Paris itself

But it does have its charms: the antique shops around the Plaza Dorrego, a quiet, tree-shaded square that shelters a Sunday flea market; the charming La Boca area down by the waterfront, home to many thousands of Genoese immigrants whose style has imposed itself in the form of brightly painted houses and murals; and the "Greenwich Village" atmosphere of San Telmo where innumerable bars and nightclubs keep the place swinging from evening to early morning.

You should certainly look in at the Union Bar or the cavernous El Viejo Almacen (tel: 33-1407) next door, on Balcarce Street in the San Telmo area. Here you can sample the classic "tango" entertainment, a nostalgic mélange of strings, accordions and old-fashioned stage dances of the type that made hearts zing back in the thirties. There are nightly shows (minimum $2.50) at 11:00 P.M. and 1:15 A.M.

For a great lunch, in pseudo-Tudor pub surroundings, drop by the London Grill whose ambience (and cheap prices) is enhanced by such English-type staples as Welsh rarebit and chicken pie. In many little ways, Buenos Aires is the most European of all South American cities.

At dinner you might like to check out the currently "in" eating place, Clark's, on Junin Street, where lots of plants and a big cozy bar contribute to an atmosphere that would be admirable anywhere in the world. Prices have risen sharply of late, however, and the celebrated Argentine "two dollar steak" is a thing of the past. Now it's about three dollars!

Buenos Aires also offers all the usual tourist diversions: a free zoo at Lastteras & Ave. Sarmiento open daily until 7:00 P.M.; wild animal preserves, one on the road to Lujan and the other near Berazatequi in Pereyra Iraola Park; a free Botanical Garden at Las Heras and Santa Fe; a planetarium (open Fridays and weekends) at Ave. Sarmiento & Belisario Roldan; an amusement park at Ave. de Libertador & Callao Street (till 9:00 P.M. weekdays, 2:00 A.M. Saturdays); and a scaled-down "Children's City" in the nearby town of Gonnet. You can rent bicycles (Figueroa Alcorla 3600, Palermo Park area), cars (Avis, Sheraton Hotel), or horses (Chaco Penaloza, La Pampa 1231), and take a motor boat ride (Ar Bo Tours, via any tourist office) up to the Delta where the Parana and Rio de la Plata rivers meet.

Obviously, too, there are plenty of theaters, movies, and nightclubs in which to spend your evenings and the most comprehensive list of these can be found in **"Buenos Aires Night and Day,"** which costs about 40¢ at almost any newsstand.

Three theaters—the architecturally fascinating Colort (Tucuman 1111, tel. 35-1430); the Coliseo (Marcelo T de Alvear 1111, tel: 42-0242); and the Cervantes National Theatre, (Liberatad 15, tel: 45-4224) all offer serious music and/or ballet and opera, and there are various cabarets with late shows, among them the three K's-the Karim (Carlos Pellegrini 1143, tel: 44-0884); Karina (Corrientes 636, tel: 40-1708); and King (Cordoba 937). For a taste of local folklore try El Palo Borracho (Corrientes 2166, tel: 941-0164) open every night but Monday.

The city's most interesting museums are the Historico Nacional (Defensa 1600, tel: 26-4588) open Thursday through Sunday afternoons; the Historico de la Ciudad Museum (in General Paz park off the motorway of the same name, tel: 572-0746) open Tuesday through Sunday afternoons; the Railroad Museum (Libertador 405, tel- 31-9021) open a day Monday through Friday.- and the Gaston Maspero Archaeological (San Martin 274) open Saturdays only, 4:00 to 7:00 P.M.

The most significant reason for the existence of Buenos Aires is its situation on the banks of the immense Rio de la Plata whose mouth forms the largest natural harbor on South America's Atlantic coast. This river is fed by half a dozen others of which the two largest, the Parana and the Uruguay, stretch for thousands of miles to the north, up through Paraguay and into Brazil.

The Guarani Indians formerly lived on the islands at the mouth of the Parana river where it joins the Rio de la Plata. The original Guarani had become extinct by the end of the seventeenth century but were mentioned by most of the early chroniclers, in part perhaps because of their barbarous customs. They ate a lot of fish and also favored human flesh.

Three or four communal houses arranged around a square or rectangular plaza was a characteristic Guarani village plan. Like the former headhunting Jivaros of Ecuador, the Guaranis trained their sons from an early age to be avengers who would capture prisoners and ritually sacrifice them in return for past defeats the tribe may have suffered. They were ingenious warriors being one of a handful of tribes who used flaming arrows to set fire to their enemy's village and force them to come into the open. But once the battle was won they made short work of their enemies in cannibalistic feasts after which Guarani women made necklaces out of the leftover teeth.

The modern Guaranis, distant descendants of those early Rio de la Plata, settlers, now live in scattered groups in southern Brazil and across the Chaco in the foothills of the Andes.

The Guarani became familiar with the virtually uncharted plains of the Chicago-the first white man to cross it, a shipwrecked Portuguese sailor named Aléjo Garcia, accompanied one of their expeditions in 1521, and there is some discussion among the anthropologists about whether the tribes who were the Cuaranis' contemporaries might have ended up there under other tribal names. It would account for the apparent disappearance of such tribes as the Querandi and the Charrua, both of which were numerous on the shores of the Rio de Is Plata at the time of the Conquest.

Much of the area between the subsidiary rivers that flow into the Rio de la Plata is a vast forest and swamp-filled plain that includes portions of all four countries (Brazil, Paraguay, Uruguay, and Argentina). It was this region, the Chaco, that the invading Spaniards, in the sixteenth century, searched tirelessly for a way west to the fabulous land which they believed must be the source of the gold and silver treasures possessed by the Guarani tribes. It was 1548 by the time they eventually penetrated the inhospitable Chaco as far as Peru, and by that time they were too late. Pizarro and his companions had managed to conquer that rich coastal land from the Pacific side.

In their contact with the Indians, the newcomers found, as conquerors all over the world have discovered in similar circumstances, amazing analogies between their own religion and those of the "superstitious" natives. Fasting, baptism, confession, and penance had their counterparts, even if human and animal sacrifices to appease divine ire had been replaced by more symbolic equivalents.

Common to most of the tribes of the Chaco was an evil spirit called *Avacua* or sometimes *anacua* or *ananga*. Another name, still in use today among the Indians of the Chaco, is *gualichu*, but whatever name it is known under, it is basically the evil spirit that brings sickness and sometimes death.

AN OCCULT GUIDE TO SOUTH AMERICA

It is also responsible, in native belief, for entering the moon and breaking it up at the time of a lunar eclipse. Attempts to drive it away, both from human bodies and the moon, took the form of throwing stones, firing guns, throwing lighted torches into the air, and in general creating as much pandemonium as possible. This custom is still in practice among many South American tribes.

The indispensable member of the community at times like these, has always been the shaman or witch doctor, to whom all human ill is attributable to witchcraft and must be combated in like manner.

The witch doctors of the Rio de]a Plata fired their spirits with abundant libations of chicha, shouting, grimacing, going into contortions like one possessed, imitating the roaring of tigers and terrifying cries of other animals," wrote Daniel Granada in 1896.

"They were the arbiters of both good and evil, of life and death, of the power of the elements; they could cause storms, alter the seas, dry up rivers or flood the fields. They could so enchant a person that he could neither move, eat, drink, sleep or talk unless they so commanded. To receive the power to perform magic they had to fast, and underwent corporal penitence, abstaining from ablutions of any kind. They lived naked and solitary in places cold and far away. They ate nothing save maize and hot peppers."

Dragons and demons guarded hidden treasures in the area of the Rio de la Plata and especially rampant was the *culebra de fuego* or "serpent of fire" which might be found anywhere that imaginary treasure were said to exist. "Demons, genii, winged serpents or *[these creatures of fire]* all had the same cause and origin and represented the same thing to the imagination of primitive man: the mother of gold, the force of the earth, the enchanted mountain that trembled, lighted up, thundered and lightning, the living earth of the Indians," Granada comments in **Superstitions of the Rio de la Plata** (Guillermo-Kraft Ltd-, Buenos Aires, 1947).

For 250 years, until they were expelled from the country, the Jesuits exerted the greatest influence for humanity among the Chaco Indians. Because these often hard-working and selfless priests didn't exploit the natives commercially, they were in sharp contrast to the *encomenderos* or Landowners; although the Jesuits tried to win the Indians away from pagan religions, they also supplied them with food, tools, and protection from human predators.

AN OCCULT GUIDE TO SOUTH AMERICA

The concept of "magical sites" is not one that is prevalent among hard-headed Argentinians and most natives would find it difficult to identify any such places in their own country. But archaeological excavations in the northwest, in Salta province near the Chilean border, have uncovered the site of a short-lived civilization (from the eleventh to fourteenth centuries) that has excited anthropologists because of its unmistakable links with the region's present-day peasant culture.

Best known is the ancient town of Tastil, a community of about 25,000 inhabitants that may have been a satellite trading post for the highly developed Inca civilization in neighboring Peru. The evidence of three strains that were indigenous to Central American cultures—witchcraft, the use of hallucinogenic drugs and the celebration of the jaguar cult—indicate links between the societies existing simultaneously in Mexico and Guatemala.

The approximately 25 percent of the site that has been uncovered so far demonstrates that a social stratification of different clans (probably priests and peasants) lived in separate unequal quarters. Jaguar symbols have been found on stones and hatchets.

When the Spaniards first invaded neighboring Chile they encountered fierce Indians of the Diaguita tribe who had infiltrated across the Andes from Argentina, bringing with them, among other things, representations (on pottery) of jaguars, an animal not found in Chile. The seventeenth century Jesuit missionary Father Nicolas del Techo reported that the Diaguitas worshipped the sun, an opinion confirmed by another missionary, Father Pedro Lozano a century ago, and also that they rendered homage to thunder, lightning, and "trees decorated with feathers".

One of the curious customs which has survived to this day is the practice of flattening the head of certain people (cranial deformation" is the technical term) by strapping boards to the skull from early childhood onwards. Hundreds of skulls deformed in this manner and a few of the boards used have been found in graves; the practice was so widespread that examples have been found in other regions, including Ecuador.

In Quito's archaeological museum, examples of both deformed skulls and the boards are on display. Recently an old Indian woman in southern Ecuador was found applying a similar device to her own child. When asked why she was doing so, she replied that her ancestors had always done it and she believed it increased the size of the brain.

AN OCCULT GUIDE TO SOUTH AMERICA

About 50 miles northeast of Salta, excavations have revealed remains of a relatively sophisticated community with motifs of humans and animals painted on cave walls. There are even "musical" stairs, stone steps that ring melodically when struck with wooden staves.

Anthropologists have been fascinated to uncover all the now-familiar examples of syncretism in the present-day peasant society: the identification of the Incas' earth mother, Pachamama, with the Christians' Virgin Mary and the whole ancient pagan calendar now irretrievably intermingled with twentieth-century church festivals.

Evil spirits figure prominently in rural beliefs, many of the medical practices, as we have noted, being based on the feeling that unspecified sickness is directly traceable to demons having taken possession and the consequent need to exorcise them. Trepanation, the custom of cutting holes or making incisions in the head, was one method of allowing the spirits to exit, although as practiced among the Incas it was more usually a surgical necessity, a means of relieving pressure on the brain among victims of battle-induced skull fractures. (In modern times and more "civilized societies, trepanation has been tried as a means of emulating the "third eye" or even as a means of maintaining a permanent state of euphoria).

An ancient form of communism is still practiced among the semi-nomadic tribes of northern Argentina, as in many other rural communities. The land, incidentally, is communal but the cattle are not, and when animals are branded at ritual ceremonies, water offerings are made to Pachamama Or Mother Earth entreating fertility for the coming season.

What was possibly the biggest pagan festival has totally fused with the Christian Easter, and it is at this time that the intermingled customs are most fascinating to observe. The Christian custom of giving alms to the poor is the latter-day counterpart of the ancient northern Argentine ceremony at which the more affluent members of the community redistributed some of the wealth they had accumulated by passing it along to the less fortunate, they received in return prestige and loyalty that emphasized the "godfather" nature of their relationship to the community at large.

The fear of being cuckolded, common to much of Latin America, may also have had some of its origins in the custom of this region of placing a horn outside the home when the husband was away and the wife alone. Naturally any stranger visiting the house at this time was regarded with grave suspicion.

The dwindling Diaguita tribes, who resisted the Spaniards fiercely, were spread over this area of northwest Argentina until about a century ago. They decorated themselves with feathers, painted their faces, and were proficient with a bow and arrow. They were also ingenious in their fighting methods, on more than one occasion they diverted the course of rivers to starve newly established Spanish cities into submission.

A curious cult that has spread throughout the length and breadth of Argentina is that of *Le Difunta Correa*. It is based on a legend ascribed vaguely to that period of "the civil wars" and deals with a wife and mother who, separated from her husband, decides suddenly to overcome all odds and rejoin him. The woman sets off on her Journey with a babe in arms (or still unbom) and succumbs to the inhospitable terrain alone, dying of cold and starvation in the wilderness. By some miracle, however, the baby survives, suckling at the dead breast for days, some say weeks, until rescued by passersby.

Basically, that is all there is to the story; nothing more is known about what happened to the baby, the husband or even more specifically where the incident happened. But the legend has been the subject of books, magazine stories and word-of-mouth embellishments, especially by truck drivers, traveling salesmen, tourists, and other motorized missionaries who have built simple shrines to *La Difunta Correa* all over Argentina. These are simple brick structures with roof and space for offerings but containing no image of any kind. The legend is believed to have originated in San Juan, near Mendoza at the Chilean border, and that is where the largest shrine is. In 1975, a fictionalized version of the story was a paperback best-seller.

In a recent article in the Buenos Aires newspaper **La Gaceta**, Bernardo Canal Feijoo suggested that the durability and popularity of the legend was a -latter-day manifestation of the earth cult," a throwback to the worship of Pachamama, the earth mother.

A seven hundred-mile paved road crosses the undulating pampa to connect Buenos Aires with Mendoza, Argentina's gateway to Chile. Here the mountains begin, the fabulous Andes, which dominate most of the countries on the remainder of our trip and which have always been reverenced right up to our own time.

Primitive man's imagination was always inspired by mountains, which he associated with thunder, lightning, and the mysterious tremors that so terrifyingly and unpredictably shook the earth from time to time. In the caverns among these elevated mountain peaks dwelt the *madre de oro*, the "mother of gold," who protected the precious metals that lay hidden there. "The mountain is angry," was a popular explanation for the thunder and lightning that resulted, as the Indians thought, from adventurers trying to steal these riches. "They believed that gold contained a deity," wrote Daniel Granada, "doubtless emanating from the Sun, whom they adored."

"And so, according to the Indians, the peaks, the cordilleras, the mountains, rivers and lakes get angry by releasing thunder and lightning, covering the sky with clouds, churning up the waters, blowing with great form, releasing tempests",

El Trovador, a snow-covered mountain in the west near Bariloche, owes its resounding name to the thunderous roars that are frequently produced by massive landslides.

Enchanted lakes, usually guarded by demons and serpents, were closely associated with mountains among which they appeared and reappeared with astonishing frequency like perennial Brigadoons. The Cuarani Indians who lived along the Parana river spoke reverently of the teyuyagua, a creature composed partly of fire, which they believed to be one of the manifestations of the *madre doro* and which lived in the nearby mountains.

But now that we have reached the Andes we must familiarize ourselves with the coca plant which has played such an important part in the lives of the natives of these regions for so long. In an area where food is scarce and where weariness from climbing in high altitudes is endemic, a substance that can postpone fatigue and hunger is well worth its weight in gold, and so it is hardly surprising that the natives regard it as a magic plant.

Coca, a bush about three to twelve feet high which thrives in the wettest part of the eastern slopes, was well known for centuries before the Incas incorporated it into their own religious ceremonies and restricted its use to the upper classes. Coca leaves, harvested three or four times each year, were used for divining and burned at sacrifices. When chewed with a little lime, the leaves liberate a small amount of *cocaine* which dulls the appetite, as well as giving the chewer more energy.

The Spaniards were quick to see the advantages of a mild drug that postponed fatigue, and their soldiers used it to assist them on their long marches into the mountains. They also enlarged the coca plantations, thereby spreading the use of the drug through all classes of society.

Coca leaves are sometimes used as currency and this is apparently an ancient practice. "It is the money of the Indians," wrote the sixteenth-century Spanish official Juan de Matienzo, "and with it they carry on business among themselves; to ask there should be no coca is to desire that Peru should cease to be."

Coca originated near Cuzco, according to legend, when a beautiful woman of loose morals so scandalized the community that it was deemed necessary to make an example of her. She was killed and buried in the fields and from her grave issued the coca plant.

The Indians collected the leaves, dried them in the sun, and were able to recognize the plant's virtues, writes Daniel Granada, adding, "The generous earth covers and purifies all, transforming the most impure into exquisite fruits and beautifully scented flowers.

He recounts a strangely similar story about the reputed origin of the mandioca or manioc root which is used almost all over South America as a basic breadlike food.

Although a virgin, the daughter of an Indian chief (so the legend goes) gave birth to an enchanting baby girl who, in a manner of months, could speak perfectly. They named her Mani but she died within a year of no apparent cause. Watering her grave daily according to age-old custom, the family soon noticed a plant springing up which gave fruit. The birds who ate of it seemed to be drunk, a phenomenon then unknown among the Indians. Digging up the plant they discovered a root whose shape they fancied represented the dead Mani. They tried eating the root and also made of it a fermented beverage. This became their wine.

There are scores of varieties of manioc but basically they fall into two classes, bitter (poisonous until the juice is squeezed from the pulp and then widely used to make bread or cakes) and sweet (*aypi*). Manioc can be planted any time of the year but grows fastest, obviously, in the rainy season. It takes eight months from planting to harvesting, and a single Indian woman can harvest as much as 25 pounds a day. This she converts into a flat, circular cake. Manioc can also be made into a kind of tapioca porridge, a dried flour called farinha, and a version of the basic, everyday Indian drink called chicha.

AN OCCULT GUIDE TO SOUTH AMERICA

Chicha, which can also be manufactured from such plants as quinoa, oca, and the red berries of the molle tree, is made by the simple process of having women chew the pulp and spit the resulting mess into jars of warm water or a communal tank. Here it is allowed to ferment; additives to assist in fermentation include palm stems, sugar cane juice, and occasionally goat dung.

Enormous quantities of chicha are drunk to celebrate hunting or fishing trips, harvest festivals, councils for war or peace, and magical ceremonies. Sometimes the sprees last for days and end in drunken fights, orgies or killings, but Spanish objections to these periodic jags among the Indians apparently stemmed more from a fear of the pagan associations than the actual drunkenness.

We are about to leave Argentina and shall cross the border into Chile in the company of a dignified English gentleman. W. H. Koebel, whose account in *Argentina: Past and Present* (Kegan Paul, London) was written in 1910 but is still an effective description of the Andean-crossing railway route of today.

"Then into a realm where the rock, soaring now in tremendous peaks towards the sky, breaks out into brilliant and unexpected coloring of its own. Black, red, orange, mauve, pink, green, violet—there is scarcely a tint that is not boldly painted upon the enormous confusion of facets, while the pure white of the topmost snow peaks hang tremulously above. Well past the famous natural bridge, the Puente del Inca, the solitary stations crouch, lonely and infinitesimal specks clinging to the mighty terraces that bear no other tokens of humanity except the rails themselves, and the few stray crosses that each mark the death of a human being."

In the old days, Koebel wrote, the line ended up here, beside the jagged peaks of Las Cuevas, the passengers being bundled out of the train to spend the night at an elevation of 10,000 feet before being transported across the mountains in the morning by mule. But then the tunnel was cut through the Andes.

"Now the traveler undisturbed, keeps his seat in the railway carriage and the train rumbles on, plunges into the depths of the great tunnel, emerges onto the cuttings upon the Chilean side, and rolls downwards sedately to the shores of the Pacific."

AN OCCULT GUIDE TO SOUTH AMERICA

Chapter 7

Chile

Mana vs. Christianity

Santiago, Chile's capital, is built on a smaller scale than Buenos Aires and thus it is easier to get to know. At first it seems somewhat shabby, in fact badly in need of a facelift, but on closer acquaintance it exudes a low-key charm.

Its suburbs are newer, and consequently are virtually in the countryside; its buildings are smaller; and the omnipresent mountains—the city lies in a valley, like a bowl with steep sides—seem to change color according to the time of day and position of the sun.

About one-third of Chile's population of 11 million lives in Santiago; almost 50 percent of the country's residents live in the temperate central zone of which the capital is part. Some of the rest live in the area abutting on the arid Atacama desert, with its copper and nitrate mines, to the north; the remainder in the colder south, among the lakes, farmland, and trees which produce vast quantities of cattle and newsprint.

Santiago is a city of many parks and the first-time visitor couldn't do better than to make an early acquaintance with the most prominent of them: Santa Lucia park, wrapped around a lofty hill in the center of the city. A winding road leads to a terrace overlooking the city and this terrace is also accessible via broad steps leading up from the Alameda Bernardo O'Higgins. An eternal flame bums on the terrace; the area is always thronged with locals strolling, drinking sodas, or just admiring the view.

A statue of Pedro de Valdivia, who founded Santiago in 1541, can be seen on the hill. Valdivia established his first fortress up here, meeting determined resistance from the fierce Araucanian tribes who had been warned of his approach by the Incas to the north. Valdivia hung on at Santiago until 1545, but came to a bad end eight years later when captured by the Indians. He was bound and forced to drink the molten gold which had for so long been the Spaniards' preoccupation.

You might find it pleasant to stay at the hotel Riviera (Miragores 106, te): 31176) which is opposite the park and costs around $15 for a double. At the upper end of the price scale is Cerrador Sheraton, in midtown, but there are a number of much cheaper hotels in this same area. (Recommended is the hotel Kent at Huerfanos 886, tel: 34026, about $12 for a double.) You should certainly plan to stay somewhere around the midtown area, near all the cinemas and the theaters which offer the characteristic folklore shows. Since the new military regime imposed a midnight curfew, night life has been somewhat restrained.

Before you leave the Santiago airport (limousines to town cost 75 pesos) stop at the tourist desk and study the list of hotels and prices.

Another Santiago park, whose main entrance is off Ave. Matta in the southern section of the city, is named after the ubiquitous Bernardo O'Higgins, the bastard offspring of an Irish father and a Chilean mother who led Chile's revolt against Spain in 1810. In this park is a newly constructed "Pueblo Village" which consists chiefly of handicraft shops, cafés with live combos for dancing, and dozens of different restaurants. This, of course, encroaches upon only a tiny section of the park.

While in this general area be sure to admire the incredibly graceful eighty-year-old buildings of the Club Hipico, the local racetrack (race meets Wednesdays, Saturdays, and Sundays), which justifiably claims to be the finest in South America.

The most fascinating of the numerous museums is the Museum of Natural History (open Sundays 10:00 A.M. to 1:00 P.M. and 3:00 to 6:00 P.M.) in Quinta Normal Park. There is a wide collection of pottery, baskets and artifacts from local Araucanian tribes as well as displays from other Indians in various parts of the subcontinent.

At one time, the territory of the Araucanians covered a vast area comprising most of central Chile and part of neighboring Argentina, and their strength was such that their influences were felt far and wide. They shared many of the beliefs of other South American tribes in that they trusted in omens, sacrificed llamas at special ceremonies, and deemed evil spirits to be the cause of most illnesses.

Despite their reputation as warriors they were virtually unique in their shamanistic practices, since their medicine men were (and still are) women. In earlier times, John M. Cooper tells us, they were commonly transvestites, dressing as women and practicing sodomy.

"The few scattered references to the character of shamans," writes Alfred M4étraux in his classic essay on the subject, "describe them as particularly gifted, intelligent men; there are hardly any allusions that could lead one to consider them neurotic personalities. But here again, the Araucanians were exceptional, for during the 17th and 18th centuries they generally were recruited among *berdaches*, those with effeminate characteristics and persons afflicted with mental or nervous disorders. Any boy who seemed delicate or effeminate was dressed as a girl and from an early age prepared for his future profession."

There are four general types of shamans, according to Silvio Alvear in his book, **Shamanismo en el Reino Quito** (Editorial Santo Domingo, 1973), who has them as: the *omus* or enchanters who cured with ayahuasca, tobacco, and various herbs; the *condeviecas* or *abagos* whose specialty was predictions made by "reading" ears of corn or small rocks; a similar type of soothsayer, the *achico*, who made interpretations from such diverse things as animal sounds, the entrails and excrement of llamas, the flight of birds or butterflies, and the study of spiders and black beetles with strings tied to their legs; and finally the *jambi camayocs* or *shagras* who included the witch doctors who affected to suck the evil 'spirits from ailing bodies. *Jambi* is an Indian word which means both poison and core, so the *jambi camayocs* or *jambi camascas* were also the tribal poison makers.

Some of the shamans' magical resources, Alvear says, included large golden breastplates as insignia of their majesty and magical powers, especially in Ecuador's metallurgically rich Esmeraldas province. Snakes adorning the head, chest, or arms were an additional symbol of magic power used by the shamans of the Manabita and other tribes.

"Illnesses, caused either by magic or various natural accidents, were of three types: a 'Foreign body' (darts, rocks, thorns, fire); an emanation or bad air belief common to all primitives; and finally the "loss of spirit or soul, characteristic of consumptive illnesses such as fright which could cause the soul to leave the body or cause the body to be susceptible to the attacks of 'bad air.'"

Enrique Oblitas Poblete's book, ***Magia, Hechiceria y Medicina Popular Boliviana*** (Ediciones Isla, 1971) is a fascinating six-hundred-page collection of remedies, most of them still in use today, based on the herbal knowledge of Bolivia's ancient Callawaya (or Kollawalla) tribes. The Callawayas, he says, inherited the medical secrets of the Incas, and possibly of the Tiahuanacus and Khollas who preceded them. Some of their discoveries have counterparts in modern science: the use of penicillin and terramycin, for example, and the administration of quinine to alleviate malaria. They could predict death by mixing a patient's urine with milk and noting that it failed to coagulate because it lacked the necessary acidic content. They performed trepanation operations much admired by modern doctors (who have inspected the skulls in museums).

Wandering Callawayans can still be found today, in small towns from Ecuador to Argentina, offering magical talismans such as puma claws or vicuna fetuses as well as more conventional herb cures and always offering their services as coca leaf diviners to solve thefts or give hope for the future.

The Araucanian shamans blew tobacco smoke toward the enemy's land and recited charms before the warriors rode off to battle. Tobacco smoking is common to most South American tribes, although when the white man first arrived, he found its use was mainly magical or medicinal and in some places still is. Medically, its uses range from relieving fatigue to curing headaches or dysentery.

Unlike most tribes, the Quechua never used tobacco for magical or pleasurable reasons, but for medicinal purposes only. The Chibcha shamans used it to foretell the future. Among the Tucuna it played a part in men's initiation ceremonies when their voices changed: they were secluded and took some tobacco snuff before being presented to the sacred trumpets.

The Guajira of Colombia divine the future by burning tobacco and watching the way the smoke drifts, but the most common use of tobacco among shamans is to blow the smoke on objects or sick persons as a cure-all. Among the Jivaro, who have what John M. Cooper describes as a well-defined concept of a tobacco spirit, the drinking of tobacco water to induce nausea is part of the preparation for shamanship, and "drinking tobacco water, squirting juice in the nose, smoking large cigars, swallowing smoke and painting the body with tobacco juice are prominent features in initiation and marriage ceremonies, victory feasts and other rites."

Particularly popular with the shamans of certain tribes in the northern part of Chile was the inhalation of a hallucinogenic snuff made by collecting the seeds of the *piptadenia* tree. The impediments used in these rites included long, thin pipes inscribed with mythical figures.

In some tribes the hallucinogenic snuff was taken as an enema, in others, blown or sniffed into the nostrils. In both cases the effect was approximately the same: a temporary intoxication that often produced strong visions or spirit visitations. The drug was used for different purposes by hunters to improve alertness and vision, by warriors for stimulus and by medicine men to assist in divination. Among the Lule Indians it was believed that snuff taking would encourage rain.

The stellar attraction of Santiago's Natural History Museum is the hunched-up, mummified body of a ten-year-old boy in a black woolen robe, kept in a glass-fronted refrigerated display case. He is believed to have been a sacrificial victim to the Sun God in some ceremony five or six centuries ago; when found atop the 5,000-foot El Plomo Mountain in 1954, his body had been preserved in snow and ice for at least five hundred years. This is not, actually, as remarkable as it sounds, because many similar mummies have been found preserved, not only by the dry sands of the desert but also by the dry air in rocky mountaintop tombs.

Whatever may have been the customs before their time, the Incas institutionalized sacrifices, just as they brought order to almost everything else. Llamas and other animals were sacrificed in great numbers at least a score of times each year, including the first day of each month. Human sacrifices were rare, but took place on such occasions as famine, defeat in battle, outbreaks of plague, or the coronation of a new emperor (when two hundred children were killed). John Howland Rowe, an anthropologist with Boston's Peabody Museum who has written extensively on Incan culture, says there were three types of victims:

"When a new province was conquered, a few of the handsomest inhabitants were brought to Cuzco and sacrificed to the Sun in thanks for victory. All other victims were boys and girls collected from the provinces as part of the regular taxation, or offered by their parents in time of terrible need. They had to be physically perfect, without marks or blemishes, the boys about 10 years old, the girls 10 to 15. The children were feasted before being sacrificed so that they might not go hungry or unhappy to the creator; older children were usually made drunk first.

"The victims were made to walk around the image or cult object two or three times, and were then strangled with a cord, their throats cut, or their hearts cut out and offered to the deity still beating. With the victim's blood, the priest drew a line across the face of the image or royal mummy bundle from ear to ear, passing across the nose. Sometimes the blood was smeared all over the body of the image and sometimes it was poured on the ground.

"When an Indian was very sick, and the diviner told him he would surely die, he sometimes sacrificed his own son to Viracocha or to the Sun, praying that the god be satisfied with the life offered and spare his own."

Also preserved in Santiago's Museum of Natural History are less gruesome relics, among them a couple of rare *rongorongo*, the ancient wooden tablets from Easter Island and found nowhere else in the world, bearing hieroglyphics which nobody has been able to decipher. *Rongorongo* were once commonplace on the lonely island but many (having been "preserved" by islanders in secret caves) have rotted away, been burned in fires or just lost, and now only a score of surviving tablets are known, scattered throughout the world's museums. They are inscribed in a rarely seen manner known as "reversed boustrophedon," which means that the sequence is of a zigzag nature; this involves constantly turning the tablet upside down to read alternate lines.

For those who care to spend a lazy day in Santiago, a pleasant hour or two can be spent around the indoor swimming pool (*piscina*) of the hotel Carrera Sheraton where, incidentally, mail can be picked up c/o American Express at Turismo Cocha in the downstairs lobby. The *piscina* is on the seventeenth floor and offers a nicely detached view of midtown, and especially the spacious *Plaza de la Constitucion* adjoining the hotel (once known as the Carrera Hilton). Afternoon tea is served up here from about 4:00 to 6:00 P.M., dinner after that. It's a good spot for drinks at any time of the day.

Visitors to Chile are usually urged to absorb some of the country's musical heritage by attending one of the colorful Pena Folklorico shows; these can be enjoyed at several midtown theaters of which the most popular is El Pollo Dorado (closed Sundays). But if you want genuine folklore, you're advised to skip the more obvious places and seek out a little café called La Fragua, above a bar in the Galeria Santiago (the covered arcade adjoining the Santiago Cinema at Merced and San Antonio streets.

Here, in a room scarcely bigger than your lounge, a group of young singers and dancers merge with and reemerge from the audience with such finesse it's often hard to tell who is entertaining whom. The audience, too, is invariably young (Chileans refer to young people slangily as lolos and lolas), a crowd, one suspects, that is not altogether sympathetic to Chile's right wing dictatorship, although this is admittedly speculation.

The performers sing and play, occasionally solo, but mostly in a laughing, bantering group, and their songs are so infectiously rowdy that soon everybody in the place is stamping feet and clapping along with them in riotous abandon. Many of the songs and dances are derived from old Indian folklore; some of the others you'll recognize as Chilean versions of internationally known laments, but when they laugh and the audience laughs with them, you'll laugh too. Language is no barrier to warm, human feelings that spring from the heart.

The show begins about 10:00 P.M. and lasts well into the night on Saturdays, although the weeknight curfew begins at midnight. (Yes, that's right, there's actually a curfew in Santiago, where anybody still wandering the streets is likely to be at least stopped and questioned.) La Fragua has so few tables it's advisable to arrive early enough to bag one and make a start on the food (steak, chicken) and drink (wine costs $2 a bottle) of which each person must consume a minimum 20 pesos' Worth. Surely an unbelievably bargain price for one of the most enjoyable evening's entertainment you could find.

A pleasant excursion from Santiago is the 20-minute drive out to El Arrayan, a tiny riverside village which is almost a suburb, in the foothills of the surrounding mountains. Amid lots of willows and other hanging trees, are numerous restaurants and cafés, as well as handicraft shops, all offering some of the flavor of rural Chile. If you have time you can go farther afield: to the village of Pomaire, renowned for its handicrafts, to the Laguna de Aculea for sailing, fishing, or water-skiing; or to the impressive mountain canyon called Cajon del Maipo which cuts deep into the heart of the Andes. For those with the time and the inclination, the tourist office will arrange trips to nearby vineyards to sample the justly renowned Chilean wine.

And then, of course, less than 80 miles away is Valparaiso, Chile's second largest city, its premier port, and an oasis offering all the usual attractions of any seaside resort.

Trains and buses run regularly to Valparaiso, to the northwest. (You can also take a $12 tour via Turismo Cocha in the Carrera Sheraton hotel.)

Valparaiso (pop. 260,000) was founded in 1536, four years before Santiago itself, and was under British rule during its early years, as can be detected in the style of some of its buildings (although few of the original buildings have actually survived the scores of earthquakes). Its main square has four statues, one at each corner, symbolizing the different seasons.

It sits on the coast about 10 miles south of a famous Araucanian Indian landmark called Con Con ("water water"), a pun referring to where the Aconcagua river meets the Pacific Ocean.

With its twenty-seven hills rising sharply from the shore (and a score or so separate funiculars rising to adjoining heights), Chile's second largest city is lashed by a cold sea for most of the year. Swimming is for Spartans because the cold Humboldt Current passes offshore, the same greedy tide that siphons off the moisture from Peru's coastal desert to the north. There are 2,500 miles of Chilean coastline; almost all of them are too cold for sea bathing.

Downtown, along the coast, is Valparaiso's business district with banks, shops, and businesses, but atop each separate hill (reached from one side by funicular, the other by road) is an independent community, self sufficient with church, shops, and school. The houses are a rich mixture of different architectural styles and periods, with here and there an especially eye-catching eccentricity. For the photographer they offer a boxful of sorted props-gingerbread wooden mansions with fretwork fringes, narrow winding streets prowled by cats, harbor views framed by cable cars, and flights of steps which can be juxtaposed at will.

Considering that Chile has almost five hundred earth tremors each year, with a severe quake around every fifty years or so, it's amazing how many of the charming old buildings are still standing, because both Valparaiso itself and the more picturesque Vina del Mar up the coast bear the brunt of most of the tremors.

AN OCCULT GUIDE TO SOUTH AMERICA

Vina del Mar is the port's less commercial and more touristy suburb. It earned its name from a vine planted in the sand ("vine of the sea") which flourished and eventually developed around it the colorful little town that exists today. You could stay at the Colonial-looking hotel Espana on a quiet side street near the station or at the O'Higgins hotel, named after the same early nineteenth-century independence fighter whose name is immortalized by so many Chilean streets. Both these hotels are convenient to the main square, Plaza Vergara, as is the elegant seafront gambling casino.

North of the town, overlooking the sea, are the $25,000 homes of some of Chile's upper income group, a tiny percentage in a country where most of the middle class is lucky to earn $250 per month.

The trip to both these coastal towns takes about two hours from Santiago, passing close to the city's airport whose name, Pudahuel, is one of the few reminders that the region was once dominated by the fierce Araucanian Indians. (The name Pudahuel and that of the Curacavi ["stone and water"] Valley are both from the almost-forgotten Indian language Mapuche.)

When the Spaniards first arrived in Chile in 1535, led by Diego de Almagro on an exploratory trip from Peru, the Araucanians numbered at least half a million, but although they fought harder against the invaders than almost any of the other Indian tribes on the continent, they were eventually dominated and their numbers reduced rapidly. Slave labor, white men's diseases (smallpox, cholera, etc.), and heavy drinking all took a punitive toll.

The Araucanian Indians of the Curacavi valley venerated and hung offerings on the sacred canelo, tree, burning tobacco as incense and watering it with chicha. They used a branch of the tree to preside over their feasts, ceremonies, and healings. The "bark was used as a laxative, the wood for building, and victory celebrations were held in an open field with a canelo tree in the center.

Valiant warriors, they had a well-established ritual for battle, the fighting men preparing eight days ahead by shaving their heads, abstaining from sexual relations, and eating and drinking sparingly. To summon their armies, the Araucanian headman would send a messenger carrying an arrow to which was attached the finger of a slain enemy, and when all the groups were assembled, a black llama would be killed. All would dip their arrows

79

and spears in the llama's blood, and cat a piece of the animal's heart to signify their united purpose.

Because of the scores of Spanish priests who investigated their lifestyle and the continuing interest in them by anthropologists of today, the Araucanians have been well documented and there must be little about their habits that has not been reported. A great many of their magical practices have been recorded, Cooper says, and (quoting references) lists. "Eating parts of an animal to acquire its qualities; rubbing the body with otter genitals as an aphrodisiac; transferring disease by bodily contact to a lamb, dog or chicken and then killing the animal; using bones and stones as talismans; depositing offerings in certain cupped rocks; dissolving scrapings in water and having horses drink the mixture to make them swift in battle; and passing feathers of certain birds over the body and feet of horses for the same purpose; and using hairs or bits of clothing of a person to harm him."

Before leaving the Santiago area, visitors with some mobility might consider staying in this pleasant valley, the Curacavi, between the capital and the coast where vestiges of the still-extant Araucanian culture still remain. About 20 miles west of Santiago on the road to Valparaiso is a charming hotel, the Ingles ($4 for a single, $5 for a double) with logburning fireplaces, flower garden, and swimming pool. It's a peaceful place to be away from it all, and to sample the sparkling young crop, chicha, of Chile's fine wine.

Brief mention should be made of the southern portion of the subcontinent, even though 99 tourists out of 100 never bother to go there. (This may change as the area continues to be opened up with better roads, new accommodations, and more frequent flights.)

The southern section of both Argentina and Chile are known collectively as Patagonia, and the region is largely inhospitable for settlers because of both terrain and climate. The ground is mostly too parched for agriculture; strong winds and, on Chile's coast, heavy snows for part of the year discourage its use for almost everything except sheep raising.

The Patagonians got their name from the explorer Ferdinand Magellan who first encountered the natives at San Julian in 1520 on the Argentine side. Since then the common supposition has been that the name came from the Spanish word *patagones* ("big feet") but the Encyclopaedia of Philosophy & Religion says modern explorers have theorized "that the name is a contraction of patak ("one hundred") and a native word *Aoniken*, the original "Patak-Aoniken" being an administrative division imposed on them by their Quechua rulers.

The encyclopedia adds: "They are, as a rule, very robust and muscular; they have long faces, straight or aquiline noses, reddish yellow skin and smooth, straight hair. They are hospitable, very good to their children, of a calm disposition and very inclined to sadness. They are taciturn and seldom laugh. Under the influence of alcohol, however, they become irritable and quarrelsome, and many of their feasts, which are accompanied by libations, end in sanguinary battles."

The Spaniards in Chile didn't penetrate the southern half of the continent too deeply, except for occasional expeditions, but, by the late nineteenth century the Tehuelche Indians had been driven back from their ancient lands and Europeanization had changed most of the culture. An eighteenth century traveler, Thomas Falker, wrote after his visit in 1773 that each family group—and there are said to be three men for every woman—regarded itself as belonging to a species of animal: ostrich, puma, etc.

In 1902 Hesketh Prichard (***Through the Heart of Patagonia***) wrote that the shammu or sorcerers who were both men and women derived their power from small perforated stones that were handed down from generation to generation and guarded jealously. But sometimes, in cases of sickness, everybody would practice sorcery, the whole family of an invalid gathering around him shouting and yelling fiercely to scare the evil spirit out of the body. "Sometimes they send the invalid out on horseback, quite naked in intense cold, for according to the Patagonians the best remedy for all ills is great noise and great cold."

There are no cities or large towns, the largest communities being Commodoro Rivadavia (pop. 70,000) in a natural harbor on the Atlantic coast, not far from Argentina's main oil fields; and Chile's southernmost town of Punta Arenas, about the same size. Because of Punta Arenas' incredible location, center of the area's vast sheep farming industry, it is where most adventurous travelers head for if they come to this part of the world. There are daily flights to and from Santiago.

Across the strait from Punta Arenas is Porvenir on the island of Tierra del Fuego, which is half owned by Argentina. Ushuaia, on the Argentina side, is the world's most southerly town.

AN OCCULT GUIDE TO SOUTH AMERICA

The triangular island, about 240 miles at its southern base and 170 miles from north to south, used to be the habitat of a tribe called the Ona who numbered about two thousand just before the end of the nineteenth century but were virtually extinct by the 1930s. They seemed to possess an easygoing nature, dividing the island between two score extended families who hunted on their own land and rarely bothered their neighbors. When the white men arrived in the 1880s, gold seekers and sheep ranchers began to exterminate the Ona, and diseases, epidemics, and internal feuds pretty much finished them off.

Our next stop entails a long trip, more than 2,000 miles across the Pacific Ocean to Easter Island, said to be the loneliest populated spot on earth. Everything is expensive there because it comes by plane (there are boats about twice a year), so you might want to prepare yourself with a few luxuries for your stay. And be sure to buy Easter Island postcards in Santiago before you leave. They'll cost twice as much on the island itself!

For five hours out of Santiago the Lan Chile 707 heads across an empty sea with nothing but an occasional ship to break the monotony. And then, with a perceptible change in the engine's tone, the plane starts to descend and through the clouds appear the first signs of land: Easter Island, *Te Pito o Te Henua*—"the navel of the world"—as the natives refer to their home.

The island is small, about 14 miles long by 7 miles wide, and before landing the aircraft makes a complete circuit. Triangular in shape, it is marked by an extinct volcano at each corner— Rono Kau to the southwest, Maunga Terevaka to the northwest, and Poike on the east. There is little sign of life except for a small community along the southwestern shore. A small plume of smoke is rising from one portion of the rolling grasslands but closer inspection reveals this to be a grass fire. The volcanoes are long extinct- although it was their presence, and the lava they produced more than one thousand years ago that originally formed the island—and if not for their distinctive shape, the surrounding landscape might well be Scotland. There is no sign of the immense, inscrutable statues that have made Easter Island— *Isla de Pascua*, famous throughout the world.

On the ground, beside a single black airstrip in contrast to the red earth surrounding it, smiling faces watch expectantly as the plane unloads. Most of the passengers are *Pascuenses*, natives of Isla de Pascua, coming home after a visit to the Chilean mainland, 2,300 miles away. They are bearing gifts, usually necessities, for their friends and families. Virtually everything the island needs must be imported via the twice-weekly Lan Chile flight, and airfreight is expensive. It almost makes more sense to take a holiday trip to Santiago, buy what's needed, and bring it back in person.

The airport boasts but a single, one-story building and the luggage is brought to a thatched lean-to and checked meticulously against passengers' tags. While waiting, the handful of newcomers are solicited, in a mixture of Spanish and English, by guides and householders anxious to get a share of the obvious income to be derived from these human sheep waiting to be sheared. A room without meals in an island home can cost as little as $5 per night but the more usual tariff is $15 per person per day including meals.

With no formalities whatsoever, the passengers are cleared and pile into VW buses or jeeps for the one-mile drive into the island's only town, Hanga Roa. Actually, most of the newcomers will have made a choice between the expensive hotel Hanga Roa ($30 per person including meals, tour prices commensurate) which is owned by the Chilean government, and the friendlier hotel Hotu Matua (half the price) which is a definite bargain. In its bar, the Hanga Roa offers a nightly three hours of bad Spanish movies on closed circuit television; the Hotu Matua counters with a library of free paperbacks and the occasional barbecue staged by its genial manager, Orlando. Both hotels are about one kilometer from town.

There are no movies, almost no entertainment, few shops, only one merely passable beach a long way from town and no fascinating little tours to adjoining places, the nearest of which, Pitcairn Island, is a formidable 900 miles to the west. Easter Island is a lonely place, one of the loneliest in the world, and its attraction for tourists is its mystery, bred by the very isolation which keep so many visitors away.

Of course it is the massive statues that have always intrigued outsiders the most: towering redstone figures as high as 30 feet and weighing up to 80 tons. They have impassive, almost stern, faces and are often wearing 10-ton hats or topknots carved from a different colored stone. Whoever built them and when, or even why, it was an impressive engineering feat, and these questions have never been answered to the satisfaction of the world's curious anthropologists and archaeologists who have been coming here for almost a century with their contradictory speculations.

The present-day Pascuenses have no tradition of massive stone-carving nor even much interest in the statues (apart from their proven tourist value) and when the Norwegian explorer Thor Heyerdahl first visited the island in 1955 not a single one of the massive figures was still standing.

Although an English sailor, Edward Davis, was the first seafarer to report a visit in 1687, the island first came into the world's consciousness from a report by the Dutch admiral Jacob Roggeveen who was sent there on an exploration by the Dutch West Indies Company and anchored off the "navel of the world" on Easter Day, 1722. He observed that most of the island's inhabitants lived in straw huts with stones for pillows, cooking their food over hot rocks. They cultivated sugar cane and potatoes but apparently were unfamiliar with metal. Some natives had long ears from which pendants were hanging.

Half a century later the island had another visitor, the Spanish captain Felipe Gonzales, who estimated the population to be about three thousand, many of whom lived in holes in the ground. Gonzales declared the island to be the property of the Spanish monarch Charles III and enticed some of its mystified residents to scrawl bird-like figures, which he assumed to be their signatures, on a treaty which only the Spaniards could read.

Next, in 1774, came Captain Cook, who looked over the by-then famous statues and concluded that the present residents did not regard them as idols. But he added: "They must have been a work of immense time and sufficiently show the ingenuity and perseverance of the islanders in the age in which they were built; for the present inhabitants have most certainly had no hand in them as they do not even repair the foundations of those which are going to decay."

During the subsequent century, Easter Island's contacts with the outside world gave "civilization" nothing much to be proud of. In 1808 an American ship dropped anchor, enticed some of the natives aboard, and enslaved them for a seal-catching expedition; in 1825, during a visit by an English ship, a local chieftain was shot and killed; in 1862, Peruvian seal hunters kidnapped almost one thousand Pascuenses to work in coastal guano mines. Although the handful of survivors (most had already died of disease, malnutrition, and homesickness) were returned after international protests, they brought back with them smallpox germs which virtually decimated the rest of the population.

Exploitation continued for the rest of the century: in 1868 British adventurers removed a stone statue to send to the British Museum; in 1872 French marauders acted similarly; in 1877 and 1882 there was more foreign pillaging. Finally, in 1888, a Chilean warship arrived and Commander Policarpo Toro Hurtado formally took possession of the island on behalf of the nearest mainland country.

The Easter Island of today, though dependent on Chile for many of the luxuries which we have come to regard as necessities, is pleasantly self-sufficient in a few small ways. Lobsters are so numerous that visitors are likely to be served them almost every other meal; they are huge and of a tasty, succulent variety, lacking the big claws of lobsters in other parts of the world. They are boiled, split down the center, and served with lemon, sometimes reheated over glowing coals as the *piéce de resistance* of a local barbecue.

Fruit is plentiful—oranges, watermelons, lemons, bananas, and the yellow-skinned guavas whose delicate pink insides are faintly reminiscent in flavor of strawberries.

The enormous herd of sheep was recently reduced because the animals were destroying all the greenery, but wild horses are so numerous that islanders whimsically list the population as "1,400 people and 4,000 horses." Recently a band of wild horses were rounded up and shipped to the mainland, to be traded for cattle of which there is still a shortage on the island.

The Encyclopedia Britannica says Isla de Pascua "represents the easternmost outpost of the Polynesian island world" and describes its population as part of a basically Polynesian subgroup. But some investigators have pointed out that certain of its archaeological features are more common to the South American continent. The encyclopedia identifies distinct cultural periods on the island: The early period is characterized by a solar observatory, megalithic walls of exquisitely fitted stone masonry astronomically oriented to the annual movements of the sun, and a heterogenous variety of small to medium-sized statues in human form."

Later, the encyclopedia continues, the existing temple terraces were destroyed and rebuilt with no regard for solar orientation but for the sole purpose of supporting the ever greater statues which eventually reached the enormous height of more than 60 feet.

Thor Heyerdahl and Edwin Ferdon in their **Archaeology of Easter Is-**

land argue that while fitted masonry blocks or slabs can be found sporadically throughout Polynesia, they do not correspond with the slightly convex ones on Easter Island which are, however, to be found in Peru. Similarly, some of the ancient stone houses with corbel-vaulted roofs are of a basic type found along South America's west coast.

As for the solar observation device and the adjacent fire pit which suggested the ceremonial significance of fire, these were also common throughout Peru. There are other parallels, among them the similarity of a "Bird Man" cult with ones that resemble it at Tiahuanacu in Bolivia and in Peru's ancient Chimu culture; the custom of cremation which was known in Ecuador and Chile but only occasionally in Melanesia; and, finally, the rafts made from totora reeds which were found around both Lake Titicaca and Easter Island's volcano craters.

The island's natural habitat tends to prove very little because much of it—chicken, sheep, yams, and other vegetables—was introduced in relatively recent times. Mainly of volcanic origin, the island is mostly too bleak for cultivation and is largely based around the solitary town, Hanga Roa, in the southwest. Its climate is subtropical with an average annual temperature of about 73°F; the rainy season occurs between May and July.

There is a weekly market in Hanga Roa plus a handful of shops, a post office, a bank, a seldom-open museum, a school, and a few dozen shabby houses along a central, red-earth avenue lined with wilting plants. But what might be considered the town's center is a small square at the top of the hill dominated by the spacious Catholic Church, an undistinguished flat building like an aircraft hangar containing simply carved wooden pews. There is an open square, on a slant, in front of the church and a rickety bench encircling the solitary tree.

Adjoining the church is a tiny graveyard in which is buried the island's most famous resident, Father Sebastian Englert, a German Franciscan priest who began his career serving as a missionary to Chile's Arancanian Indians and then worked as Easter Island's solitary priest for thirty-five years, almost until his death in January 1969. He died at the age of eighty while on a visit to the United States where he was helping with an exhibition of the island's mysterious artifacts.

It was Father Sebastian who did the most to uncover the tangled history of the isolated island that he chose for his home. He documented the legends and laboriously tramped around listing the hundreds of statues, painting numbers on them which are still clearly visible. He speculated on who the early Easter Islanders might have been, outlining on the one hand the view of Sir Peter Buck that the influences (and thereby the skill to carve the statues) came from Polynesia in the west, and on the other, Thor Heyerdahl's theory that at least some of the original settlers came from South America (and more specifically from Peru) to the east.

But it was his perceptions of the nature of magic, or what the natives understood as magic, that made Father Sebastian such a valuable witness to the continuity of ancient belief. He discussed the concept of mana, that supernatural power possessed by persons of high rank (*ariki*), which enforced prohibitions and ensured bountiful crops and good fishing. He pointed out that even after death the *ariki* were believed to retain magical powers, their skulls being specially marked, and sometimes placed on plantations or in chicken houses to increase fertility.

"This," he wrote, "is a significant key to understanding the true nature of mana. It existed completely outside the volition of the possessor who was essentially its receptacle or vehicle."

The notions of mana, he added, were still appreciated by many islanders but its potency was felt to have been diminished by the introduction of Christianity. Nevertheless, it was mana, in the opinion of the most superstitious of the islanders, that had enabled the fifty-ton statues to walk the long distances from the quarry on the side of Rano-Raraku where they were carved, to the sites on which they are now found several miles away.

According to the oldest island legend, the first inhabitant was a king named Hotu Matua who arrived in the twelfth or thirteenth century from a barren and to the west after being beaten in battle. Hotu Matua and his two hundred followers disembarked in Anakena Bay, in the north, unloaded plants and animals, established their homes in caves, and carefully preserved banana leaf scrolls on which ideograms were inscribed. These were later copied, on the king's orders, onto wooden scrolls known as rongorongo for safe preservation. King Hotu Matua had five children, of which the eldest, Tuu-Maheke, succeeded him as a king; at this time the island was divided up between the five offspring, forming the original tribes.

This sketchy history of the Pascuenses' distant origins receives confirmation, of a sort, from twentieth-century carbon datings which have established from ancient cooking fires that the enormous altars (ahu) which line the island's cliffs—there are almost 250 *ahu* altogether—were probably constructed between the ninth and thirteenth centuries of our era. Built with basalt rocks, they obviously had religious significance because apart from acting as platforms for the immense statues (*moais*), most were also used as ceremonial burial places, and even today scores of skulls and bones remain buried in nooks, crevices, and caves around such sites. Pierre Loti, a young French midshipman who explored the island extensively in 1872, suggested the prevalence of skeletons might indicate that human sacrifices took place. He wondered, considering how many idols and monuments could be found in some a relatively small area, if the island might not have been a sacred one to which people came from afar to take part in religious ceremonies.

The Argentinian writer Jorge d'Amato says that the statues' builders could not have come from Polynesia because Polynesians, though expert wood carvers, had no experience with stone work. And he, like Heyerdahl, suggests that immigrants from the Incan empire visited the island bringing their long experience of carving monoliths with them. Loti, however, wrote that he detected the style of the Maori race in the statues along the cliffs which appeared to him to represent "the spirit of the sands" and "the spirits of the rocks."

Whatever their origins, the method of the statues' construction is still clear for all to see. On the outer slopes of the defunct volcano Rano Raraku, the quarry where the statues were carved from solid rock is silent and undisturbed; unfinished statues, body and features carved but the backs still attached to the cliff face, lie around in profusion.

Apparently the figures were completely finished before being lowered down the inner rim of the volcano and then transported, without wheels, and without being damaged, many miles to where they were eventually erected. Many of the figures were eventually capped with the cylindrical topknots, themselves weighing several tons each, which were carved and brought from a totally different quarry at Punapau in the island's southwest interior.

Inside the volcano, scores of other statues lie around, apparently awaiting shipment through the gap on the west by which the volcanic lava originally flowed to the sea. More statues stand in asymmetrical rows on the lower slopes out side the crater. The ground is littered with flakes of obsidian that naturally formed the black glass from which the Elizabethan magician John Dee made his magical "shew stones."

The floor of the crater has for centuries been covered by a vast lake, dry in summer, which has frequently served as a source of fresh water on an island that possesses no other supply aside from subterranean wells and rainwater. The lake's surface is thick with the pulpy, green totora reeds which are found nowhere else in the Pacific but are characteristic of Peru's Lake Titicaca; this was one of the factors that led Heyerdahl to suggest that boats made from plaited totora had brought Incan explorers here in the first place. The inspiration for Heyerdahl's earlier book, in fact, had been Kon Tiki-"Tiki of the Sun"—a warrior who was defeated in battle near Lake Titicaca and who, legend said, had built a raft on the Peruvian coast and sailed west. In 1947, constructing a raft of balsa logs, Heyerdahl sailed from Callao on the Peruvian coast, landing 101 days later at the Polynesian island of Raroia, even further west than Easter Island, without serious mishap, and proving that such a trip had at least been possible for the South American Indians long ago.

Heyerdahl's book about his months on Easter Island, with a full team of archaeologists that included William Mulloy, professor of anthropology at the University of Wyoming, was a best seller under the title *Aku Aku*, which is the local term for spirit. It was Professor Mulloy who returned to Easter Island in 1960 and organized the re-erection of a group of seven statues at Ahu Akivi. They stand there today, each about 15 feet tall with impassive faces slightly tilted towards the sky as if in anticipation of something coming. In front of their ahu or base is a terrace of football-sized boulders in rows, interspersed with thousands of small eggshaped pebbles. A breeze blows constantly around them, and apart from the ubiquitous wild horses, the undulating landscape is empty. It would be an assuredly magical spot to spend the night in the shadow of these ancient guardians.

To set these statues back on their bases, Professor Mulloy used pretty much the same method that had been demonstrated to Heyerdahl in 1955 when the then-mayor Pedro Atan, with the assistance of eleven laborers, had spent eighteen days raising a twenty-five-ton statue with two wooden levers by the method of gradually pushing more and more stones under the figure until it was upright.

AN OCCULT GUIDE TO SOUTH AMERICA

Atan, a prominent character in Aku Aku, was a self described "long ear," a descendant of an earlier racial group on the island who were massacred in an uprising about three centuries before by the "short ears" they had enslaved. Legend had it that the "long ears" were burned alive in a ditch they had constructed for their own protection on the slopes of Poike; carbon-14 tests by Heyerdahl's group in 1955 confirmed that an immense fire had indeed taken place in the ditch at that time.

Even up until the early nineteenth century, the statues were apparently still standing all over the island. But no visitors mentioned seeing any standing after 1838 (the ones standing today have all been re-erected) and historians conjecture that internal strife and civil war, probably brought about by increasing food shortages, led to the statues' destruction either as the spoils of war or, as Father Sebastian suggests, "to obliterate the supernatural power of ancestors," which is what most chroniclers have come to believe they represented.

At one of the most picturesque sites on the island, Vinapu, where the *ahu* is composed of enormous, close-fitting blocks whose construction reminds most observers of Incan sites, seven statues once stood oriented towards the setting sun, facing inland. But the tidal wave that followed a gigantic earthquake in Chile in 1960 tossed the statues about, scattering and breaking them. At Tonga Riki, an inlet that forms the lowest part of the island, dozens of other forty-ton statues were tossed around by the tidal wave and carried inshore for hundreds of feet as though made of cork.

Most of the statues look alike, with thick torsos truncated at the waist, the merest suggestion of hands and arms by etched lines, long, flat noses, and incised foreheads. But one is different. It depicts a man kneeling, his buttocks resting on his heels and hands stretched out along his thighs. The posture is characteristic of that adapted by chorus singers in festivals known as *riu* and again, says Heyerdahl, has its counterpart in statues seen in Peru.

In his *Easter Island: Island of Enigmas* (Doubleday, 1971) John Dos Passos asks: "What did [the statues] represent to their sculptors? Is it possible that like the totem poles of the Northwest Indians they represented divine ancestors and family heroes?" And he quotes again from Pierre Loti, who twenty years after his Easter Island visit was elected to the *Academie Francaise*. "So many squared stones moved, erected and transported," he quotes the Frenchman, "testify to the presence here during centuries of a powerful race accustomed to the working of stone and having inexplicable methods of excavation. In the origins perhaps all people have gone through this megalithic stage during which they controlled forces which we know nothing about."

But we will lay speculation aside for there is still plenty to see, notably the numerous caves formed either by the action of the sea or by the expansion of gases in the volcanic lava, as the island was first being formed sometime in the last two thousand years.

At times during the eighteenth century, when civil wars had demoralized the population and severely restricted the food supplies, cannibalism became a matter of record on the island, and much of the population took to hiding in whatever secret caves they could find. Caves had always been burying grounds for the dead, and now they became homes for the living as well.

Some of them are enormous. About one kilometer south of the statues at Abu Akivi, a cluster of banana trees marks the entrance to one of the longest and biggest. It is high enough to walk upright, wide enough for several people abreast, and winds around to an exit several hundred feet farther away. Despite its size it would make a good hiding place, situated in lonely countryside where only the cry of an occasional keening hawk is heard (there are no seagulls on the island because the hawks ate all their eggs) and where the only passerby is a random rider with lasso ready, galloping in western style after a wild horse.

Another cave, typical of many, is hidden amid the black lava rock of fields to the northwest of town. This has an entrance just wide enough to lower oneself, opening up into a broad passageway that branches in two directions, ending in wide openings high on the cliffs above jagged rocks. In the olden days, Heyerdahl writes, many of the island families maintained their own secret caves in which they kept priceless relics and carvings, some of which he inveigled out of their owners to take back and enrich the world's museums.

Even today not everybody lives in houses. At some tiny bay, where a decline in the cliff allows boats to land, an isolated family group will be living gypsy-style beside the sea, their belongings divided between cavelike cavities in the rocks, a tattered tent, and perhaps a makeshift hut constructed from planks and strips of tin. Invariably somebody will be playing an accordion, a fisherman will eventually land with lobsters in a sack, and chickens, barefoot children, and pipe-smoking sailors will leave their smoky pots steaming atop a driftwood fire and make their way to the water's edge to inspect his catch.

Many of the island's fishermen take off from the pink, sandy beach at Ovahe, a charming cove to which a bus runs on Sundays and at which mid-week visitors are apt to find the fishermens' clothes hung up on rocks awaiting their late afternoon return.

Apart from the statues, which after all can be found almost everywhere around the island, Easter Island's most mystic spot is undoubtedly Orongo, a series of what an 1886 visitor, U.S. paymaster William Thompson, called "burrow-like dwellings" and which were in use only once each year, during the "Bird Man" (Tangata-manu) ceremonies at the spring equinox (September).

At this time almost all the island's able-bodied men gathered to compete for the honor of finding the first egg laid by the flock of sooty terns that annually returned to nest on the neighboring rocks of Motu Kau Kau and Motu Nui. Father Sebasdan speculated that the man who received the first egg and climbed the cliff with it safely in his mouth, might have been regarded as the reincarnation of the god Makemake, whom tradition said had first brought the terns to the island. Obviously, in a community where food was often scarce, a fresh supply of nourishment in the form of eggs would be a welcome addition to the regular diet.

The winner of the annual race, that is to say the first man to return safely with an egg, became symbolic king of the island for the forthcoming year. His head was shaved and painted, his right hand was considered sacred and unusable, he was confined to a specially constructed hut on the slopes of the volcano where he remained in solitude until his term was over. The "Bird Man" cult is believed to have begun early in the eighteenth century and died about the middle of the nineteenth.

The site of Orongo is magnificent. On one side is the almost perfectly circular crater of Rano-Kau, its entire amphitheater a sunken lake which is a mass of reeds and foliage in different shades. The sides are almost sheer and on the narrow pathway between its rim and the sheer cliffs which drop hundreds of feet into the sea it is easy to imagine the strong wind plucking you suddenly from the edge and dropping you on either side. The white waves crash onto the reefs and it must have taken intrepid swimmers indeed to plunge into those boiling waters and struggle to the rocky islets across the channel.

Orongo, high on the cliffs at the outer edge of the volcano Rano-Kau, is a rich field for the investigator into ancient customs. In addition to the numerous sculptured rocks, carved with the half-human, half-birdlike figure representing Makemake, great spirit of the sea, there is also to be seen a kind of primitive sundial composed of a rock with holes. A pole thrust into one hole casts a shadow in a direct line over another hole at summer solstice, and so on with other equinoxes around the clock.

The ground all around the top of the volcano is still littered with ancient bones, remnants perhaps of long-distant massacres, and the crater itself, according to Pierre Loti, "is the widest and possibly the most regularly shaped in the whole world."

Faster Island has still one last mystery with which to baffle a fascinated world, and this one may never be solved. It concerns the wooden tablets, rongorongo, mentioned earlier in this chapter and which, legend relates, the first king, Hotu Matua, ordered to be made to preserve the ancient wisdom.

Within living memory there were islanders who claimed to understand the meaning of these tablets, but as the Last people who knew for sure were among those captured during the Peruvian invasion more than a century ago, the key to the mysterious hieroglyphics has been lost forever. About twenty of the original tablets remain, a few of them on tablets on the toromino wood that was once indigenous to the island where it grew in the volcanic craters. Most of the tablets are in European museums, two are in the tiny museum at Hanga Roa. A few others may remain undisclosed in private collections on the island. Some of the tablets were said to have been destroyed by the early missionaries as artifacts of the faith that Christianity had replaced.

Most of the symbols on the tablets are unidentifiable and although Makemake is recognizable, others represent forms not known locally, so their translation would be a big step to establishing from whence the original settlers came. The tablets range from about 5 $^1/_2$ inches long by 4 inches wide to more than 5 feet long by 7 inches wide, although reproductions offered for sale on the island are always of the smaller dimensions.

It is not only the symbols themselves that scholars find unusual but the style in which they are written—the zigzag form mentioned earlier is found only on these tablets and a few similar fragments from Tiahuanaco and other parts of pre-Incan Peru.

At present, Lan Chile is the only airline with rights to Easter Island although applications are pending from other lines and it seems likely that in any case there will be more development, more hotels, in future years.

Lan Chile files from Santiago twice a week—one trip stops en route to Tahiti, making a return stop five days later; the other goes direct to the island and returns the same day—but it's also possible to include the island on one of the tours operated by Lan Chile and Air New Zealand. This twenty-day tour described as "the Exotic Triangle" is quoted at around $1,100 per person. Leaving from Miami it includes five days in Peru, three days on Easter Island, and a week or so in Polynesia.

And now, back to Santiago from which we fly over the Andes to our next stop: Bolivia. Here, for the first time, we begin to familiarize ourselves with life at thousands of feet above sea level. Both physically and mentally it is very different from anything we have experienced on our trip so far.

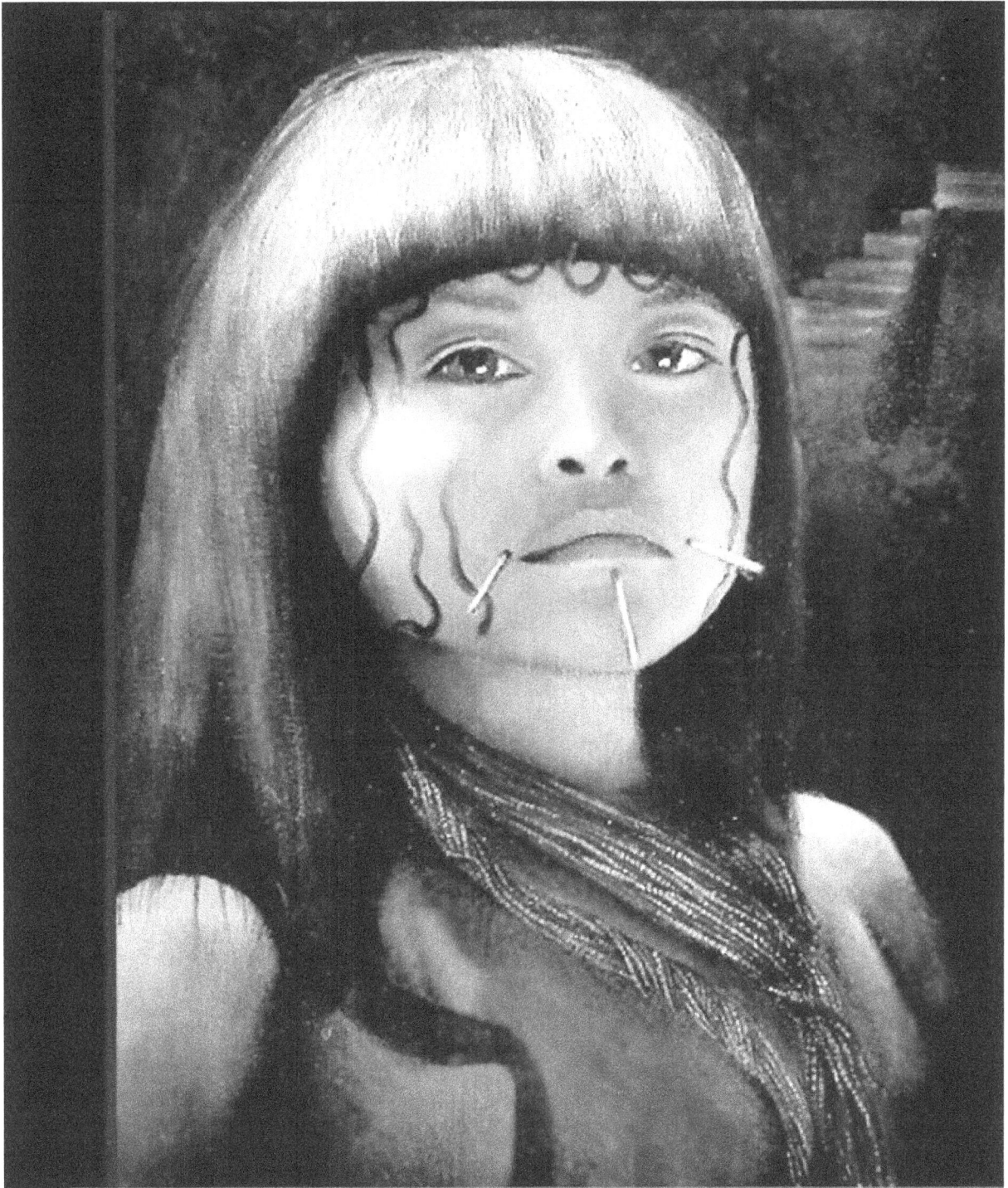

AN OCCULT GUIDE TO SOUTH AMERICA

At Manaus, Brazil, the natives build their houses on stilts at the edge of the river.

The fabulous Incan ruins of Machu Picchu, Peru.

Above, the mysterious massive Puerta del Sol (Gate of the Sun) at Tiahuanaco, Bolivia.
Below, this intricately carved monolith, relic of a pre-Incan civilization, stands on the Bolivian altiplano near Tiahuanaco.

Above, author John Wilcock stands before two of the huge stone heads to be found on Easter Island, off the coast of Chile.

Below, ancient reed boats were the models for these present-day totora craft that survive in the fishing villages around Lake Titicaca.

Spectacular view of Rio

Above, the fantastic battlements of Cartegena, Colombia, part of a chain of seven fortresses which once protected this important Spanish port.

Below, ruins atop Panecillo Hill, overlooking the city of Quito, Ecuador.

Chapter 8

Bolivia

"An Almanac of Carved Stone"

The population of Bolivia, a country without a seacoast, is significantly more Indian than white—as can be verified by a stroll through La Paz—even allowing for the vast numbers of mixed-breed *cholos* who have permeated every aspect of the country's life.

Thousands of Ayrmara Indians still live in wretched adobe huts scattered all over the altiplano, an almost treeless, scrub-covered wilderness that stretches between the parallel Andean ranges of Kimsachata to the south and Achata to the north. Kimsachata in ancient Aymara means "it has become three," and the mountain does indeed have three peaks, only one of which has proved climbable.

All of these mountains, of course, can be admired from La Paz itself, but once having climbed out of the valley in which the city sits, and over the rim, onto the famous altiplano, one is in a region so much higher that even the mountains somehow appear on a more accessible scale.

Barren as the altiplano appears to be, it is almost a paradise compared to the empty coastal desert and the entangling jungle that flanks it, and it has been settled since ancient times. More than 500 miles long and ranging from 30 to 100 miles in width, the altiplano drops gradually in height from north to south and is traversed by a handful of rivers of which the largest, the Choqueyapu, flows through La Paz and, in fact, after countless centuries of erosion, actually created the 2,600-foot deep valley in which the city lies.

Covered almost everywhere with jch'u, an all-purpose grass that is used for everything from ropes and thatch to feeding llamas, the altiplano supports a surprising amount of plant and animal life, including many varieties of frost resistant potatoes and such domesticated creatures as chickens, pigs, ducks, sheep, and cows.

Unpaved roads, whose loose rocks constantly shatter the windshields of passing vehicles, stretch across the near desert, occasionally leading through Aymara villages which are little more than groups of adobe homes gathered around a central square. The invading Spanish made one such village, Laja, their main headquarters in the sixteenth century, building a church from the stones of the abandoned Sun Temple of Tiahuanaco, (also Tiahuanacu) a few miles away. Later they moved their capital eastwards to found La Paz, following reports that the river there was washing gold down from the Andes and that it could be easily panned.

Historians are unable to agree on who built Tiahuanaco although its culture was influential and spread far to the north. The evidence of archaeology, explains the folklorist Harold Osborne, "points certainly to the existence of a highly centralized social organization whether religious or political which must have preceded the Inca regime and must have lasted many centuries."

The race which preceded the Incas was the Quechuas or Quichuas, who co-existed side by side with the Aymara (also known as the Colla). The Quichua language, already widely spoken by the time the Incas arrived, was used by them as a unifying force and became so predominant that it is still spoken by more than six million people today.

The Quichuas and the Aymara also shared the same god, Viracocha, sometimes referred to as Ticci meaning roughly "the cause" or "the beginning," and occasionally Tukupay, meaning "he who finishes or perfects." As civilizations have done before and since, the Incas (who had a habit of rewriting history to conform with their own myths) took over existing beliefs more or less intact, adding a few details of their own to enhance the importance of Lake Titicaca and the sacred island on which Viracocha, the Inca Sun God, had survived the great flood.

Garcilaso de]a Vega, himself the son of an Incan princess and a Spanish soldier, documented the legend in his famous *Comentarios Reales de los Incas*, published late in the sixteenth century: 'Seeing that the Indians believed this ancient tale, regarding the island and lake as sacred, the first Inca, Manco Capac, in his natural wisdom and ingenuity took advantage of it and created a second fable stating that he and his wife were children of the Sun and that their father had set them down in that island so they could wander the earth teaching people."

The story is amplified by another sixteenth-century writer, a native Indian named Juan de Santa Cruz Pachacuti, who said that Manco Capac's father had been presented with a *tupa yauri* (royal wand) by an elderly man with white flowing beard and long hair who appeared from Lake Titicaca. At his child's birth, the wand turned into a golden scepter and when, as an adult, Manco Capac set off on his wanderings, it was this golden staff—a symbol of the Sun's rays—that sank into the earth of its own accord, determining the site for the Incas' sacred city, Cuzco.

The description of the man with the flowing white hair and beard is significant because it conforms to all the other legends about Viracocha, whose actual name in Quicha can be translated as "sea foam."

In ***American Hero Myths*** Daniel G. Brinton emphasizes the importance of Viracocha as "creator, and ever-present active divinity; he alone answered prayers and aided in time of need; he was the sole efficient god. All prayers to the Sun or to the deceased Incas, or to idols, were directed to them as intercessors only."

One of the most reliable early authorities, Christobal de Molina (***Relacion de las fabulas y ritos de los Incas***, 1553) comments:-They did not recognize the Sun as their Creator, but as created by the Creator, and this creator was "not born of woman but was unchangeable and eternal.

Brinton says that in 1571 the Spanish viceroy held an inquiry at which many of the oldest Indians, especially those of noble birth, were questioned specifically about just what the old religion was and all were in agreement: "On this point the statements were most positive. The Sun was but one of Viracocha's creations, not itself the Creator." The writers who have called the Inca religion "a sun worship," therefore, have been led into exaggerating its significance.

As for Manco Capac, when his work was done, "he did not die, like other mortals, but rose to heaven and became the planet Jupiter, under the name Pirua. From this, according to some writers, the country of Peru derived its name.

Some idea of just how tangled Christian and pagan beliefs have become can be gleaned from the old folklore of countries where the Spaniards imposed their new religion atop ancient superstitions. In the three-volume set of tales, **Brujerias Tradiciones y Leyendas** (Difusion Ltda, La Paz, 1969) by the Bolivian writer Antonio Paredes Candia, it is surprising to find how many similarities exist between the folklore of the Old World and the New, and at this late date it is probably impossible to determine how many of the tales existed before the two cultures collided. What is the difference, for example, between the Scottish tales about the kelpies of water spirits (or the Loch Ness monster, for that matter) and the *lichi* which is supposed to protect Bolivian lakes and occasionally lure the unwary within reach, dragging them down into the depths from which they never return? Evil (and sometimes beneficial) spirits of the water are widespread, and turn up in many different cultures.

More specific to the Andean area is the legend of the magic lake which shelters a golden city, reminiscent of the El Dorado fable which lured the Spaniards (and many who came after them) ever southward from Panama in search of it. In its purest form the legend concerned a gilded king—El Dorado—whose body was washed with powdered gold in a lake into which gold offerings were thrown every year by his faithful subjects. A serpent was said to rise to the surface to receive the offerings.

Colombia's Lake Guatavita was the origin of the legend, but gradually many different locations were claimed to be the true one and hundreds died over the centuries pursuing the El Dorado quest in mountain and jungle. The Chilean folklorist Julio Vicuna Cifuentes wrote that the legend was widespread in Chile, and Candia's nomination is the Golden Lagoon of Corocoro in western Bolivia.

Buried beneath this lagoon's waters, he reports, is an enchanted city whose houses are all made of gold or silver and which, on the nights of the waning moon, rise to the surface. The lake can be seen from far away because it shines more brightly than the sun; but no one who has seen it has ever returned alive because "the lagoon is guarded by unique sentries who are visible only to punish trespassers and treasure hunters. One is an immense golden lizard, while, within the lagoon itself during the nights of the full moon, swim two ducks made of gold."

When the Spaniards first arrived in Bolivia in the early sixteenth century, this was the type of story that confronted them, and it was a long time before they were able to sort out fact from fiction. One thing that did become evident, though not for some time, was how much mineral wealth lay under the Bolivian soil. The conquistadors had almost given up on this apparently barren land when, in 1544, they discovered the rich silver deposits at Potosi. These were exploited for two decades and when seemingly exhausted were given a new lease on life when Viceroy Francisco de Toledo devised a method of extracting the lower-grade silver by the introduction of mercury into the mining process.

Sometime early in the conquest, the invaders stumbled upon a site of even greater consequence, from an archaeological point of view, Tiahuanaco. They were astonished at the size of the ruined temple. "Indeed the buildings are the most spectacular of any in this kingdom," wrote the Jesuit priest Bernabé Cobo) and even more amazed by the fact that local Indians had no memory or legends of its creation.

One explanation for this, according to Harold Osborne (*South American Mythology*, Paul Hamlyn, London, 1968), is that the people who built up the influential and widespread Tiahuanaco civilization "were overthrown by warlike immigrants who wiped them out and liquidated their culture and traditions." Supporting this theory is the fact that many of the buildings were left unfinished; that there is a legend that two local chieftains made war upon each other, thus undermining the kingdom and leaving it ripe for Incan conquest; and the other legend about the existence of a "white and bearded race" which disappeared without trace many centuries before.

The anonymous author of a *History of South America* (Central Publishing House, Cleveland, 1913) says there were three central structures: the fort, the temple, and the palace of the Inca, the last of which was misnamed: "neither built as a residence for an Inca nor used by any as such."

Because of the depredations by natives over the centuries, both before and after the Spaniards removed many of the stones for other building projects, Tiahuanaco is not wildly impressive today. Some believe, however, that it was the site of the greatest sun temple in the world—an almanac of carved stone," as Professor Arthur Posnansky described it in his book, *Tiahuanaco*, first published in 1914. This classic work, "the fruit of a lifetime spent in study," was republished in 1945 (J. J. Augustin, New York) in large format with hundreds of pages of bilingual text plus color plates, drawings, diagrams, and charts. (The English translation is by James Shearer.)

AN OCCULT GUIDE TO SOUTH AMERICA

Professor Posnansky believes that Tiahuanaco was "the cradle of American man—the foundation of South American culture," and suggests a date for its construction as far back as 15,000 years ago, a date that some investigators regard as outlandish. Be that as it may, almost everyone agrees that the sacred site dates to the pre-Christian era and was a sophisticated observatory to measure the sun and moon phases, as well as the eclipses. This would have been in an epoch when a bad agricultural year—especially if not foreseen by the Khollas, the sacerdotal caste that ran things—would have been not only catastrophic to the people at large but would have had unpleasant repercussions among the godlike upper classes.

Even today, the deserted and abandoned temple of Kalassasaya is still oriented more or less on the meridian, its length and width conforming to the maximum angle of solar declination between the two equinoxes. The sun rises exactly in the main gateway on the morning of the spring equinox in September, for this is south of the equator.

The major landmark in this solar temple observatory of Kalassasaya is an immense Sun Door whose lintel was broken in two at some date after the sixteenth-century Spanish occupation. When the indefatigable Spanish traveler Cieza de Leon visited the site in 1640, the Sun Door was presumably still buried in the ground, because he fails to mention it. But he remarked on the fact that great walls and ramparts were still standing. Most of these, except for the lengthy wall of tight-fitting blocks that surrounds the temple, have since disappeared.

It is the massive Sun Door which—broken lintel notwithstanding—has now been re-erected that Professor Posnansky focuses upon. The central figure, that of Viracocha, the Sun himself, has a head larger than his body; his feet rest on the "staircase sign" motif that may have been derived from the agricultural terraces with which, since ancient times, the Indians have covered their hillsides; and his extended arms hold scepters representing command and power.

Around the god are symbols representing the lunar months, with September predominating since it is the month of the spring equinox—thus the beginning of the earth's most fertile period, and the time when an important festival was dedicated to Pachamama.

"The ground, the food-giving earth goddess was Pachamama"; wrote Professor Posnansky, "the moon, Paximama; the lake, Cochomama. Even the wind was a divine being called Huayra-Huirakjocha. The hills and especially the volcanoes were also considered to be divinities and were called *Achachilas*—an Aymaran word meaning 'grandfathers'."

The month's thirty days are represented by moons, only twenty-four of which are shown. Professor Posnansky theorizes that the six days of the "invisible moon" are depicted by the six puma heads, in line with the ancient folklore (still prevalent today) that the celestial puma eats away gradually at the moon and then allows it to grow back gradually.

About one kilometer southwest of Kalassasaya and the sunken temple it adjoins (a replica of which can be seen in La Paz) are the remains of a smaller temple, possibly one dedicated to the moon. It was constructed of enormous blocks of red sandstone; the Indians living in the area today call it Puma-Punku, the door of the puma.

How old, actually, is Tiahuanaco? Experts disagree, but the professor bases his case for real antiquity on several factors. In the first place, he says, there is nothing in local folklore that relates even remotely to the origin and object of "that magnificent metropolis" It was already ancient and long abandoned by the days of the Spanish conqueror, at which time Indians averred it had been built by a race of giants before *Chamak-Pacha*—an Aymara word that means "period of darkness" and could refer to a glacial epoch when the sun was rarely seen.

There is evidence suggesting that the altiplano, being near the equator, did not endure a glacial period as long as other parts of South America, and as a result harbored human life from an earlier date. But the oceans, of course, were much higher, and Lake Titicaca itself (now 11 miles away) may have stretched to the very walls of the temple, as can be verified by the traces of marine fauna discovered both in the lake and in the subsoil of the surrounding countryside. In any case, Posnansky says, the climate must have been much more agreeable than it is today to support the kind of civilization that made Tiahuanaco possible.

Encyclopedia of Philosophy & Religion comments that the building of Tiahuanaco "'necessitated a great population, mechanical skill—the result of long ages of civilization—and abundant supplies of food."

In the center of the vast project, overlooking temples, a series of underground caves in which the priests may have lived and also the nearby village—is a pyramid-shaped hill called Akapana. The word may have been corrupted from the Aymara term *Aka-Kjahuana* which roughly means "the place from which one sees." As the highest point in the neighborhood—the altiplano is consistently flat—it may well have been the fortress from which the temples were guarded.

For the past half-century at least, it has contained a water-filled crater resulting from excavations by the Spaniards who removed the fortress block by block. Its pagan stones formed the base for the church in the nearby village of Tiahuanaco.

Dominating a spacious plaza surrounded by nondescript two-story houses, the church is today flanked by two enormous pagan deities taken from the temple area centuries ago. The village is visited once a week by a train from La Paz and on which, half a century ago, most of the treasures from this "almanac of carved stone" were carted off to the big city. Of all the spirits that influence the lives of the Aymara, the *achachilas* which inhabit lakes—and especially the surrounding volcanoes, Illimani, Illampu, Hake-Hake, Soraka, Huayna, Potosi—are considered the most important. The higher the mountain, the more influence its spirits are presumed to have. The Andean peaks, in Indian belief, have relationships of love, hate, and envy just as men do, and the monarch Illimani (23,000 feet) is said to have been sufficiently disturbed by the effrontery of Mururata at challenging its height that it complained to Viracocha demanding justice. Whereupon the god loaded his slingshot and decapitated the audacious Mururata, kicking the head into the flat Oruro plain with the shout "Go Sojama"—a name the former mountaintop still bears.

The Incas began to move southwards into the altiplano area about 1430 during the reign of the Incan emperor named Viracocha, when the fierce Lupaca tribe (who drank the blood of their enemies) were in residence. Both the Lupacas and the nearby Pacaje (who "devoured the beating hearts of those they had conquered") were reputed to be offspring of the marriage between Mount Illampu and Lake Titicaca.

At its height, the Incan empire stretched 2,500 miles, from southern Colombia to central Chile, with a population of more than four million. The last uprising by the Incan chief Tupac Amaru was not crushed by the Spaniards until as late as 1782 although, by then, almost all of the Incan empire had been under Spanish rule for two centuries.

The Lupaca and the Colla Aymara tribes, who were rivals in the Lake

AN OCCULT GUIDE TO SOUTH AMERICA

Titicaca area, vied for Incan backing which the former won. The colla attacked first but were beaten in a battle at Paucarcola. Later the Lupaca revolted against the Incas but were defeated by a force headed by Topa Inca himself, who went on to conquer the rest of Bolivia and part of Chile (where he was blocked from further southern expansion by the fierce Araucanians) before devoting the rest of his reign to governing. He died in 1493 after twenty-two years on the throne and was succeeded by his son, Huayna Capac.

Huayna Capac extended the Incan empire even further, setting up the northern boundaries north of Quito on the Ecuador/ Colombia border and subduing the coastal area around Guayaquil and the island of Puna. Not far south of Puna is Tumbes, where Pizarro's exploratory expedition first touched down. Word of this landing was brought to Huayna Capac just before he died near Quito in 1527.

At one of the Lupaca towns on the western shores of Lake Titicaca are traces of the ancient lunar cult which preceded the solar cult. The town is called Pomata which means "residence of the puma" and here the slinky felines were raised to honor the goddess.

It is hard to explain the significance of Lake Titicaca to anyone unfamiliar with the reverence the natives of the area express toward it. Perhaps Luis E. Valcarcel's summary in his **Mirador Indio** is best. "All the legends of Peru," he writes, ..are prisoners of the lake and reflourish in a climate of eternity. It is the colloquy of the mountain, the Olympus of the Sun and Lightning. Thus it was understood by the ancient Incas. In its magical geography it is the land of the Chimera, the land of the Gods, the origin of the Celestial Bodies, the Matrix of the Creation!"

Some writers have suggested that there were parallels between the Tiahuanaco carvings and those found in the Chavin culture which was based on the northern Peruvian religious site at Chavin de Huantar as far back as 800 B.C. A motif often referred to as "a feline deity" dominated Chavin sculpture, and anthropologist Edward P. Lanning comments that the central figure on Tiahuanaco's Sun Door has a feline mouth and "is so similar in concept and associations to the old Chavin Staff ", that he is very likely a later representation of the same deity." Pondering why this should happen, long after the presumed extinction of the Chavin cult and outside its sphere of influence, he comments, in his book **Peru Before the Incas** (Prentice-Hall,

1967)- "Though there is no proof of what happened, it is fascinating to speculate that the Chavin cult survived as a minority religion, and that it again took root—after a long time and a great deal of stylistic change far to the south of its original homeland."

Harry Tschopik, Jr., the Harvard anthropologist who has studied the local Aymara extensively, refers to their present day culture as "apprehensive" and adds: "The great bulk of Aymara magic is oriented toward controlling natural phenomena to assure economic security." Both public and private ceremonies, he explains, are designed to produce general prosperity, better crops, larger flocks, or more fish, and economic gain underlies most cases of witchcraft, the chief medium through which aggression is expressed."

Llamas play an important part in magical ceremonies, being sacrificed on important occasions and at other times, mated with special rites and an accompanying fiesta. Llama fetuses serve as offerings, being produced by abortion. "All llamas, alpacas and vicunas are thought to be owned by a certain mountain spirit to whom some blood is offered whenever a llama is killed."

The llama is the Andean Indians' all-purpose beast and plays a large part in everybody's life. Victor W. von Hagen says, llamas have, like the camel "an amazing ability for adaptation; they can live in a range of perpetual glaciers at 17,000 feet altitude or acclimatize themselves to the desert. Normally a llama loaded with half its weight will walk between six and twelve miles a day; if pressed it will travel longer. As the camel was to the Asian, so the llama was to the Inca; its wool was used mostly for heavy blankets, strong cords, sacks for cargo (its wool is very greasy); its dung, like that of the camel, was a fuel, and was gathered in their communal voiding places."

In Aymara tradition, when a human dies a rope is placed in the corpse's hand and tied around a llama's neck; the animal is then sacrificed so that the dead person may have company on the way to the next world. Funeral ceremonies are elaborate, with the mourners turning their clothes inside out, washing their mouths and hands, and returning to the dead person's house by a different route "to avoid misfortune and prevent the ghost from following them." Women who die in childbirth, witches, and suicides are buried fiace down.

Diviners (yatiri) play a big part in the community life, being consulted before virtually every important decision, from choosing a bride (much love magic is practiced) to making a journey.

Coca also plays a large part in the magical ceremonies, the leaf usually being offered in groups or multiples of three perfect leaves. Coca diviners who study the leaf for color and texture are commonplace and confine themselves to simple tasks such as predicting whether a sick person will live or die, locating stolen property and divining the outcome of a marriage or business venture. Even the birth of a baby provides an opportunity for divination, with the midwife floating a piece of the placenta in a bowl of water and watching its movement to predict the child's future.

Other divinatory techniques include the observation of the flights of birds, the direction of smoke, the movement of flames, position of stars, and the study of dreams. There seems to be a clear distinction between the black and white magician, the latter's major functions being the offering of sacrifices for the benefit of the crops, the placating of spirits to cure disease, and especially the apprehension of thieves.

Not long ago Harry Tschopik, now assistant curator of ethnology at the Ameriem Museum of Natural History, lived for a couple of years at the lakeside town of Chucuito. an almost totally Aymara town where he and his wife were known as 'Senor and Senora Gringo." The local customs, he averred in a National Geographic article, were much as they have always been: a llama sacrificed and its blood scattered around to appease the evil spirits at the dedication of a new house; an evil spell planted on the family by a neighboring witch who thought she had been ridiculed; and the reading of coca leaves and subsequent ceremonies to counter the spell.

At the southern end of the Aymara's altiplano lies Bolivia's capital, La Paz, a city certainly like no other. For the short term visitor, it can be both interesting and invigorating, but the whole place gives the impression of a city that has accepted twentieth-century customs on a trial basis and might at any time renounce them all and revert to the practices still prevailing on the surrounding altiplano.

There can be few major cities where modern ways have blended so incongruously: the sixteenth century cathedral, resplendent with treasures of silver and gold (and a mint with a blue neon halo) is partly constructed with enormous blocks dedicated to another god, brought from the sun temple at Tiahuanaco. The grotesquely carved heads of pagan figures sit impassively within arms length of all who pass through the cathedral doors.

In the adjoining streets off Calle Max Paredes, Indian women in striped rebozos, all wearing the ubiquitous bowler hats, (bombinas), sell the shriveled fetuses of baby llamas. No self-respecting builder would omit one of these from the foundations of any house if he wanted its occupants to enjoy untroubled living therein.

The stalls along Calle José Limares are piled high with incense, and the herbs which can remedy all ailments. Some stalls offer talismans, although the more common way to protect a friend—or harm an enemy—is to consult one of the many *calmelaches* who, for a fee, will prepare the right talisman for any and all occasions.

Ave. Max Paredes, a cobbled hill with stalls at both sides selling bolts of cloth, shoes, toothpaste, pots and pans, and all kinds of plastic items, leads to one of the city's major markets. Here you can become acquainted with some of the scores of different potatoes familiar to all Andean countries. One is a gray-flecked variety (*tchunios*) that is left out in the frost all night; another gets its flavor from being kept underwater for a couple of weeks.

When the Spaniards founded La Paz there had been a settlement of sorts on the site for centuries, housing remnants of the earlier Inca and even Tiahuanaco civilization. But the distinctive style of the Colonial builders stamped the city with a character that it retains today. Off Calle Catacova are numerous little alleyways that have barely changed in four centuries, and on one Colonial-style street, the former house of Bolivian hero Pedro Domingo Murillo with its wrought-iron railings, lanterns, and charming balconies is better preserved than most.

Murillo was one of the revolutionaries who was killed in 1809 during Bolivia's lengthy fight for independence from the Spanish (the street, Jaen, on which he lived is named after one of his fellow revolutionaries), and there's a statue of him in nearby Plaza Murillo where the presidential offices and currently unused Congressional Palace (Bolivia is another military dictatorship) are situated.

The Tiahuanaco monoliths and artifacts are maintained in a sunken plaza—a replica of the "underground" temple at Tiahuanaco itself—in Plaza J. C. Tejeda Sorzano where the central attraction is the twenty-foot-high statue of Pachamama, or earth goddess, whose carved multiple braids have their counterpart in the hairstyles sported by the almost extinct Chipaya Indians of today.

In the 1930s there were only about three or four hundred Chipaya left, and their numbers are not likely to have substantially increased. Linguistically, they are identical with the Uru Indians who live at the northern end of Lake Titicaca, and culturally, they are similar to the Aymara Indians who are all around therm. But being more isolated, their beliefs have been less subject to outside influences and some rites are better preserved. Pachamama, for example, is a deity important enough to be associated with virtually every Chipaya ceremony when, according to the anthropologist Weston La Barre, she is offered coca, libations of chicha, "and grease balls decorated with plants and silver paper.

"Llama foetuses are burned in her honor and whenever an Indian drinks he makes a libation for her. At the end of a feast, the Indians kiss the earth to show their devotion to her.

During harvest time Pachamama receives special attention throughout most of the Indian communities in South America, even though in many places her worship has been fused publicly with that of the Virgin Mary. There are fiestas in the fields, which are sprinkled with alcohol or the blood of sacrificed animals, and chicha, coca quids, or samples from the new crop are dedicated to the god. When the weeds are burned to clear a new field for planting, the direction of the smoke is noted as being an indication about the future harvest. Seed potatoes are taken from the sack two at a time, and it is considered that good fortune is on the way if an even number remain in the bottom of the sack. Another good omen is an eagle or condor flying over the field during planting.

The plaza sheltering the Pachamama statue (and some others which, unlikely as it seems, appear to have been influenced by Assyrian and Egyptian carvings) is called Sorzano, and the street leading downhill from it, Servedra. Both of these are the names of former Bolivian presidents of which there have been a tremendous number in this country's turbulent history. In fact, there have been about 160 presidents altogether, which is slightly more than the number of years that Bolivia has existed as a republic. Sometimes, it seems, an erstwhile "president" issues a proclamation or grabs a microphone to announce a personal coup that hasn't entirely taken place. One day in 1970, for example, there were six claimants to the presidency in twenty-four crowded hours.

AN OCCULT GUIDE TO SOUTH AMERICA

Heading south out of the city down Ave. Siles (the name of another former president) we start by following the course of the Choqueyapu river on our way to visit the Valley of the Moon. It was this river that washed the grains of gold down from the Andes and caused the Spaniards to abandon their earlier settlement at Laja, on the altiplano, and set up a capital here in the valley. The river, contrary to logic, flows not west into the sea but east into the Amazon.

Temporarily we lose its course, turning right on Calle Arequipa (beside the monument to the explorer Humboldt) and then right again down Benito Juarez, before turning left and rejoining the river at a point where the Indian washer-women have laid out their clothes on the bank to dry.

The Choqueyapu continues onward to fertilize a lush green valley, but our route twists and turns past a cactus farm and through archways cut from the solid rock into a fantastic world of millions of giant caveless stalagmites, where nothing but small lizards live. The peaks rise from a few inches to 20 or 30 feet above ground, and are constantly changing their size and shape from the action of the wind and rain on the soft stone from which they are composed. The trip to the Valley of the Moon must be made by taxi or on a tour, as there are no buses. It is possible to get there by walking, which would take about an hour starting from the Humboldt statue.

The favored hotel in La Paz is El Sucre (Ave. 16 de Julio 1636, tel: 55080), which ranges from about $8 for a single without bath to around $20 for a double with. It's central, on the main street near all tourist and airline offices, and has an excellent restaurant and bar, comfortable lounge, and convenient ground floor coffee shop. There are cheaper hotels nearby and a Sheraton, about six blocks to the south, will be ready shortly. Be warned that a 28 percent tax is added to all hotel bills. And try to arrange your trip from the airport in a shared taxi—in which case the rate will be around 30 pesos per person. There are no airport buses.

There's a city tourist office right opposite the Sucre, but for tours to outlying points check out Valsa (Ave. 16 de Julio 1787, tel 54049), whose genial, English-speaking manager, Jean Jacques Valloton, also operates the new hotel El Dorado.

Because of La Paz' altitude (at 11,000 feet it is the world's highest capital) most visitors are affected by *soroche*, a mountain sickness characterized by headaches and sleeplessness. Hotels keep tanks of oxygen on hand to revive the most serious cases. You can also consume quantities of a pill called Micoren 100 (manufactured by Geigy), but the best advice is to take it easy, never overexert yourself, and don't eat or drink too much. It takes a day or two to get used to the altitude, by which time your headaches should go away, as should your difficulty in breathing.

During the week, night life in La Paz is almost nonexistent; on weekends you should enjoy some of the typical folklorico, of which the best example can be seen at Club Kori Thika (Calle Juan de la Riva 1435, tel: 52151).

Actually, you may want to retire early, if only to be able to rise with the sun and take a bus or car up the winding road northward to the rim of the valley. From here, the city becomes a sea of twinkling fights in a basin whose upper edges are etched against the pale sky. Outstanding is 21,000 foot Illimani, topped by a black halo of cloud. From the city it appears to be the backdrop to every southern street, although it lies at least 50 kilometers away.

The airport is up here on the northern road, at the edge of the altiplano, and the road that leads to Tiahuanaco forks off to the right and crosses the barren plain to the shores of Lake Titicaca almost 100 miles from the city. Cement bridges are being constructed across the trickling streams that traverse the altiplano (in the rainy season they become raging torrents), and beside almost every waterway a small community has arisen. Otherwise the region appears deserted, apart from the random homesteads, always surrounded by high adobe walls, and the tiny figures, usually carrying sacks or leading sheep, who can be seen tramping across the plain.

For a few months of the year, during the rainy season, the land is green, but for most of the time it is a parched wasteland suitable only for growing potatoes and nourishing a few livestock. The roads are almost always dusty, and to follow another car or bus too closely means to be permanently enveloped in choking clouds of dried mud.

Some of the Aymara huts boast a cross rising from their thatched roofs but almost as frequent is the woven "god's eye" which, common to many aborigine cultures, has always been regarded as "a benevolent instrument that brings divine attention to the successful performance of tasks," in the words of the nineteenth-century Norwegian anthropologist Carl Lumholtz.

Because of the altiplano's great height (its average altitude is 12,000 feet) and dry, chilly atmosphere (average temperature: about 50°F, the air is extremely rarefied. It is thus possible to see for miles. Not that there is very much to see. It is only when one nears the lake that the bleakness gives way to a more gentle terrain: a land more fertile with trees, the first sight of llamas, and a tiny farm with a cow or two.

Lake Titicaca, at more than 11,000 feet above sea level, is the highest navigable lake in the world. Because of its size (125 miles long, 30 miles wide), it's easy to see how the ancients might have regarded it with awe: a tremendous "sea" high in the mountains that may well have once stretched to the holy walls of Tiahuanaco itself.

About 40 percent of the lake is in Bolivia, the rest in Peru, and the entry into the latter country is made by lake travelers at the tiny town of July, from which transport northward to Puno, at the lake's northwestern edge, is accomplished by road.

The easiest way to make the trip between the two countries is by hydrofoil (the *Titicaca Arrow* or *Arrow of the Andes*) plying from the town of July to Huatajata and back. Make a booking through one of the tourist agencies in La Paz to avoid difficulties, not the least of which is coping with the unnecessarily complicated procedures of Peru's customs and immigration department. "I learned that one of Bolivia's popular sayings is that the law should be used, not obeyed," wrote William E. Carter in **Bolivia; A Profile** (Praeger, 197 1). It's best to change your Bolivian money into Peruvian soles (the latter worth about half the former denomination) before leaving La Paz, to get the most favorable rate.

The hydrofoil leaves Huatajata, on the Bolivian shore, at 8.30 A.M., but the trip there from La Paz takes at least one and a half hours by tourist coach. Breakfast is served at lakeside, and everybody takes pictures of llamas and alpacas that some of the tourist-conscious Indians have brought to the dock to meet the daily batch of foreign visitors. If you regard this as a sort of local folk show, you might want to slip the lady shepherd a few pesos for her thoughtfulness.

Also paddling nearby is a colorfully dressed Aymara in one of the lake's characteristic *totora* reed boats of the type that Thor Heyerdahl constructed to prove their oceangoing capabilities. The pulpy, dark green reeds are made into cigar-shaped bundles about ten feet long, two of which are used for the bottom of the boat and two others lashed to the sides. They are propelled by poles and occasionally equipped with sails. If the anthropologists and archaeologists are correct, these boats, whose basic material grows only here and in the crater lakes of Easter Island, have played a major role in ancient history, transporting monoliths so huge that even today their movement from one place to another would present a major logistical task. The boats can still be seen all around the edges of the lake, where they are used for fishing.

Crossing Lake Titicaca takes from 8:30 A.M. until midafternoon because the tourist-attuned hydrofoil makes several stops, dodging the ferries in the narrow straits of Tiquina, skirting historic Moon Island, and touching down at the boomerang-shaped Island of the Sun, birthplace of the legendary Incan Sun Cod. The Incas believed that Father Sun spent the two days of the equinox living here among his subjects. During his visits he was said to have impregnated women to bear divine offspring, and one commentator, Zelia Nutall, speculated that the time between the two days of the equinox on Lake Titicaca was nine months, or the period of human gestation.

In support of their case that the Sun Cod visited the island in human form, present-day Indians sometimes show off what appear to be two huge "footprints" in a rock pavement.

The hydrofoil makes the briefest of landings on the Island of the Sun, long enough for everybody to taste of the sacred spring whose waters legendarily promise eternal youth. Once back on board, the passengers are "baptized" with water sprinkled from a leafy bow and presented with scrolls reading: "I, Manco Kapac (the founding Inca ruler, a demigod who turned to stone), King of the Incas and Lord of the Sacred Lake Titicaca, hereby certify that M .... has crossed my territory on the——of—, has tasted the sacred water on the Sun Island and has received the blessing of the Sun Cod."

Garcilaso de la Vega wrote that the Incas built terraces on the island on which "by dint of great care" they grew a few cobs of maize. These were distributed to chosen Virgins of the Sun and also sent to other temples and convents throughout the Inca empire "so that all might enjoy the grain sent from heaven. "

Once back on the lake, the traveler first starts to notice that the surrounding hillsides are agriculturally developed in a narrow terrace style, which has been known in these parts for centuries. They will be seen increasingly from here northward, wherever Andean terrain restricts the land available for cultivation. The guide, aware of the headline-attractiveness of the Incas, points to them as a product of that relatively recent civilization, but this method of using every inch of available land is literally as old as the hills.

Professor Posnansky, whose research on Tiahuanaco was quoted earlier, believes that these terraces were the origin of what he calls the "staircase sign" motif that dominates so many blanket designs throughout Mexico and Central and South America.

The sign, he says, is often seen under the feet of animals, idols, and men to denote that they are resting on the ground. It appears on the famous Sun Door at Tiahuanaco "and shows how the earth receives the heat of solar and lunar rays transmitted to it by the condor heads with which it is interspersed."

A penultimate stop is made at the little town of Copacobana. Its importance as a pagan religious site in Inca times was cleverly buttressed by the Spaniards, who turned it into an important center for pilgrims after an image of the Virgin, manufactured by a local Indian, acquired the reputation of performing miracles.

At the time of the conquest, Lewis Spence says in **Myths of Peru and Mexico**, Titicaca and Pachacamac were the two cardinal shrines of the Incas-those of the creator and the sun, respectively. "A special reason for pilgrimage to Titicaca was to sacrifice to the sun as the source of physical energy and the giver of long fife. He was especially worshipped by the aged, who believed that he preserved their lives."

Houses were built at Capahuana (now Copacobana) to shelter these pilgrims who, before visiting the Island of the Sun, were obliged to confess their sins at each of the three sculptured doors which had to be passed before reaching the sacred rock. The first door bore a figure of a puma; the other two were ornamented with feathers of the various birds who were sacrificed to the sun.

Despite the Spaniards' greed for gold, much of it escaped them, according to Garcilaso de la Vega who says the Indians hid "a great quantity of treasure" in lakes, caves, and mountains from which there was no hope of recovering it. At Copacobana, for example, he quotes Father Blas Valera as saying that there was as much gold and silver left over as had been employed in the budding of the temple. When the Indians heard of the Spaniards' relentless search they threw this stockpile into the lake.

Another lake, in the Orcos Valley about 20 miles south of Cuzco, is supposed to be the hiding place of an immense gold chain made on the orders of Huayna Capac. In 1557 a group of Spaniards tried to drain this lake by tunneling in the mountains under it, but had to abandon the search after striking rock.

The week-long fiesta of Carmen, which is celebrated in Copacobana at the beginning of August, has enticed as many as 50,000 people to the small town. The shrine built with their offerings seems disproportionate to such a small place, although how many of the Catholic worshippers are in actuality partaking in ancient fertility rites could probably never be established.

The little town is awash for much of the year with young bearded travelers complete with backpacks. They cluster around the charming plaza with its statue of Manco Capac and bed down at cheap pensions. The Residencial Portenita and hotel Playa Azul are fine, each charging about 30 pesos per person.

A late lunch is served at July after crossing the lake, and then it's onwards by car to Puno, a couple of hours' drive along the western edge of the lake. The countryside is gentler than on the Bolivian side, although it is populated mostly by the same tribe, the Aymaras. The journey is enlivened by frequent appearances of llamas, alpacas, sheep, cows, and an occasional flock of pink flamingos.

AN OCCULT GUIDE TO SOUTH AMERICA

AN OCCULT GUIDE TO SOUTH AMERICA

Chapter 9

Southern Peru

The Children of the Sun

For visitors entering Peru via the land route around or across Lake Titicaca, Puno (pop. 35,000) is the first major stop. It's a small town consisting of little more than a grid of six or seven streets, running north to south beside the lake, plus a dozen other streets bisecting them. The main road into town runs nearest to the lake; on it are the railroad station and the hotel Ferrocarril across the street. The State Tourist hotel (about $10 for a single) is the most luxurious; it adjoins the dock, from which bouts leave on lake trips.

Three blocks further up into town, behind the Ferrocarril, is one of Puno's two main plazas, and it is here, and on the street connecting it to the other plaza, that most of the action takes place. Shops are open til 7:00 P.M., the most popular being the bookstores (Marxist works are prominent) and record shops which attract the young crowd because of their habit of booming loud tapes into the street. The Hosteria Colonial between the two plaza is pleasant and inexpensive.

Each November 3, Aymara Indians still gather on the shores of Lake Titicaca at Puno to await the return of their legendary ancestors, Manco Capac and Mama Ocllo. "Unlike any other folkloric manifestation, not a murmur can be heard from the crowds as they wait for the fabulous apparition from the direction of the Island of the Sun," reports Simone Waisbard.

The most popular trip from Puno is a boat ride on the lake to visit the Uru Indians who are famous for their dependence on the totora reed. They live on raftlike islands made of the sturdy plant in this northern section of the lake and some are said never to set foot on shore. The totora reed, platted together to form the floating base of their community, also provides the basic material for their homes, boats, and even some of their food, as the pulpy inside of the root is quite nutritious,

The Uru language, widespread throughout Peru in Colonial days, is now confined to a small arm mostly around the take where the existing Uru Indians also speak Aymara. Dr. Weston La Barre, who says they claim to be "the oldest race on earth, antedating the sun," adds that their main festival, at the vernal equinox, has been changed to coincide with a Christian celebration of nine days earlier. On this date they blow pipes, sing, dance, and sacrifice a llama, smearing its blood near the entrance of each hut.

Nominally they are Catholic, but they worship Pachamama and believe in dream interpretation, meteorological signs, and omens.

The Uru have not been popular with anthropologists who, almost without exception, have referred to them in such terms as "mistrustful," "suspicious," avaricious," and "stupid." The word Uru, La Barre adds, was commonly used in the seventeenth century to mean "dirty, ragged, rustic" and although La Barre refrains from making the connection, he includes (under data on their dress habits) that Uru women "wash their hair in fermented human urine." One community of Urus can be visited on three-hour tourist trips from Puno. What the visitors see is a handful of Indian families, along with their pigs, centered around a small visitors' area which serves as the focal point of the community and at which souvenirs (made out of—guess what?—totora reeds) are sold. The Uru, who also knit caps, mittens, and socks made from the soft down of lake birds, don't much like being photographed, but are willing to accept it, especially when mollified with a few Peruvian soles.

From Puno the visitor has a choice—north following Manco Capac's route to the sacred Inca capital of Cuzco or west to where even more ancient civilizations have left innumerable traces of their cultures: the Nazcas, lcas, and Paracas. The trip to Arequipa, only about 100 miles west of Puno, takes a whole day whether made by rail or road; travel on present-day roads is not appreciably faster than in the days of the Incas because the rugged terrain is almost more suited to runners (with strong hearts) than to automobiles.

The Incas' much-vaunted road system, said by some observers to be the finest since the Romans, centered around two main highways which ran the length of the empire—one along the coast and the other high up in the Andes. The latter began at the present Colombia-Ecuador border and ran south through Quito, Huancapabamba, Cajamarca, and southeast via Vilcas to Cuzco, south of which it split to circle Lake Titicaca. It then continued down through Bolivia and into Mendoza, Argentina.

The mountain highway zigzagged up steep hills, and in marshy country rested on causeways. The coastal road was wider—up to 13 feet-except where it crossed steep hills, and wherever possible was accompanied by a channel of water and overhanging fruit trees offering shade. Scores of subsidiary roads connected the main ones, and no town remained unlinked to one major highway or another.

The road between Puno and Lima still utilizes remains of the Imperial Route to the Sun, along which the Incas traveled to reach the farthest points of their empire, which comprised the modem republics of Ecuador, Peru, and Bolivia. "The road was paved and carefully maintained, with every last bit of straw and small rock swept away when the gold litter of the supreme Inca was passing," says Simone Waisbard in *Tiahuanaco* (Editorial Diana, Mexico, 1975).

For centuries treasure seekers and grave despoilers have passed along this road, searching for anything of value, at whatever destructive cost to history. They have overturned graves, wrecked ancient homes, and tunneled into the adobe walls of countless pyramids; yet much still remains undiscovered.

The paved road ends at the small fishing port of Camana from which a narrow dirt road winds up into a realm of snow-covered volcanoes. A few years ago aerial photographs revealed the existence of stone steps on the steep slope of one of these volcanoes, Coropuna, which Incan traditions say was the site of the marvelous Temple to the Sun. It has never been explored.

A similar pyramidal fortress, notes Simone Waisbard, has been seen from the road between Arequipa and Cuzco on the slopes of the volcano Chachani.

In 1963, a group climbing the Coronado Grande stumbled upon a "map" drawn on rocks which suggested further exploration higher up. Sure enough, 2,000 feet higher they discovered an Inca burial ground, covered with volcanic ash, which when excavated revealed forty human skulls, all trepannated, placed in a perfect circle around a golden idol.

"They symbolized a ritual known in Arequipa province as 'sacrifices to the goddess of the snows.' A very demanding goddess, more than 3,000 years old, she is one of the Apus, the tutelary divinities to which the ancient peoples of the Andes made human sacrifices," writes Waisbard

"Every year on a date fixed by the sages who could read the stars, each clan organized a monumental procession sometimes hundreds of kilometres long to the top of the volcano they worshipped. There they deposited the young virgin being offered, along with the necessary paraphernalia of a sacrifice—food for the final journey, small gold figures, bone carvings, incense burners."

There is widespread belief in the Peruvian Andes that mountain peaks guarded by Apus and their fellow spirits, *aukus*, have concealed within them great palaces and haciendas, together with herds of livestock, according to the anthropologist Bernard Mishkin. Among these animals are condors, vicunas, llamas and—most feared of all—the Ccoa, a black-striped, gray, cat-like animal with phosphorescent eyes. The Ccoa, who brings lightning and hail, destroys the crops, equips some believers with the power of sorcery and ruins others.

One of the highest peaks in southern Peru, Ausangate, is reported to be the Ccoa's home. Here, in the wet season, he begins to collect rain for later transformation into hail to ruin the crops.

In 1969, in a mountain-ringed valley near Ayacucho, at about 9,000 feet above sea level, archaeologists discovered stone tools and the bones of an extinct ground sloth which, when carbon tested, were revealed to be around 14,000 years old. Writing about the finds in the Scientific American (April 1971), Richard S. MacNeish suggested the artifacts could represent "the earliest stage of man's appearance in South America."

Arequipa, Peru's third largest city (pop. 230,000), sits in an oasis valley beneath an extinct volcano, and has such a perfect climate that crops are grown the whole year around. Forty miles from the sea, it is also 7,000 feet above it, and so well placed that Cieza de Leon, visiting it a decade after its founding in 1540, commented: "Its position is so well chosen, and its climate so mild that it is held to be the healthiest in Peru and the most peaceful to live in."

AN OCCULT GUIDE TO SOUTH AMERICA

Arequipa may have derived its name from the Aymara word *ari* (meaning "peak") and the Quecha word *qipa* (meaning "behind"). It does sit behind Mount Misti, a 20,000 foot volcano whose eruptions had almost wiped out earlier settlements by the time Pachacuti's Incas arrived.

Arequipa's seventeenth-century cathedral (mostly rebuilt in the nineteenth century) dominates one side of the charming Plaza de Armas which is rich in Moorish buildings and arcades. Some of the old Colonial atmosphere has been destroyed by earthquakes but enough is left to retain what G. de Reparaz Ruiz, in his guide to Peru, calls a classic Spanish Colonial "chessboard layout." The climbing streets of the San Lazaro district, behind the Tourist hotel (a favored choice) at Selva Alegre, and the period decorations of the Santa Catalina convent (open 9:00 to 11:00 A.M. and 2:00 to 4:30 P.M.) are the major sights. Many of the numerous old churches are built from a light gray volcanic rock called sillar which has led to Arequipa's nickname of "the white city."

The twelve-hour train trip between Puno and Arequipa offers spectacular views, as does the route between Arequipa and Cuzco. There are flights from Arequipa to both Cuzco (twice a week) and Lima; comfortable buses and colectivos also connect Arequipa and Lima.

For many days now we have been in the mountains, ever since our first splitting headaches (remember *soroche*, the altitude sickness?) in La Paz. Crossing the Bolivian altiplano we have considered the theory that the ocean once lapped at the shores of Tiahuanaco. But if that ever happened it was thousands of years ago, and today Lake Titicaca is almost 12,000 feet above sea level.

Across the lake at Puno we began to climb over the Andes and now, at Arequipa, we are still 7,300 feet above sea level. But we are about to enter a very different world: the coastal desert.

This is not the scrubby, comparatively fertile altiplano, but real desert, desert so hot and dry that the bodies of people who died two or three thousand years ago are still intact, preserved like dried fruit. And the way they lived their lives is spelled out by the objects still set beside them, the pictures they drew on pots and the palaces they built of mud.

Since Max Uhle set up a meaningful structure for archaeology in the 1890s, Peru has been dissected by hundreds of experts, not only archaeologists but also anthropologists, linguists, ethnologists, social scientists of every kind, who have given a remarkably clear picture of what the lives of these early people were like. They were among the first people to come to terms with nature and the rules they set down have remained the guidelines in places where magic is still being practiced, quite literally, just as it was thousands of years ago.

A number of the periods the experts have defined are understandably uncertain—some say a culture may have influenced or overlapped another, others disagree. After we've taken a look at these early cultures to the west and noted that the last in the pre-Colonial period was the Incan race, we'll, metaphorically speaking, skip back over the mountains to Puno.

From Puno we'll head for Cuzco, in the steps of Manco Capac who, as the first Inca, began a line of regal men/gods, his descendants extended the empire to the border of Colombia in the north and far into Chile and Argentina in the south.

But we are getting ahead of our story.

From Arequipa a northwesterly course towards the coast, and eventually Lima, will take us through some of the most heavily excavated archaeological sites Peru has to offer.

Nazca (pop. 20,000) is a green oasis 2,000 feet above sea level in a desert that stretches 40 miles west to the ocean. The State Tourist hotel has a swimming pool and there's also an interesting city museum. Most tourists visit Nazca to inspect the ancient ruins in the surrounding area, not the least of which are the mysterious markings that stretch for miles in the desert.

The Nazca culture is dated to somewhere between AD. 300 and 900, and Nazca art, while not rated quite as highly as the superb Mochica culture with which it was roughly contemporaneous, is nevertheless highly regarded. Its ceramic ware and its embroidered textiles are multicolored and realistic. Sometimes as many as eleven colors were used on a single piece of pottery, with red usually predominating. Trophy heads are often depicted on pots.

Little is known about Nazca architectural styles because very few traces of any buildings have been discovered. One explanation for this absence of monumental architecture, suggests Federico Kauffman Doig, might be the lack of an authoritarian government to fortify their communities. "It is considered that the Nazcas formed a peaceful people, in general term, especially if we compare them to the Mochica," he writes in *Manual de Arqueologia Peruana* (Ediciones; Peisa, Lima, 1969).

Most of the highly polished, brightly colored ceramics (made by the coil technique) were found in almost circular underground graves. The largest such collection, discovered in twenty-five tombs excavated by Max Uhle at Ocucaje, was sent to the University of California.

Playful birds, mice, or monkeys are a frequent theme on the pottery, with llamas, fish, and bats also fairly common. In the more serious works, birds or monstrous whales are depicted portraying mythological beings, and warriors are shown carrying the crescent-shaped knives with which they were prone to chop off prisoners' heads.

Vases in the shape of shrunken heads as well as pictorial representations of such heads with skewered lips have been found in the Nazca area, but never any of the heads themselves. However, in 1940 Julio C. Tello described some especially well-preserved full-sized heads he had unearthed, and he also explained how they had been originally prepared. The skin had been peeled from the skull, cleaned of all organic matter, and cured, then stretched back over the skull and sewn up. Tello found no evidence that might explain what purpose these preserved heads served.

Pampa Colorada is the name for the flat plain stretching between the towns of Palpa, Nazca, and Poroma on which, over 500 square kilometers of desert, enigmatic lines, and figures were cut or marked by unknown people at an unknown date. Cieza de Leon, in 1548, referred to them as "signs pointing out the way" but omitted to mention what they pointed to.

The Peruvian Air Force has mapped and photographed the pampas area between the mountains and the river Ucayli fairly thoroughly and giant blow-ups of their pictures were recently on exhibition in Lima.

The photographs show gigantic lines, some miles in length, ending in claws, concentric circles, enigmatic fish figures, a circle with arms coming out of it and a tail. Among the pottery on display in the Nazca Museum is a piece which could be interpreted as a space man in a helmet and this has strengthened the theory that the lines may have marked a landing strip for visitors from outer space.

Because the lines are best seen in perspective and in some cases can only be interpreted from the air, it has been suggested that they were originally created by people who could fly—i.e., visitors who came from another planet. There is no evidence for this theory but it cannot be completely discounted. It has been proposed, in fact, in connection with other sites, notably some of the enormous stone circles in such out-of-the-way places as Callanish in the Scottish Hebrides.

The Nazca lines have generated growing interest in the past couple of years with a large-scale exhibition of photographs held at the ICA Gallery in London and an expedition to the site by members of the International Explorers' Society who made a test right above the desert in a smoke filled balloon of a type they believe might have existed centuries ago. One of the IES team, Bill Spohrer, has suggested that some of the lines may have traced flight paths made by these ancient "airmen" and that other signs were "ritualistic shaman symbols" of significance to the pilots.

The figures and lines, which were first discovered in 1939 by a New York professor, Dr. Paul Kosok, who called them "the largest astronomy book in the world," were marked out in various ways. Most of them are shallow furrows in the dark surface, exposing the lighter subsoil beneath, as in the hillsides; others are shaped from lines of rocks of contrasting hues.

The designs include gigantic trapezoids 2,400 feet long; a 600-foot lizard, bisected by the Pan American Highway; sets of parallel lines, some almost 1.5 miles long, others running up a steep slope; spirals and geometric patterns; indefinable figures, and almost a score of birds. The bill of one of these birds points to the rising sun on December 31, the summer solstice in lands south of the equator.

A German mathematician and geographer, Maria Reiche, is probably the foremost expert on the Nazca lines, having spent more than two decades investigating them and making calculations. Concluding that they are the key to some ancient "calendar science," she compares them to Egypt's pyramids, with the difference that they can be best appreciated by looking down on them from a great height instead of looking up.

Ms. Reiche suggests that ancient Peruvians may have had equipment or instruments that we have never learned about to make their calculations, which she thinks were related to the solstices.

In any case, she says, the process of planning and converting one scale into another "presupposes a highly developed faculty for abstract thinking

AN OCCULT GUIDE TO SOUTH AMERICA

... which we would never expect in a primitive people.

"December is a month of expectation in Nazca. People watch eagerly the dry riverbeds which are due to fill with water which can be conducted over the fields to cover again the dry, barren lands with luscious green, Ms. Reiche writes in **Mystery on the Desert** (Hans Schulz-Severin, Stuttgart, 1968). "The sun's rising and setting points, oscillating like a pendulum over east and west, could be employed as a giant time-measuring device on which to read the return of the fruitful season and the intermediate epochs."

A recent report in a Lima newspaper said that Maria Reiche, after spending almost thirty years on the Nazca pampa, is now in England studying Druid circles where, she says, the same unit of measurement has been used as in the Nazca drawings.

How long have the lines been there? A carbon-dating by Dr. Duncan Strong of the rotted remains of a piece of wood found below the surface (possibly the remains of a sighting pole) gave an estimate of A.D. 450 to 600. As mentioned, the pottery and textiles of the Nazca period have been dated at anywhere from A.D. 300 to 900.

An explanation for the durability of the lines, at least, is that the climate of the region is one of the driest in the world, with a short rainfall only every year or two, and a cushion of warm air created by the surface stones offering shelter from the winds.

A few tours go to Nazca, which is not easy to visit on one's own because of the difficulty of ensuring a flight over the area. The lines can be best seen in perspective from the air but in Lima there is inadequate information on making such flights. One tourist agency that does include a flight over the Nazca lines in its two- or three-day tours is Peru Chasquitur (Rufino Torrico 868, Lama, tel. 289845).

Some of the Lan Chile tours of South America include a three-hour flight over Nazca by private aircraft. It also takes in a similarly mysterious sight in the vicinity: the 800-foot high Candelabra of the Andes etched into a hillside near the sea at Pisco. A few miles outside Pisco is the Paracas peninsula, site of another ancient civilization which is described more fully in the section on Lima.

North of Nazca is the pleasant town of Ica (pop. 80,000), beside the Ica river at the head of a valley that was populated several hundred years before the Incas arrived. The civilization has given its name to a culture that is associated (and sometimes confused) with the Nazca epoch that preceded it. Judging by pottery finds, both the Icas and late-Nazcas were influenced by Tiahuanaco styles.

But the later Icas were also influenced by their conquerors, the Incas, because among the pyramids with their stairways and terraces were buildings with distinctive Incan wall niches and some of the pottery had the characteristic Incan pointed base. Textiles tended to concentrate on geometric patterns and were similar to Chimu pieces from the north, implying steady contact.

Near Ica is Cachiche, a so-called "witches' village," where many people come to consult *brujas* about the future.

From Ica it would be logical to follow the early trade route north to Lima but for clarity's sake we will hop back to Puno. From here we make the trip northwards to Cuzco—a city that two out of every three tourists to Peru make sure to visit. Our visit to Lima will be made after a side trip to Peru's most glorious sight: the Incan mountaintop city of Machu Picchu.

Puno, incidentally, is the major stronghold of the Aymara language. Although Quechua replaced many local tongues under the Incan empire, becoming widespread even in Ecuador to the north, there are still enclaves here and there where older languages have retained their hold.

The train from Puno to Cuzco leaves at 6:40 A.M. every day (notwithstanding the information in that otherwise indispensable guide, **The South American Handbook**). It's best to stay at the hotel Ferrocarril in Puno in order to get your ticket early when the station across the street opens at 6:00 A.M. Pay extra and travel in the buffet car; it's worth it for the company. Second-class is acceptable for those on rockbottom budgets but everyone is advised to take along some fruit or sandwiches to supplement the fairly unexciting lunch offered in the buffet for 150 soles. The first-class fare is 520 soles; second class is a mere 200 soles.

The trip takes about twelve hours up into the magnificent Andes with occasional stops at remote villages where items of wool and fur are offered by natives with friendly weatherbeaten faces. The prices are not always bargains.

It's a romantic trip through the mountains to Cuzco, following what must have been a similar route to that taken by the first Inca, Manco Capac.

In front of the buffet car, on a swaying platform in the wind, it seems, for a moment, as if one is at the center of the world. Dusk falls, the Andes seem to change shape and color with every passing kilometer and the magic of Peru truly captivates the spirit.

The story of Cuzco is basically the story of the Incas, those children of the sun" who dominated Peruvian history for about five centuries until the arrival of the Spaniards. As we have seen, many of their ideas may have been borrowed from the civilizations that preceded them but it was their particular genius for absorbing and improving upon such ideas, together with brilliant organizational talents, that put them on top and kept them there so long.

Because the Incas had no system of writing, what is known about their era has been painstakingly put together from oral tradition and the artifacts they left behind. The earliest Spanish historians were able to see some things for themselves, others interviewed articulate survivors, among them the *quipucamayoc* or record keepers. The best-known Incan chronicler, Garcilaso de]a Vega, being half-Inca himself, called upon his family to fill in details—some of which later historians have found to be suspect.

At any rate, ironic as it might be that a race which lacked writing should have so much written about it, there is plenty of documentation about the last great pagan empire to inhabit the western hemisphere.

John Howland Rowe of Boston's Peabody Museum lists the Incan emperors chronologically as Manco Capac (about A.D. 1200), Sinchi Roca, Lloque Yupanqui, Mayta Capac, Capac Yupanqui, Inca Roca, Yahuar Huacac, Viracocha Inca, Pachacutec (around 1438), Topa Inca (1471), Huayna Capac (1493), Huascar (1527), and Atahualpa (1532).

When the Spanish invaders first arrived, the Incan empire had probably reached and passed its greatest heights. Like empires before and since, it had overreached itself territorially, and dissensions were being felt at home. The greatest of Incan rulers, Huayna Capac, had just died and divided the swollen empire between his natural son, Huascar, and an illegitimate one, Atahualpa. In the inevitable civil war that followed, the latter gained the upper hand.

It was in 1524 that Francisco Pizzaro first left Panama to explore the rich lands to the south, but various hardships ended both this expedition and a subsequent one in 1526. In 1531, however, with royal permission from Spain to explore and conquer Peru, he finally reached the northern Peruvian city of Cajamarca and, despite being greatly outnumbered, managed to trick the Incan ruler, Atahualpa, and capture him, massacring hundreds of Atahualpa's subjects in the process.

Although ransomed by his subjects with millions of dollars worth of gold, Atahualpa was accused of treachery and murdered by Pizarro's men on August 29, 1533. The Incan empire, already badly divided, greatly underestimated the fighting qualities of the Spanish and armies of Indians were beaten time and time again by a handful of mounted Spaniards. Within two years, Lima had been founded as the seat of the viceroyalty of Peru and the pagan Incan empire totally subdued.

The able-bodied Incan workers, *puric*—the ones between twenty-eight and fifty—were the basis of the Incan labor force and they were organized on a decimal system, with one hundred *puric* under the direction of a *Pachacacamayoc*, and these in turn answerable to chiefs, all the way up to four provincial governors who reported to the Inca himself. Land was communal but the produce was divided between the people, the church, and the government which used its share to organize relief in time of famine.

The Incan system worked well within its limitations, because in return for giving up their independence and freedom of movement, all subjects had security and freedom from want. Wherever the children of the sun labored, wrote Sir Clements Markham, "the eye of the central power was ever upon them, and the never-failing brain, beneficent through inexorable, provided for all their wants, gathered in their tribute and selected their children for the various occupations required by the State according to their several aptitudes."

Indeed, Sir Clements explained, the system was true socialism, such as dreamers in past ages have conceived. It existed once because the essential conditions were combined in a way that is never likely to occur again. These are an inexorable despotism, absolute exemption from outside interference of any kind, a very peculiar and remarkable people in an early stage of civilization and an extraordinary combination of skillful statesmanship."

Incan subjects were organized according to *ayllus*, which might be described as tribes or extended families grouped together and counted decimally.

Each *ayllu* worshipped its particular *huaca* or sacred object and all, in addition, paid tribute to both the Sun and a certain *huaca* at Huanacauri. This was a stone which, according to legend, was the petrified remains of one of the four brothers who were the first followers of Manco Capac. The *huaca* was said to be three miles from Cuzco but its site is now unknown.

Huaca is an all-embracing term used by the Incas and present-day Peruvians to signify anything sacred; this could be any of the nature gods or spirits that haunted local takes, springs, hills, caves, etc.

In Incan society the *mallquis* or bodies of ancestors were preserved and respected, often being kept in caves or preserved in towers called *chulpas*. Usually the deceased's possessions, or at least things that would have been useful to him alive, were buried along with his body. This custom still prevails in some parts of Peru today. Nothing, it seems, can completely eradicate the belief that souls as well as bodies, have their needs.

The Cuzco of today, a lovely city, is dominated by a giant Christian cross on the hills above it, as if to reaffirm that its pagan origins are a thing of the past. Its population of around 100,000 is about half what it was at the height of its glory and, judging by the impoverished look of many of the barefoot Indians around town, its lower-class citizens are not appreciably better off than they were then.

Emperor Pachacutec (1438-1471) had the entire city rebuilt when it became the center of the Incan empire and the 50,000 laborers who were brought in to accomplish that task did such a good job that much of their work stands today and, by law, can't be demolished—not that pulling it down would be easy.

All over the city remains of the Incan stonework still stand and apparently will for centuries more. Massive, close-fitting blocks are its central motif with the distinctive arched doorways in which the lintel-covered top is narrower than the bottom. (The Incan architects were not familiar with arches so the narrower the opening, the better the side pillars bore the weight.) We can see examples of these walls in side streets off the main plaza, particularly Callejon Loreto, the site of the Compania church, and, in what remains of the pagan Temple to the Sun (now partially restored), incorporated into the Santo Domingo convent, with its charming sunny patio. Everybody always points out the "stone with 12 corners" which forms part of a wall on

Calle Triunfo, two blocks from the plaza.

The beautiful Plaza de Armas is the place you'll find most memorable in Cuzco. It was the central square in Incan times, and continued as such through Colonial clays up to the present. It's dominated by a large seventeenth-century cathedral at one side, the attractive Iglesia de la Compania church on another. There are arcades with souvenir shops and two hotels: the expensive Hostal Viracocha, and the bargain hotel Virrey (400 soles for a single, 550 soles for a double) where the manager, Hugo Mocoso Mar, is extremely helpful. The Virrey is usually booked solid; if not, try to get a room overlooking the plaza. Just off the plaza is the pleasant hotel Conquistador, its doorway usually blocked by a souvenir seller *con llama*. The Cuzco Tourist hotel, not quite so central, is the city's best. There's also the modest hotel Continental near the station. A friendly, knowledgeable guide, Professor Oscar Nin Echegaray, can often be found at the Cuzco hotel and he'll organize private tours for you if you're in a rush.

There were colorful celebrations in Cuzco every month of the Incan year. The first month, June 22 to July 22, was called *Inti Raymi* and was a time of many ceremonies and sacrifices of llamas to the Sun. More sacrifices accompanied the following month's festival of *Chahuarquiz*, the plowing time. Then came *Yapaquis*, the time for sowing, and after that the August festival *Coya-raymi,* held when the rains commenced, bringing with them much sickness.

"Four hundred warriors stood in the great square [at Cuzco]," the **Encyclopedia of Philosophy & Religion** tells us, "a hundred facing each of the cardinal points. The priests shouted, 'Go forth all evils' and the four parties started in four directions shouting 'Go forth all evils.' They ran until they came to rivers, where they bathed and washed their arms. The Inca and the people also bathed and there were ceremonies for driving away sickness at the doors of all the houses.

"Such was the ceremony for driving the sicknesses out of Cuzco," said Cristobal de Molina, whose account was written between 1570 and 1584. The reason for bathing in these rivers was because they were rivers of great volume and were supposed to empty themselves into the sea and to carry the evils with them.

Afterwards there was dancing, the passing around of great torches of burning straw, feasting, and the ceremonial application of a ground maize pudding called *sancu* to faces, door lintels, and the bodies of the dead "that they might also enjoy the benefits of the feast."

Cuzco's glorious Sun Temple, called Coricancha, forms the foundation of the present Santo Domingo church, just as the former Palace of the Inca Viracocha is buried under the cathedral.

The interior of Coricancha in Incan times was "literally a mine of gold," reported William Prescott. "On the western side was emblazoned a representation of the deity, consisting of a human countenance, looking forth from amidst innumerable rays of tight which emanated from it in every direction, in the same manner as the sun is often personified with us. The figure was engraved on a massive plate of gold of enormous dimensions thickly powdered with emeralds and precious stones.

"It was so situated in front of the great eastern portal that the rays of the morning sun fell directly upon it at its rising, lighting up the whole apartment with an effulgence that seemed more than natural and which was reflected back from the golden ornaments with which the walls and ceiling were everywhere encrusted. Gold, in the figurative language of the people, was 'tears wept by the sun" and every part of the interior of the temple glowed with burnished plates and studs of the precious metal."

Adjoining the temple were others dedicated to the Moon, "the deity held next in reverence, as Mother of the Incas", the Stars, the Thunder, and Lightning, and to the Rainbow. All the plates, ornaments, and utensils were of gold or silver and twelve immense silver vases stood filled with maize. The gardens sparkled with gold and silver flowers and animals including a beautifully constructed llama with a golden fleece.

Most of these treasures were carried off and melted down by the Spaniards but some of what remained can be seen in Cuzco's present-day Archaeological Museum on Calle Tigre. The city's other main museum, the Art Museum (Calle Hatun Rumioc), specializes in the Colonial period. Their opening hours are not listed here because they're unreliable, rarely opening when they're supposed to. Good luck.

The city's colorful market is beside San Pedro church and the railroad station. Go early. The Barrio de las Artistas, near San Blas church, is a nice undisturbed blend of Colonial and Incan, and repays a casual wandering.

There are occasional folklore performances at the Cuzco Center of

Native Art (Calle El Sol 604, tel: 3708) where the instruments are authentic and the costumes dazzling.

On June 24 of each year, Cuzco stages a folklore festival meant to capitalize on the ancient Incan festival of *Inti Raymi* which was held at summer solstice. Similarities between the ancient and the modern, understandably, are few.

At *Inti Raymi*, reported William Prescott in his classic **The Conquest of Peru**, "when the Sun having touched the southern extremity of its course, retraced its path as if to gladden the hearts of his chosen people by its presence ... the Indian nobles from the different quarters of the country thronged to the capital to take part in the great celebration.

"For three days previously there was a general fast and no fire was allowed to be lighted in the dwellings. When the appointed day arrived, the Inca and his court, followed by the whole population of the city, assembled at early dawn in the great square to greet the rising of the Sun. Eagerly they watched the coming of their deity and no sooner did his first yellow rays strike the turrets and loftiest buildings of the capital, then a shout of gratulation broke forth from the assembled multitude, accompanied by songs of triumph, and the wild melody of barbaric instruments that swelled louder and louder as his bright orb, rising in above the mountain range towards the east, shone in full splendor on his votaries."

Inspiring as all this sounds, there was a grimmer side. One of the Incas' less admirable habits was to make the stomachs of their enemies into drums and arrange the hands of the corpses so that they appeared to be drumming on their own bellies.

Garcilaso de la Vega flatly denies that the Incas were guilty of making human sacrifices but most other authorities contradict him and Prescott attributes his error to an honorable wish to absolve his race "from so odious an implication." Human sacrifices by the Incas, however, do seem to have been reserved for especially important occasions.

At the enthronement of a new Inca as many as two hundred children were slaughtered as sacrifices, if not by strangulation then by having their hearts extracted.

At Cuzco's *Inti Raymi* festival it was usually a llama that was sacrificed and its entrails inspected "to read the lesson of the mysterious future."

AN OCCULT GUIDE TO SOUTH AMERICA

Prescott comments that such reading of entrails was unusual in the New World, though familiar in Europe, and goes on to draw another comparison with ancient Rome by pointing out that a sacred fire was then kindled by means of the sun's rays on a concave mirror. Plutarch, he says, in his life of Numa, describes the reflectors used by the Romans for kindling the sacred fire as concave instruments of brass, though not spherical like the Peruvian, but of triangular form.

When the fire was lit a burnt offering of the dead llama was made on the altar and then more beasts were slaughtered to provide a feast in which the nobles and the common people joined. The day's revelry was closed with music and dancing.

A bread made from maize kneaded by the Virgins of the Sun supplemented the fare and afterwards the Virgins, whose duty it was to watch over the sacred fire obtained on this day, went back into seclusion. The maidens were watched and guarded at all times. If one of them was caught in an intrigue she was buried alive, her lover strangled, and the town or village to which he belonged was razed to the ground and sowed with stones."

In his book, **The Pre-Columbian Mind** (Academic Press, 1972), F. Guerra reported that priests were occasionally punished because they had heterosexual intercourse with the maidens but "sodomy could be committed with therm without loss of virginity which was of paramount importance in their office as maids of the Sun."

Carcilaso de la Vega reported that there were "no less than fifteen hundred maidens of royal blood" in the establishment at Cuzco and that the low buildings, surrounded by high walls, in which they were lodged were embellished as lavishly as the palaces of the Incas.

"Yet the career of all the inhabitants of these cloisters was not confined within their narrow walls," Prescott comments. "Though Virgins of the Sun, they were brides of the Inca and at a marriageable age the most beautiful among them were selected for the honors of his bed, and transferred to the royal seraglio. The full complement of this amounted in time not only to hundreds, but thousands, who all found accommodations in his different palaces throughout the country. When the monarch was disposed to lessen the number of his establishment, the concubine with whose society he was willing to dispense returned not to her former monastic residence but to her own home; where, however humble might be her original condition, she was maintained in great state, and far from being dishonored by the situation she had filled, was held in universal reverence as the Inca's bride.

The duties of these Virgins included spinning, weaving, and making the fine clothes the Inca and his wife wore and the garments offered as sacrifices to the Sun. The nuns also made the bread (*cancu*) for the sacrifices at the great festivals and brewed the drink (*aca*) consumed by the Inca and his family,

Other houses throughout the country operated in similar fashion except that they were open to beautiful women recruited from all classes and formed a pool from which the Inca was routinely supplied with additional wives.

Cuzco itself was planned as a calendar city, with an exterior outline in the shape of a gigantic puma whose stone head was formed by the fortress of Sacsahuaman on Hawks' Hill and "the martial outline of the first wall of the plaza represented its pointed fangs, while its blazing eyes were the towers faced with gold sheets, shining in the sun."

The puma city, wrote Manual Chavez Ballon in **Notes Cuzquenas**, was a temple to time, its twelve districts counted clockwise and represented the twelve months; each district had three main streets, each of which was equivalent to a week of ten days, and the seasons were embodied in the four quarters (*Tahuantinsuyu*) which met at the great central plaza.

An interesting side trip can be made to the village of Pisac with its Incan ruins, the beginning of a chain of fortresses that protect the Urubamba river valley. The ruins lie at the top of a hill outside Pisac and present a steep climb which is worth making for the magnificent view. Buy a handful of coca leaves and lifka (a catalyst for chewing same) at a small *abarrote* (grocery store) in the village.

One of the noblest examples of the Incan building technique can be observed at the fortress of Sacsahuaman, on a hill overlooking Cuzco on the road to Pisac.

The road leading up from Cuzco is lined with eucalyptus trees planted by the Spaniards, and all the way out to the fortress, young purplish eucalyptus shoots are evidence of the reforestation currently taking place.

Sacsahuaman, built in the fifteenth and sixteenth centuries by Pachacutec and Topa Inca, with three zigzagging walls to give a clear view of any attackers, is composed of enormous stones—one weighing a fantastic 300 tons—brought from as far as 15 miles away, pushed, pulled, assembled, shaped, and fitted together by a work force of 20,000 Indians under the direction of a trio of Incan architects. Many of the boulders are 15 feet high by 12 feet wide, cut and elaborately fitted like a jigsaw puzzle assembled by a race of giants. The huge stones are convex, uncemented, and fitted so closely together that "you can't fit a knife blade between them," as the oft-repeated cliché goes. There are solid stairways and big, classic Incan doorways in the familiar Incan pattern: the heavy lintel resting across a space narrower at the top than at the bottom.

Brown birds with yellow chests inhabit the ruins and are known locally as "stone-peckers" for their habit of living among the rocks and jabbing away at the insects that infest the niches.

The Spanish chronicler Pedro Sancho wrote that many Spaniards who had visited other foreign kingdoms "say they have seen no other building like this fortress, nor any castle more secure. These walls are the finest construction to be seen [in Peru]. They are built of stones so large that nobody who saw them would think they had been placed there by human hands-they are like great mountain crags."

But in 1536, after fearful battles, the Spaniards captured Sacsahuaman, and the surviving Incan leaders fled north, first to the fortress of Ollantaytambo in the Sacred Yucay Valley and then to that hidden city in the mountains which Hiram Bingham later theorized must have been Machu Picchu.

Cieza de Leon bemoaned the destruction of Sacsahuaman, adding: "I hate to think of the responsibility of those who have governed here in allowing so extraordinary a monument to be destroyed. The remains of this fortress ... should be preserved in memory of the greatness of this land." Carcilaso de la Vega, who ranked it as one of the wonders of the world, said that all buildings above the ground were destroyed by 1560.

Around Sacsahuaman (which guides often pronounce as "sexy woman'), the countryside is marvelously lush and enticing with little valleys, ridges, and clusters of trees sheltering an occasional home. Potatoes, barley, and wheat grow readily in this fertile region which is one of the reasons the Incas chose it for their center.

On the road between Sacsahuaman and Pisac are other sites. Not far from the fortress, offering a beautiful view of Cuzco's red-tiled roofs, is Kenko (Quenco) with its open amphitheater containing niched stone seats for spectators when sacrificial ceremonies were conducted. Behind the rock pile is an immensely complex series of eaves, stairs, and tunnels with a big central altar rock (and a groove for the blood to flow down). Mummies that were found here can be inspected in Cuzco's Archaeological Museum. There's a tiny museum at the side (key at the house next door); its chief contents are stone pots with pointed bottoms, pieces of obsidian, brooches, and a rusty *tumi* or ritual surgeon's knife which might have been used for sacrifices.

Two other nearby sites are the fortress of Puku Pukara ("Red Tower," named for the stones of the watchtower) which dominated the approach to the capital up the eastern valley; and Tambo-Machay, a shrine to which the Incas came to worship water and the sun. Partly reconstructed, it rises from a pile of huge stones numbered with white paint among which hard-hatted Peruvian laborers are working. Streams of crystal-pure water flow down grooved stone channels onto the terraces. It must have offered a charmingly peaceful respite from the rigors of the capital a few miles away.

About 40 miles south of Cuzco at the town of Paruro, an annual ceremony takes place, symbolically representing a historical event that never happened: the defeat of the Spaniards by the Indians. It would be wistful if it were not so bloodthirsty. The ceremony is the Yawar Fiesta, held in September, when a giant condor—captured on a hazardous expedition into the precipitous Andean peaks-is sewn by its claws to the back of a *salqua misitucha*, a wild, bad tempered bull with killer horns.

The condor, always a sacred bird to the Indians, is their champion against the bull who represents the might of imperial Spain; in this unequal championship it is the condor who always wins. "There is both glory and terror in the drama which unfolds in the ring," writes Alfonsina Barrionuevo. "Basically it is a revenge in which the Indian compensates himself for centuries of injustice."

Ms. Barrionuevo's book, **Cuzco, Magic City** (Editorial Universo, Lima, 1968), is a compilation of fascinating legends concerning Huaro, the town of the witch doctors in Quispicanchi province; the mountain Pachatusan where the Incas placed the imperial mummies to dry in the sun; and the enchanted city of Piuray, submerged beneath a lake off the road to Chincheros.

In the early morning (5:00 A.M.), trucks leave Cuzco's market for

AN OCCULT GUIDE TO SOUTH AMERICA

Chincheros, about a two hours' drive to the northeast. The town, which appears almost unchanged from Incan times, has a good Sunday market where you can buy beautifully woven belts from the Indians and there are views of the magnificent 20,000-foot Vilcapamba peaks.

The three-hour trip to Machu Picchu begins and ends with a zigzag series of bends—first as the little orange train swings to and fro, climbing the hills out of Cuzco itself before descending to the plains of Anta, the dried-up bottom of a former lake. The last leg of the journey is a bus ride up the steep mountain from Machu Picchu station on a road that offers a series of 180-degree bends.

Virtually every seat on the morning train (the station is next to the Cuzco market) is occupied by tourists of all nationalities who sit together in chattering groups. There is no buffet car, but an energetic Peruvian vendor doubles back and forth along the length of the train offering first soft drinks, then sandwiches, finally cookies and candy.

Once into the Urubamba valley, it's not far to Ollantaytambo, the mountain fortress to which the fugitive Incas fled from Pizarro's pursuing army after being forced out of Cuzco. Unconquered, the fortress is an unspoiled Incan monument, and fascinating to explore. But the train won't wait for you, so if you have time, get off today, stay overnight in one of the local homes (cheap and primitive), and resume your journey to Machu Picchu tomorrow.

At about the halfway point between Cuzco and Machu Picchu, where guides point out the remains of an Incan bridge across the river (adjoining a modern bridge), the train halts at one of the few sections of double track, to allow the Cuzco bound train to pass. While waiting, the passengers alight to stretch, take photographs, and buy some of the celebrated giant sweet corn husks for which the village was famous even in Incan days.

From here onwards the train parallels the course of the turbulent Urubamba river, spanned occasionally by small bridges, but even more often by a primitive, hand-operated cable device by means of which a person can pull himself through the air to the opposite bank, riding only a few feet above the raging waters.

There are few homes in these parts, and the gorgeous river valley is almost without sign of human life apart from the occasional minuscule communities squeezed between the railroad track and the river.

AN OCCULT GUIDE TO SOUTH AMERICA

At Machu Picchu everybody has been told to alight quickly because there are insufficient buses to carry passengers to the top (elevation: 7,900 feet). So the moment the train halts, there's a mad rush to join the lineup. Eventually all are deposited beside the Machu Picchu hotel (about 700 soles for a single, 1,100 soles for a double; advance reservations essential) where a simple lunch is served around noon before tour parties set off to look around the ruins. These are closed at 5:00 P.M., but the view up here is so magnificent and the silence so overwhelming that people who have stayed at the hotel overnight regard it as a once-in-a-lifetime experience. The sunrise alone well justifies the extra day.

Archaeologists have concluded from the ruins, and what has been found in them, that the city of Machu Picchu was built around A.D. 1420 during the reign of Pachacutec, the Incas' ninth emperor.

But if the historians are correct, this most hidden of the Incan cities didn't fulfill its potential until more than a century later.

In 1535, Manco II, one of the sons of Huayna Capac who had been crowned as a figurehead by the Spaniards, rebelled, and with 20,000 Indians put Sacsahuaman and Cuzco under siege. After a six month struggle the Incas were once again defeated and Manco II fled into the jungle, setting up headquarters at Vitcos (today known as Chuquipalta) and establishing an empire which history calls the Empire of Vilcapamba.

Vitcos became a refuge for Spanish deserters and refugees and was often visited by missionaries, but its very existence was a threat to Colonial rule, and eventually the Spaniards penetrated the river valley and destroyed it, killing most of the people and taking the last emperor, Tupac Amaru, back to Cuzco where he was executed.

But further up the valley somewhere, was the legendary Vilcampamba, and the Spaniards never discovered it. Nor did anyone else until, in 1911, Hiram Bingham was led to it by Indians after he had spent many months in the jungle inquiring about the location of the lost Incan cities.

In his book, ***Lost City of the Incas*** (Atheneum, 1963) Bingham says the ruins are called Machu Picchu ("the old mountaintop") because nobody knew what else to call them, though no one now disputes that it was the site of the ancient Vilcampamba. 'The sanctuary was lost for centuries, because this ridge is in the most inaccessible corner of the most inaccessible section of the central Andes. No part of the highlands of Peru is better defended by natural bulwarks—a stupendous canyon whose rock is granite and whose precipices are frequently a thousand feet sheer."

The Urubamba river makes a horseshoe curve at this point, almost encircling the Machu Picchu site, to form a natural moat. A dry moat running downhill separates the terraces from the city proper, a sort of Gnat line of defense if attackers managed to climb the mountain.

A population of approximately 1,400 was about the maximum that Machu Picchu could support at any one time but the community was self-sufficient in food and water. It was probably for this reason that its presence remained a secret all through the remaining years of the Spanish occupation of Peru.

The major points of interest are the series of cultivated terraces with layers of earth atop clay; the semicircular tower under which is what's been described as "the royal tomb," although the flat, altarlike stone it contains is more likely to have been used for sacrifices; the palace of the princess (which Hiram Bingham thought to be the residence of the chief priest); the Incas' palace; the main temple with its altar of granite blocks; and, up a flight of steps and atop a hill, a stone pillar known as *Inti-huatana* which is a type of sundial found in other parts of Peru and is used to measure solstices and equinoxes (this one pointed north). The literal meaning of *Inti-huatana* is "hitching post for the sun" and it was the place to which the priests tied the sun at the point of its furthest distance from the southern hemisphere (winter solstice) so that it would begin to come back again.

In Cuzco two sets of pillars called *pachacta u nanchac* were erected on hills in the direction of sunrise and two sets towards sunset to mark the extreme points of the sun's rising and setting. When the sun rose and set between the middle pair in each group, the solstices were known to have arrived.

Louis E. Valcarcel feels that the forest around Machu Picchu still holds many surprises which have yet to be revealed. For example, he asks, what happened to the old people who died there? He finds it mysterious that of the 135 skeletons found in the tombs, 109 were of young women, and that no gold ornaments were found in the tombs or temples. And if the city was ready to be defended, he reasons, why were no weapons found?

In his **Machu Picchu** (Editorial Universitaria de Buenos Aires 1973) he maintains that the site was undeniably a sacred one. "A constant rule observed by the Incas was to construct, in every city of any importance, a temple to the sun, a house of chosen virgins and a royal palace. But, in Machu Picchu, we encounter many more than merely these three buildings (of obvious official importance) which stresses the difference between this and other Inca cities."

When excavations were begun on the terraces, it became clear that even the sod and clay had been specially brought here from afar to provide an element in which crops could grow without having the water' run off too quickly. By an ingenious system of channels it flowed from one terrace to another, keeping the whole complex fertile.

A series of pools, each overflowing into the one below it, ensured no wastage of water which was collected and channeled in pools at the top of the hill. The present-day hotel gets its water in a similar manner.

About 3.5 miles away across the mountains may be found more Incan ruins known as Huri Huyan.

The Incan tribes, according to legend, had come from a place called Tampu-Tocco and had once before been established at Cuzco but had been forced to leave after an invasion of hordes from the south and east, preceded by comets, earthquakes and divine divinations," Once the Incas were restored in Cuzco, wrote Hartley Alexander in **The Mythology of All Races** (MacMillan, 1948), the ancient home of Tampu-Tocco "became no more than a monumental shrine where priests and vestals preserved the rites of the old religion and watched over caves made sacred by the bones of former monarchs." The discovery of Machu Picchu revived the old legends of Tampu-Tocco, many historians believing them to be one and the same.

The Machu Picchu station is not quite the last one on the railroad line, but people interested in exploring the jungle that lies further east usually prefer to make the onward journey by car rather than by train. (Another way to visit the jungle is to fly, from Lima to Iquitos, on the Amazon.)

Souvenir sellers and stalls offering various products of llama, vicuna, etc. surround the station and as the return train doesn't leave till 4:00 P.M., there is ample time for shopping or mailing postcards from the tiny booth that acts as a post office.

The late-afternoon return journey is even more enjoyable than that of the early morning. The mountains look more and more romantic, the river even more torrential, as dusk falls and the flat wail of the train's horn arouses the spirits of the valley.

Nearing Cuzco the train swoops down over the city from on high, offering an unexpected aerial view similar to a plane about to land. Then, as if on a giant string being dangled from one side of the valley to the other, we are flashed back and forth, each swing bringing the city appreciably closer, until we are near enough to see the flickering TV sets in people's houses.

Although $20 tours to Machu Picchu eliminate all the annoyances, it's certainly cheaper to make your way to the station (be there by 6:00 A.M. and try to get a seat on the left) under your own steam. First-class round-trip fare is about $2, to which you'll have to add bus fare (about $1 up the hill from the Machu Picchu station), plus entry to the ruins (another $1.50), and whatever you spend on food. Of course, you're dispensing with the guide service which is included in the tour, but perhaps you can eavesdrop on one of the many groups.

Another alternative is to alight from the train at the 88-kilometer stop and walk the 25 kilometers of the "Inca Trail." There is a student train some days (ask the tourist office in Cuzco for a schedule and map of the walk) that is cheaper and earlier than the tourist train. The hike takes three days (backpack and camp in the woods) and brings you out at the entrance gate to Machu Picchu itself.

AN OCCULT GUIDE TO SOUTH AMERICA

AN OCCULT GUIDE TO SOUTH AMERICA

Chapter 10

Northern Peru

Pyramids and Pottery

Lima (pop. 3.5 million) is Peru's capital and although it was once famous throughout the world as the base of Spanish power on the subcontinent, it's pretty dull today. If your time is limited, be advised to save most of it for more interesting places.

The city is rich in elaborately decorated churches and Colonial homes but most of what is most fascinating about Peru dates to before the time of the Spaniards, and there is little of that to be found here in Lima. The area around Lake Titicaca, Cuzco (with, of course, Machu Picchu), Arequipa, Nazca, and the northern ruins of Chan Chan all have more to offer.

Lima's best hotels are the old, worldly Gran Hotel Bolivar (Plaza San Martin), the equally posh Hotel Crillon (N. de Pierola 589) or the slick, American-modern Sheraton (Pasco de la Republica). All are expensive (from about $25 for a Single, $35 for a double) and somewhat overrated. Slightly less expensive but possibly offering better valve are the hotels Savoy (Gailloma 224) and Alcazar (Carriana 564).

If you stay at the Gran Hotel Bolivar, comfortable but a bit snooty, you may prefer to forego the expensive dining room in favor of the English-style Colonial Bar where the vegetable soup is first rate and the potato chips are the finest south of the Santa Monica pier. The Sheraton has the city's only hotel swimming pool.

A logical sightseeing tour of Lima on foot might begin at the Plaza de Armas, created by Francisco Pizarro as the Colonial center, and include some of the historical homes and churches. You should see the eighteenth-century Palace of Torre Tagle (restored in 1954, and now the Ministry of Foreign Affairs); the Inquisition Building on Plaza Bolivar ,and one of the world's oldest buildings (and adjoining museum) at Acho in the Rimac District. San Isidro is a suburb with elegant, modern homes and also an immense step pyramid (Choquehuanca Street) which can be inspected en route to the Miguel Mujica Gallo Museum. This is most conveniently seen on a tour paired with the equally fascinating Larco Herrera Museum. Lima is rich in museums and almost all of them are worth seeing.

There's a pre-Incan *huaca* or Indian burial ground to be inspected in San Isidro, at the corner of Nicolas de Rivera and Rosario avenues. Open from 9:00 A. M. to 12:30 P. M. and 3:00 to 5:00 P. M., it includes a tiny museum containing some of the artifacts found on the site.

The name Lima is a corruption of Rimac, the name of a valley in which a pre-Incan oracle was stationed. Garsilaso de la Vega says the idol was "in the shape of a man which spoke and gave answers to questions, like the oracle of the Delphic Apollo." The word Rimac, he explains, means, "He who speaks."

There are plenty of tour agencies, the best known being Lima Tours (Ocona 160, tel: 27-6624) which is right behind the Gran Hotel Bolivar and acts as the local American Express representative. Among the excursions offered are an afternoon visit to the Larco Herrera and Gold museums; a daily tour to Lima's nearby port, Callao, with a stop at a bustling Indian handicraft market; and excursions to Pachacamac (plus a visit to the National Archaeological Museum) and to 15,000-foot Ticlio pass, high in the Andes. There are also longer excursions to Cuzco and Machu Picchu; to Trujillo and Chan Chan; to Iquitos on the Amazon; and up into the mountains via railroad to Huancayo.

Huancayo (which has a tourist hotel) is the most important market town (on Sunday) in Peru. It can be reached by car or a spectacular train ride that at times reaches a height of 15,800 feet above sea level.

It is difficult to track down the infrequent tours to Nazca to inspect the desert markings there. One such agency is listed in the discussion on Nazca in the previous chapter, but most travel agents seem to operate tours only when there is enough demand.

Because the museums will probably consume most of your time—they are far apart—we'll deal with them fairly fully before recommending the out-of-town spots that should be visited, and Ill try to give you some background on the various exhibits as we go along.

The National Museum of Anthropology and Archaeology (Tuesday to Sunday 10:00 A.M. to 6:00 P.M., closed Mondays) fills in the details about many subjects we have touched upon elsewhere. For example, there's a large-scale model of Macho Picchu which is really impressive and which seems to reproduce virtually every building and tree at the site. It conveys a much better overall view than can be gleaned at Machu Picchu itself.

In the lobby of the National Museum is a large chart comparing the different time and culture periods so that you can confirm (for example) that the early Chavin period (around 800 B.C.) coincides with that of Mycenae, Assyria, and Babylon on the other side of the world. You can inspect the realistic Mochica pottery (about 200 B.C. to A.D. 700), among which is a case full of mythical beasts, as well as examples from the earlier Chavin, Paracas, (600 B.C. to 300 B. C.) and Nazca cultures.

Paracas pottery was rather nondescript, in dull colors, but the cloth-covered mummies unearthed from their cavelike tombs demonstrate their skill and artistry in weaving tapestry. The Paracas were also experts at trepanation, proved by the skulls which have been preserved.

The Smithsonian's T. Dale Stewart says trepanned Paracas skulls are the earliest examples of this type of operation, the reason for which was not always apparent. Sometimes sawing, grating or drilling (the surgical instruments were usually obsidian or quartz flakes), the top of the head was a necessary operation when somebody had been injured by a blow on the skull; at other times it must be presumed to have some relationship with magical ceremonies. "The rate of survival from this primitive surgery was surprisingly high," he comments, observing that investigators had noted "advanced healing of the bone" in up to 63 percent of the cases.

The Paracas culture stems from a peninsula of the same name just south of Pisco on the coast. Here there are graves cut into caverns, and also subterranean tombs made from stones and adobe bricks. The two types represent different periods, called respectively Cavernas and Necropolis with nobody quite sure which came first, although Cavernas seem to have the edge. Necropolis textiles and pottery are superior, as befits chronological development, and somewhat resemble those of the nearby Nazca culture.

The famous Paracas textiles found in graves, says A. L. Kroeber, are unsurpassed in fineness and richness of design and color. "The most sumptuous are rectangular mantles, bearing aligned, isolated figures of gods, impersonators, demons or warriors, either in a wide border surrounding an empty panel or in the panel itself." Often they are a mixture of wool and cotton, and in many instances decorated with beautifully colored feathers from such brightly plumaged birds as the macaw.

The Nazcas, who followed the Paracas, were more sophisticated in their pottery, using a wider range of brighter colors.

The museum devotes a special display to the Nazca Lines, those mysterious tracings in the desert laid out with such mathematical precision and oriented to the stars.

The distinctive black on white pottery from the Chancay valley, just north of Lima, can be seen surrounding a macabre, dried-up mummy in the foetal position. His hands are tied, possibly for sacrifice; maybe whoever buried him didn't want him coming back after death and causing trouble

It was at Chancay that a rare specimen of the Incas' *quipu* was found, a specimen now in New York's Museum of Natural History. (Another *quipu* can be seen in this museum.) The *quipu*, probably in use in South America since early times but refined by the Incas, was a sophisticated counting device which recorded numbers by means of knots tied into strings of different colors and lengths. These strings all hung from a thicker, central cord, the whole effect resembling an elaborate rope necklace.

Since the *quipu* counting system is decimal, the knots in the pendant cords represent 1 to 9, with the higher numbers usually the furthest away from the main string. The whole thing is literally a symbol of power, being a record of a certain number of men, supplies, riches, etc. so that the official or chieftain to whom it was delivered held in his hand; an up-to-date accounting of whatever it recorded.

Various contemporary investigators have theorized that the colors of the different cords were significant, although this is impossible to prove or disprove. Both white and black have been variously thought to refer to time, and both white and yellow, it has been suggested, may have meant gold, with red possibly symbolizing warriors or war. Twisting different colors together, adding subsidiary cords, local variations in the *quipu's* meaning— all these factors and many others make it difficult to interpret these records today. Even in the Incas' time it was necessary for a class known as the *quipu-*

camayoc to interpret and supplement the string records.

The four-year school attended by children of Incan nobles devoted one year to the study of *quipu* (the other years being devoted to religion, Incan history, and the study of the Quecha language).

Designs resembling *quipus* have been found on some Mochica pottery and *quipus* were known to have been used by the Aymara, the Araucanians, and the Pehuenche whose red *quipus* were sent to the enemy both as a demand for reparations; and a threat that vengeance would be exacted if the account was not met.

Among the Andaqui tribes of Colombia a form of *quipu* was used by the head of the household as he went off to fight a battle- He gave his wife a knotted cord which enabled her to untie a knot each night and thus know not only when the battle would take place but also when to, hopefully, expect him back.

The *quipus*, along with other messages were transmitted in Incan times by an elaborate and highly efficient series of runners who were trained from boyhood for their arduous job. Resthouses were set along the roads every few miles where messengers waited to continue the journey, as in relay races. The men served fifteen-day shifts and rarely ran more than one mile at a time before passing on the *quipu*, thus maintaining enormously fast overall speeds. Bernabé Cobo, writing late in the last century, recorded that the average collective speed of runners was about 150 miles per day and that from Lima to Cuzco—more than 400 miles on bad roads—took Incan runners three days, a distance that the Spanish mailmen took twelve days to cover on horseback one hundred or more years later. In addition to important messages, the runners sometimes brought fish fresh from the seashore to the emperor.

The Miguel Mujica Callo Museum, located on a continuation of Avenida Primavera at Chacarilla del Estanque, tel: 25-5531, open daily 3:00 to 7:00 P.M.) houses one of the world's largest collections of gold objects and its staircase is lined with beautiful posters denoting the various countries the exhibit has visited. The museum displays objects from the Chimu, Mochica, Nazca, Taihaunacu, and Incan cultures among others, as well as a display of ancient and modern weapons ranging from Indian stone clubs to dueling pistols and bullfighting swords, from slingshots to World War II guns.

The museum, which looks like a concrete strong box, is set in a garden and guarded by old-fashioned cannons. This motif is continued in the entrance hall with suits of armor and every conceivable type of gun on display.

Gold, of course, has always been worshipped for much more than its financial value a concept that never even occurred to the Indians until the arrival of the Spaniards with their greedy western ways.

Many races believed that gold is the direct product of the sun, a sort of physical counterpart to that ageless god, dwelling under the earth rather than in the skies above it. Geber. the eighth-century Arab who might be described as the father of alchemy, suggested that gold was the only "pure" metal, a flawless combination of mercurial and sulfuric principles that were less perfectly combined in other metals.

Some of the more outstanding items in the Gallo Collection are an ancient "miniskirt" composed of thousands of gold discs sewn onto a cloth backdrop; enormous gold earrings, the size of saucers, worn by Incan chiefs; ponchos with gold belts and decorations; gold fingernails, and innumerable *tumis*, the crescent-shaped trepanation tools which are usually topped with the representation of a god.

Also on display are some outstanding Chancay and Nazca feather garments including a foot high headdress of feathers and gold, still attached to a two thousand-year-old mummified skull perforated with an arrow hole.

"The third of the important collections is to be found at the Rafael Larco Herrera Museum (Ave. Bolivar 1515, open 9:00 A.M. to 1:00 P.M. and 3:00 to 6:00 P.M. closed Sundays). This once private collection was bequeathed to the museum by a former sugar millionaire. Museum officials look very unfavorably upon cameras, especially in connection with what's termed "the erotic collection", scores of Mochica ceramics depicting sex acts-which is kept in a separate wing.

Situated in a lovely, flower-filled garden, the museum is a fascinating jumble of Peruvian archaeological treasures but is outstanding for its hundreds of perfectly preserved ceramics depicting every conceivable aspect and activity of the Mochica culture (from roughly A.D. 400 to 1100). These pieces stand six deep in floor-to-ceiling glass cases, and are so numerous that they could well be distributed to other museums around the world without appreciably diminishing the collection's comprehensiveness.

AN OCCULT GUIDE TO SOUTH AMERICA

The center of this culture was in the Moche valley and adjoining area, near to the present-day city of Trujillo in northern Peru.

Depictions of sexual acts on Mochica pottery were so graphic, reported F. Cuerra in *The Pre-Columbian Mind* (Academic Press, 1972), that the celebrated erotic sculptures at Khajuraho in India, Japanese erotica, and Roman mosaics seem like naive Victorian illustrations" by comparison. "Nothing can be found among the archaeological specimens of Middle-America comparable in sexual perversion to ancient Peru . , . normal coitus appears among them as a very neglected sexual custom when compared to sodomy or fellatio."

"Some of these ceramics are definitely made with humorous intent," the museum's curator, Rafael Larco Hoyle once wrote. "Others may carry moral implications such as scenes which depict the physical and moral destruction of a sexual pervert."

Both men and women are depicted as shamans, and the belief in witchcraft and magic is depicted in religious scenes closely tied to nature worship.

Now to the outlying places of interest. Twenty kilometers south of Lima, along a stretch of the Pan American Highway sheltering gas stations, chicken farms, and a sprinkling of light industry, the turnoff is made to Pachacamac, once the most important religious center along the coast. It was the site of one of Peru's most revered oracles, already five or six centuries old when the Incas arrived around 1400.

There isn't too much to see today except for a hilltop ruin which was once a three-tiered Temple to the Sun built on the orders of the Inca Pachacutec, and a nearby (reconstructed) House of the Mamaconas, or Sun Virgins, where young maidens were trained either for royal concubinage or for sacrifice. (Any men found within its sacred enclosure were executed in the public square.)

The city has two long, narrow streets running perpendicular to a third, and this joins a road connecting squares "that must once have been filled with pilgrims or served as amphitheaters for the presentation of dances or lyric pieces," writes Pedro Villar Cordova (*Las Culturas Pre-Hispanica del Departmento de Lima*, 1935).

The Pyramid of the Sun is 73 feet high with terraced sides and covers a total of twelve acres. There were painted designs on the upper terraces; the lower ones sheltered houses for the various pilgrims who came to consult the oracle. The terraces adjoining the pyramids were often used as burial grounds, and pyramids themselves were once commonplace, there being more than one hundred of them in the Rimac valley around Lima, until expansion of the city during this century.

Pachacamac's adobe-lined burial chambers are conical or of cylindrical shape, the bodies mummified with false heads made of different substances: wood, clay, or cloth.

The Temple to the Sun faces west, out to sea. Below is a bullring and cock-fighting arena; offshore is a small island, with the remains of some crumbled buildings. It was once a big guano-collecting center.

Millions, of years of nesting by birds of the cormorant, pelican, or guanay family have deposited vast amounts of guano on islands like this one all along the northern Peruvian coast. Guano has always been known as a rich fertilizer and was used long before the Incas enacted laws concerning its conservation and use.

The reason for so many birds gathering on these islands is connected to the nearby presence of millions of small fish, *anchoveta*, which swarm here to feed on the rich plankton brought by favorable ocean currents. When these currents shift out to sea taking the fish with them, apparently in seven year cycles, guano birds starve by the millions, and their emaciated bodies pile up all along the shore.

When Atahualpa, in captivity, was casting about for funds for his ransom from the Spaniards, he thought of Pachacamac and the gold stored there, and decided it could well be sacrificed, later explaining to Pizarro why he was so unsympathetic to the oracle and its keepers. "The oracle there had recently delivered three disastrously wrong predictions," writes John Hemming in **The Conquest of the Incas** (Sphere Books, London, 1970). It advised that Huayna-Capac would recover from his illness if taken into the sun, but he died; it told Huascar that he would defeat Atahualpa; and, most recently, it had advised Atahualpa to make war on the Christians, saying that he would kill them all. Atahualpa concluded that a shrine that was so fallible could contain no god, and Pizarro told him he was a wise man to reach this conclusion."

One of the rooms on the ramparts of Pachacamac is said to have been the place of the oracle, where a priest dreamed of a condor being destroyed by an eagle. This was subsequently interpreted as being a forecast of Peru's conquest by Spain.

The Pachacamac oracle's reputation was such that when the Incas first arrived and conquered the region they not only consulted it themselves but allowed the priests great autonomy, merely adding a new edifice to the site. Pedro Cieza de Leon in his **La Cronica del Peru** quoted a Spanish soldier as saying; "'The Incas, seeing the grandeur and antiquity of the temple, and the authority it held with the people of the region and the great devotion which everyone showed to it, dealt with the native lords and with their ministers . . . so that the temple of Pachacamac might keep its authority and service, so long as another temple for the sun be built in the most prominent place. . ."

But although an important religious center, Pachacamac gradually declined as a city; it was still substantial when the Spaniards arrived in 1533 but their disapproval (Hernando Pizarro slaughtered the priests and looted the temples) ended its influence.

Regarded as a minor tourist attraction today, the site was once the most revered one in Peru after Cuzco, according to Cieza de Leon who visited it in 1548 and reported: 'The building was on top of a small, man-made hillock of adobe and earth. . . It contained many doors which, together with the walk, were painted with pictures of wild animals. "Inside the temple," he wrote, "was an idol in front of which the multitudes gathered on special occasions confronted by priests, whose backs were turned to the idol, their eyes downcast and tremulous. Before the image of this devil they sacrificed animals and sometimes human beings."

This seems to fit with the findings of German archaeologist Max Uhle who, in 1896, discovered tombs containing the skeletons of numerous women who had obviously been strangled to death.

It was at Pachacamac in 1896 that Uhle, the father of modern archaeology, tested his techniques of "stratigraphy," a method of classifying and correlating different levels of rock and substance to delineate time periods. In his subsequent excavations up and down the Peruvian coast, Uhle classified four periods of Peruvian history: Pre-Tiahuanaco, Tiahuanaco, Post-Tiahuanaco, and Incan. This, with various subdivisions and elaborations, has been the prevailing system ever since.

AN OCCULT GUIDE TO SOUTH AMERICA

Uhle's excavations at the Pachacamac site revealed that the remains of the present pyramid covered a much older temple and that three levels, including some even older graves, denoted three distinct time periods in which different styles were developed.

A so-called Pachacamac style grew out of the site during its later, more prestigious years. Its dominant characteristic was the eagle designs which were much copied in other regions.

Most excursions from Lima are either south, like the one to Pachacamac, or north along the Pan American Highway. One short diversion to the east is worth mentioning briefly: to the small town of Chosica, about 25 miles from the capital and just high enough above sea level to be sunny most of the year, as opposed to Lima which is usually covered by clouds. Chosica, where it rarely rains, straddles the Rimac river.

The Pan American Highway, apart from a stretch between Panama and Colombia, is now complete from the Mexican border to Brasilia, a stretch of 10,000 miles that can be driven almost entirely on paved roads. Sometimes it may be necessary to make diversions because of local conditions or bad weather (not all the highway is "all-weather") but officially the road is open all the way. Back in 1927, when José Mario Barone negotiated the trip between Rio and New York, it took him two years, the Cuzco to Lima stretch alone taking him fourteen weeks (today it takes three days). If you are planning to drive on the highway write to the General Secretariat, Organization of American States, Washington, D. C., and ask for the booklet *The Pan American Highway System* which describes conditions in each country along the route.

It is this highway which we now take north out of Lima in search of the Chimu kingdom, one of the civilizations that had been flourishing long before the arrival of the Inca. It was centered at Chan Chan, along Peru's north coast, near the present city of Trujillo. An immense city that sprawled across a score of valleys and even today—at a quarter of its original size—is at least twice as big as Pompeii, Chan Chan must be one of the world's most curious sites. For it is literally a city of mud: a series of extensive palaces surrounded by high walls, and subsidiary dwellings that were built of the same baked mud adobe brick that is used so extensively for building today, seven Centuries later.

The Chimu used to post a watchman in the desert to assist travelers who might lose their way and this custom was later followed by the Incas.

According to a report presented to the governor of Peru between 1541 and 1544, the Chimus ruled an area stretching from Nazca up into what is now Ecuador until the Incas arrived to challenge their rule. The last of the Chimu line, Chimo Capac, raised a large army against the Incas but was defeated "by sheer force of numbers," wrote Philip Means in **Ancient Civilizations of the Andes** (Gordian, 1964), and the Grand Chimu was then led off to Cuzco, loaded with honors and returned to his native province to rule as a vassal to the Incas.

Flights to Trujillo are operated daily by both Faucett and AeroPeru. The latter airline has been known to postpone or cancel flights randomly, and is rarely able to tell passengers whether or not there are seats on return flights. The result (as happened to me) is that you sometimes end up buying a ticket which can't be used and which the airline declines to redeem.

If you have the time it's a good idea to drive the 300 miles up the coast, or possibly fly one way and arrange a ride back. If you wait at the gas station at the southern end of Trujillo you'll eventually locate somebody who'll be glad to give you a lift for a few dollars. The newspaper vans that deliver the papers are comfortable and reliable. There are also buses; the ones returning to Lima leave Trujillo at 5:00 A.M. and 7:00 P.M.

Because of the hundreds of miles of desert between Trujillo and Lima there's almost every possible variation of natural sand sculpture, created over the centuries with the aid of wind, rain, and earthquakes. The mountains display sand drifts in their crevices, just as higher in the Andes the crevices shelter snowdrifts. Once in a while there will be oxidized copper green hills, or iron red hills on which some patient passerby has taken the trouble to plant a name in letters of lichen.

At Paramonga, just after crossing the river Fortaleza, we reach what some archaeologists maintain was the southern boundary of the Chimu kingdom. Here a last unsuccessful stand was made against the invading Incas about 1460. A magnificent ruined adobe fortress towering above the highway marks the spot. Some say it was not a fortress but a temple; it may have been both.

In these parched coastal areas, it was the moon goddess who predominated in ancient times rather than the sun god. The sun could not be appeased; it shone constantly and ignored all sacrifices. But the moon controlled the tides and to the early coastal dwellers that meant the difference between good and bad fishing.

The Indians of the Pasamayo valley, north of Trujillo, who believed that the human race was descended from stars, worshipped the moon, which they held to be more powerful than the sun because she could be seen both by day and night. The Indians of the coastal plain believed that when the moon did not shine she was in the other world castigating thieves who had died," wrote Philip Means. "Thievery is the vice most abhorred by these people." Five-year-old children were sacrificed to the Moon, he added, and the Indians also deified three stars which they called Pata and believed to be a thief bound to his captors, sent by the Moon to lead him away to be devoured by vultures.

When thieves were in evidence but not apprehended, these Indians set up a pole from which were suspended green branches and ears of corn to make everybody aware of the danger and sacrifices were made to the Moon to ask her assistance in pinpointing the guilty.

Trujillo (pop. 200,000) is Peru's fourth largest city, the only one of any substantial size north of Lima, and relatively nondescript. Founded officially (it had already existed for a few months) in 1535 by Pizarro, it was given the name of his birthplace. Ironically enough, it was the first city to demand independence from Spanish rule four centuries later.

Many traces of Colonial building still remain, especially around the magnificently spacious Plaza de Armas on which the cathedral and Tourist hotel (about $20 for a double) are situated. There isn't much else to see, although the town is oddly more interesting by night than in daytime. Be sure to take a look at the splendid eighteenth-century house once owned by General Iturregui (who proclaimed Trujillo's independence in 1820) which is now a plush private club. It is near Socialist party headquarters which can be readily identified by the constant stream of martial music it relays into the street.

Typical small-town night life has its own attractions. Walk out of the Tourist hotel, along the top side of the plaza, proceed another couple of blocks, and then turn left for a block or two until you come to a busy intersection. This is the local equivalent of New York's Times Square: hustlers, beggar men hanging around reading papers, young couples, police, and the other characters in the nightly side show. You're part of it, don't forget, so be as unobtrusive as possible and you'll notice more.

Trujillo has a couple of tourist agencies which arrange occasional excursions (both are located near the plaza) but you may be obliged to make out-of-town trips by taxi. You'll find almost any taxi driver will be delighted to take you, but it may be cheaper if you arrange to have the same driver take you to Chan Chan and the Moche Pyramids (they're in opposite directions) rather than to make both excursions separately (around 300 soles for each trip).

It isn't a matter of which is most impressive. Both are well worth seeing, especially now you've come all this way. So it's rather a case of which will you see first. Well, that depends on how you plan to leave town. The Chan Chan ruins are relatively near the airport, whereas the pyramids are not far from the Pan American Highway south of town.

On the way to Chan Chan, you can make a brief stop to see the temple of Esmeraldas, an adobe brick structure on which is carved a frieze of unidentified animals. It is impressive in that it hasn't crumbled away to dust, but it's just a curtain raiser for the real thing.

To express the plural of things, the Chimus repeated the same word and as Chan means "sun," Chan Chan means a lot of it.

Chan Chan really is amazing. To start with, it seems to stretch forever, a mass of crumbling mud ruins and sturdy brown walls with impressively clear carvings that the occasional rains have affected hardly at all. Of course, this is one of the driest parts of the world, with showers falling about twice each century; but even so, considering that most of it was built before the fifteenth century, was conquered by the Incas in 1460, looted by the Spaniards after that, and has been rifled and robbed by hundreds of souvenir hunters since, it's amazing how much is left to see. Nobody speaks English, by the way, and all the guidebooks are in Spanish.

At the time Pizarro headed south past Trujillo in 1527, the ancient Chimu capital was still standing, according to William Prescott, "and while not as opulent as it was before the Inca conquest in 1476, it was still the chief city of a vast area; more than 50,000 people lived there. Chan Chan with its high walls and enormous Sun Temples could have been seen from the sea."

"The city reached its height of its power and influence in the mid-fifteenth century under King Minchancaman, but the Incas deposed the Chimu rulers later in that century, only a few years before the Spaniards arrived. When Cieza de Leon visited Chan Chan in 1548 it was already deserted and the buildings ruined. Even so, he wrote, "one can see they must have been exceptional."

Built of adobe blocks of exactly the same kind used today, and covered over with wet mud which was baked hard by the sun, the immense city comprises nine separate palaces each self-contained with its own plaza, cemetery, gardens, water supply. The most interesting part of the ruins is the Tschudi Palace.

Some of Chan Chan's enclosing walls are as high as 20 feet and up to 2,000 feet long and the city itself, covering at least six square miles, was surrounded by a number of hills which served as watchtowers. Planned from the first as the capital of the great Chimu empire, Chan Chan probably had a population of about 50,000 at its height, with most of its citizens cramped into the barrios adjoining the spacious, almost deserted palaces, each at least twenty acres in size, which apparently served as memorial temples for previous kings.

The last Chimu emperor, Nancen-Pinco, extended the tribe's domain along almost 1,300 kilometers of the Peruvian coast, at a date estimated by John H. Rowe to be about A.D. 1370. To exist in this deserted region, the Chimu constructed an elaborate network of channels, bringing in water from the nearby Moche river but also from rivers as far as 50 miles away. In the ruined city of Chan Chan more than one hundred wells have been uncovered where the city's water was apparently stored.

Like the Incas who followed them the Chimu had no method of writing, but some of their cultural habits and ways of life have been reconstructed from Spanish chroniclers and from the vast amounts of distinctive pottery (most of it black) they left behind. A typical native of Chan Chan, writes Dr. Alberto Rodriguez, a professor at Trujillo's National University, "decorated his image with a cap that covered his short hair, hung painted pieces of wood from his ears and colored his face, legs and feet with red achiote dust and black genipa. The face (thus) appeared like a war mask and the legs and feet seemed to be covered with long stockings. The variety of clothing colors and the use of tattoos was especially marked on holidays."

The Chimu worshipped the sea (*ni*), the moon (*si*), and great rocks (*elespong*) and their belief in the afterlife caused them to worship the dead, leaving offerings on hills and in sacred places. Religious festivals, harvests, births, and war triumphs were celebrated with joyful feasts at which much chicha was drunk.

A group of Harvard archaeologists who excavated the Chan Chan site in 1969 found not only the skeletons of llamas buried beneath some of the buildings (it is still the custom in Andean regions today to plant a llama foetus in the foundations of buildings) but also human skeletons. There were scores of them, and all were female. It seemed clear that they were human sacrifices. The Harvard team theorized that each of the separate "palaces" belonged to successive Chimu kings who, as they died. were buried with ceremony, their palace maintained permanently as a sacred shrine. The new ruler then built a separate palace of his own.

The ordinary people lived outside these royal areas, although towards the end, when the great desert empire had been vanquished, the peasants finally moved into these royal enclosures and set up their own primitive homes.

In similar manner, Chan Chan's modern neighbors have begun to encroach on the ancient city, plowing up acre after acre of the sprawling ruins. But the process of nibbling away at the site has been going on for centuries. One of the earliest grave robbers, Hans Horkheimer tells us, was Trujillo's first founder. Martin de Estaté, who found "a chair of gold and pearls" valued at 100,000 pesos (at least $300,000). Subsequent seekers, in the sixteenth century alone, found treasures totaling a further $2 million in value, and as late as 1864, a Spanish colonel found and melted down "a cubic meter of silver vessels."

"Treasure-seekers find it easy to make holes in the adobe of Chan Chan to look for new rewards," Horkheimer wrote in *Vistas Arqueologicas del Noroeste del Peru* (Trujillo, 1944). "The Chimus' building technique was excellent but they were dealing with frail material." Occasional heavy rains (especially in 1925) and earthquakes have added to the depredations of the farmers and treasure hunters.

Although the Chimus adapted some of the styles that came before them, particularly that of the Mochicas whose language was related to their own, their culture has a distinctive, dominant style. Most Chimu pottery is black with only occasional coloring; the "stirrup-spout" is characteristic, as are the "whistling" jars which, if lipped in the right manner, allow air to enter and leave, causing a musical sound.

Copper, bronze, silver, and gold work from the Chimu period has been rated mediocre by historians, compared with that of some other cultures, but a number of the potters were good enough to be invited to Cuzco to work for their Incan conquerors. The Incas may have borrowed two other ideas from the Chimus: the hierarchical differences between nobles and commoners, stabilized by a hereditary aristocracy, and the square-block town plan that Chan Chan typified (and which is still with us today).

Scenes depicted on the pottery were often very frank. "Judging by these physical artifacts," says Dr. Rodriguez, "the Chimu did not know 'shame' . . . in their ceramics one sees many poses of the practices of masturbation, fellatio, and sodomy. One must suppose the men and women led extremely erotic lives, but they also appear to have been familiar with birth control.

Adulterers, however, were buried alive, and even theft was brutally punished by cutting off the thief's hand or foot. As for the tribe's healers or medicine men, if they were unsuccessful they were punished for their negligence by being attached to the deceased and left in the open to die while Their dead "patient" was buried.

Among the more impressive things about Chan Chan are the enduring carvings and friezes on the mud walls, These depict pelicans, fish, various animals, and lines of circles that look like waves or full moons. Like most primitive people, the Chimu were close students of the skies. Instead of a calendar they were said to have judged the passing of a year by watching for the appearance and reappearance of the Pleiades (the cluster of seven stars which forms the constellation of Taurus and which in mythology were the daughters of Atlas).

A festival dedicated to the Pleiades was celebrated at Lima every June when the crops were in danger of frost. At this time, the constellation, which was believed to influence the weather, was most visible.

When the showdown with the Chimu kingdom came, it was the Incan Prince Tupac who conducted the campaign, and he was soon victorious. The Incas, following their usual custom, helped themselves to the gold and allowed the Chimu to continue worshipping their own gods. This was a pattern for Incan conquests and had a lot to do with the way they retained control over captive peoples by taking representatives to Cuzco, the capital, and incorporating them into their own nobility.

The exact birthdate of the Chimu civilization is not known. In many obvious respects it followed shortly after, or overlapped, that of the Mochica which flourished before and slightly after the tenth century A.D. (the Chavin civilization, centered near present-day Recuay, in the south, was still earlier.)

Writing about the archaeology of the central Andes, the late Dr. Wendell C. Bennett commented that the Mochica period "seems to have gradually died down until the cultures which followed were able to replace it rather than merge."

But the Mochicans left enduring monuments to their ancient civilization in the form of pyramids, two of which, the Huaca de la Luna and Huaca del Sol survive as the biggest pre-Colombian sculptures in South America. The unpaved road to these pyramids winds off the Pan-American Highway south of Trujillo through a countryside dotted with adobe huts, pigs, kids, and banana trees—a region which must look very similar to the way it did when the pyramids were built, roughly ten centuries ago. The Mochicans constructed an elaborate system of irrigation channels and aqueducts to fertilize the barren valleys in which they lived, and a great percentage of these are what still keeps the land green today.

The two pyramids lie in a once-flooded plain near the peak known as Cerro Blanco, at the foot of which is the Moon pyramid. At the edge of the plain, 546 yards west, the Sun pyramid is located. Both pyramids were constructed with millions of adobe bricks, covered over with earth, and both have suffered extensively from caves dug into the top and sides by searchers looking for treasure.

Many caches of gold idols were said to have been found by the Spaniards, but nothing much has been found since, although the smaller Moon pyramid has yielded up several skeletons from its base, indicating that it may have been a ceremonial burial ground.

The Pyramid to the Sun sits on a 60-foot-high platform about 730 feet long and 450 feet wide. An estimated 50 million adobe bricks were piled on this base in stepped terraces and a causeway, now indented with caves and holes, leads to the top. From here you can look down onto a lower terrace now studded with names spelled out by loose rocks. The Moche river runs near the pyramid's base, causing the sterile desert to change abruptly into fertile countryside covered with grass and trees. In 1925, torrential rains swelled the river to a point where it washed away part of the pyramid.

Rectangular-shaped adobe tombs in the region were sometimes found to contain the remains of what was obviously a nobleman, because accompanying the usual burial artifacts there would also be the body of a sacrificial victim, usually a young woman. In other huacas (mounds) were paintings of sacrificial victims with blood pouring from their amputated noses into a sacred cup. Sometimes the pictures showed the cups being offered to mythological creatures that resembled birds. Similar motifs are also seen on some of the Mochica ceramics.

Mochica pottery is renowned for its beauty and its realism. Hundreds of thousands of these ceramic pieces have been found (as already noted, the Rafael Larco Herrera Museum near Lima has the world's largest collection) and to the archaeologist they are among the most reliable witnesses of past events. "The knowledge derived from archaeology is more explicit than literature or oft-told tales," declares Victor W. von Hagen in his **Realm of the Incas** (New American Library, 1957). "Literary statements can be challenged, but potsherds and artifacts are tangible and visible and reveal much. Pottery, too, can become language, as one sees among the Mochicas."

The finest Mochica specimens rival those of the ancient Greeks and are highly valued by museums for their aesthetic beauty in addition to what they teach us about the Moche life-style

"Moche artists," says Columbia University's Edward P. Lanning, "portrayed the figures and scenes of everyday life and their mythology. They have left us their own view of the world in which they lived. . . . We recognize the hunter, the soldier, the weaver, the beggar, the disabled veteran, the prisoner of war, the mother with her baby, the messenger, the governor, and all the other people to be seen on the streets of a busy town.

"One remarkable Moche specimen shows a textile factory, with several weavers working under the supervision of a foreman. Other scenes show battles or the bringing home of naked prisoners with ropes around their necks. Government officials are shown carried in litters or seated on thrones and receiving messages or delegations. Every rank and class seems to have had its own distinctive dress patterns, hairdos, hats and ornaments."

Animals, birds, and plants are represented in particularly detailed fashion, showing the Mochicas' familiarity with dozens of different species.

AN OCCULT GUIDE TO SOUTH AMERICA

The Mochica deities, as seen on the ceramics, were associated with plant and animal life and sometimes came to earth in the guise of a hunter or fisherman. Dance scenes often depict winged figures and skeletons, suggesting the existence of a cult of the dead or ancestor worship. Prisoners of war, taken from the battlefield naked, were thrown from mountaintops, their bodies afterwards being quartered and taken home as trophies.

Rafael Larco Hoyle, director of the Herrera museum, speculated that the Mochicas believed that life was maintained in the bones when the flesh decayed; some tombs, he said, were found to contain hollow canes leading from the mouth of the body to the earth's surface.

"In Mochica art, the feline deity was anthropomorphized and developed into a Supreme Divinity shown as a man with great fangs, a wrinkled face and catlike whiskers spreading from the nose. The Supreme Divinity ruled the destinies of the world, but lived like people and could reveal himself as both a man and as a god," Dr. Hoyle wrote.

There are dozens of vessels showing this god sitting at the foot of a cliff and receiving the sacrificed humans who have been thrown from the cliff. He is also seen holding up a rainbow in the form of a two-headed serpent.

Lacking the potter's wheel, most South American cultures created their pottery by building coils of clay one on top of another. However, much of Mochica pottery was produced from molds, a clay model being made and fired and then a mold cast over it. When the mold was cut vertically, it yielded two "negative" casts from which subsequent vessels were created. The painting stroke, says A. L. Kroeber, was "firm, swift and sure."

The Pan American Highway south of Trujillo first traverses a flat desert dotted with mountains of sand. There are numerous chicken runs, usually just bamboo mats wrapped around poles to keep out the drifting sand. But the primitive homes of poor Indians themselves are little more than this, plus a thatched roof.

The desert-covered coastal strip is bisected by more than sixty rivers, each running into the sea through a valley that his been inhibited from ancient times. Control of the coastal region and the different tribes and civilizations that have occupied the valleys has always been in the hands of those who administer its water supply; and the Incas, with brilliant engineering skill, quickly moved to bring the aqueducts, reservoirs, and irrigation channels under state control. At the same time, they extended them as well as the subsidiary but all-important system of terrace farming on the hillsides.

The grotesque mountains-of-the-moon adjoining the Pan American Highway eventually give way to enormous sand hills, mostly with a baked-mud covering which presumably stops the gigantic piles from being blown or washed away. Here and there a wall of drifting sand has built up, blocking the valley entrance between two ranges like a curtain of dust.

The landscape is bleak with only an occasional cryptic message carved on a hillside-"**RESTAU** . . . " or "*Vinos y Piscos*" with an accompanying arrow pointing east, or a glimpse of blue sea in a tiny bay between the skyscraper-high sandbanks. The biggest of these bays shelters the major fishing port of Chimbote (pop. 130,000) which manufactures steel and is by no means a sightseeing spot. Not far south, at Casma, the turnoff is made to Huaraz, 145 kilometers east on a bad road, for those planning a visit to Chavin de Huantar, presumed center of the oldest widely documented culture in northern Peru. The ruins at Cerro Sechin and Sechin Alto, in the Casma valley, could possibly be older. Here there are slabs carved with trophy heads and upright stelae depicting warlike figures. John Hemming guesses their date as 1500 B.C., and says they are unique in Peru. The Chavin era may have begun about 800 B. C., but nobody knows for sure. They are believed to have overlapped the Paracas in southern Peru; some of the Paracas designs showed Chavin influence.

Archaeologists have been arguing for years about how widespread the Chavin culture became, because they affect to see its influence in the work of many parallel and subsequent cultures. A distinctive feline god jaguar? puma?) with a curved tail often occurs in Chavin stone carvings, and feline heads protrude from the Castillo, or ancient temple, at Chavin de Huantar. "No other design style in all of Peru is so dominated by a single concept," wrote Professor Wendell Bennett.

A sculptured monolith found at Chavin (now in Lima's Archaeological Museum) bears the representation of a deity which is very similar to the figure on Tiahuanaco's Sun Door, and carvings resemble those seen on Nazca pottery. There are also carved heads reminiscent of trophy heads.

Chavin de Huantar's ruins are chiefly composed of five platform-like buildings which seem to have been a temple of some kind. The main structure, known as the Castillo, has three floors, interior galleries, and an ingenious system of air shafts for ventilation. After centuries of earthquakes it still stands. The lack of human dwellings nearby would indicate that it was probably a religious center.

Most observers seem to agree that what gave the widespread Chavin style its unity was a dominant "stone-carving" style that, even when not actually used on stone, conveyed a certain solidity and heaviness. Chavin pottery was thick and somber with almost no painted designs. Alfred L. Kroeber mentions "the impression of terror which lurks in Chavin sculpture," and adds: "The total effect is one of slow motion, often intricate but never flamboyant, without lightness of touch, every detail seemingly significant, and impressive rather than pleasing."

The designs are intricately mixed with jaguars, condors, snakes and humans, all intertwined with representations of the previously mentioned female deity. Rafael Larco Hoyle suggests that the feline motif originated in the Nepena valley which runs down to the coast, about 60 miles northwest of Chavin de Huantar, from which it radiated all over Peru. In this area, he says, a large percentage of the offerings to the dead, found in ancient graves, were carved or sculpted representations of this god.

Claude Levi-Strauss is not alone in believing that Chavin culture bears resemblances to that of the Olmec civilization and "foreshadows the development of the Maya civilization."

Our historical diversion, however, is now over for the time being, and we are about to look at one last area of Peru before continuing our journey north. So far we have dealt with two of Peru's three different regions: the arid coastal desert and the vertical strip of mountainous Andes that adjoins it. But there is a third horizontal area to the east of that: the lowlying jungle which even the Incas were never able to completely subjugate. The origins of the Amazon are here and, alongside its tributaries, the remnants of the fierce tribes who were never quite civilized: the Yaguas, Cocamas, and unnamed Indians going under the generic term *Orejones*. The word means "long ears" and is often used to refer to tribes who pierced their ears with heavy discs which caused the lobes to stretch

The Cocama, who lived in communal huts along the banks of the Ucayali river, were still practicing head-shrinking in the seventeenth century and were wont to set off on piratical trips along the river, bringing back the severed heads of their enemies as trophies.

AN OCCULT GUIDE TO SOUTH AMERICA

Their decision to wage war, says Métraux, was made at a drinking bout, at which all the men took ayahuasca, and went into a trance, interpreting their dreams as premonitory vision. "Before leaving for battles, the men rubbed cayenne pepper in their eyes to sharpen their sight and were whipped on the legs by the chief to become more agile."

Magical powers were attributed not only to ayahuasca, which shamans drank as part of their apprenticeship, but also to powdered curupa leaves which we re blown into the nose and "provoked agreeable visions."

Ayahuasca, known also as yagé (and several other names), comes from the stem of the *Banisteriopsis* plant which is usually pounded in water or boiled and allowed to cool. Sometimes datura seeds are added, resulting in a bitter, brownish green drink that usually makes the drinker vomit before going to sleep, later to experience vivid, sometimes terrifying dreams.

Datura is even more powerful than *Banisteriopsis* and the Chibchas of Colombia used to feed it to those unfortunate slaves and wives who were condemned to be buried alive with their deceased masters and husbands.

Ayahuasca in Quecha means "death vine" and this may partly explain its extensive use by shamans for communication with the spirits of the dead. Nunes Pereira says its ingestion "causes a peculiar psychological mood with hallucinations, optical illusions and, according to some people, telepathic phenomena."

Pereira, author of **Panorama da Alimemcao Indigena** (Livraria Sao Jose, 1974), says drug usage among Indians has increased lately, with coca widely used and Indians of the Yanoama tribe using half a dozen other plant drugs. "When we were in Roraima we watched the extraction of drugs from some of these plants and were told by women of the Xiriana tribe they tried to restrain the men's use of the drug because it gave them an insatiable lust."

The Indians of the Ucayali river, in this eastern part of Peru, also had a unique way of dealing with their dead relatives, several anthropologists have reported. When somebody died under normal circumstances, the tribe first interred the corpse in a huge jar under the hut until the flesh had rotted. Then the bones were cleaned, being kept in a decorated vase for a year, after which it was buried in a special ceremony called "to dry the tears." After that the deceased's name was never mentioned.

The areas around the Putamayo river, which borders Colombia, and the river Napo, north of the Amazon are inhabited by the now-peaceful Yaguas, who fish with poison from the *barbasco*, (a plant used in the manufacture of insecticides), hunt with blowguns and curare-tipped spears, and blacken their teeth. They live in communal huts containing five to ten families, with each hut named after a plant or animal.

When a Yagua woman gave birth to a child the father was confined to his hammock for ten days, prohibited from singing, making music, or touching the yarn of the chambita plant. Yagua shamans, incidentally, were among the few who were expressly enjoined to remain silent during magical ceremonies.

Yagua legends relate that people once lived in the sky but that when the game supply there became exhausted, a brother and sister were lowered to earth and became the first Yagua.

Tourism is not exactly on a grand scale in these regions, but the little town of Iquitos (pop. 90,000) gets its share, being reachable by river from both Pocallpa in Peru and Manaus in Brazil, trips which depend on a certain amount of patient organization owing to the difficulty of getting reliable schedules. Most visitors arrive by air from Lima, Bogota, or Manaus.

Iquito, the world's farthest inland port, was a boom town at the height of the Amazonian rubber industry, when its magnificent homes were built and the streets lined with tiles imported from Portugal. Today it still lives mostly on exports: live animals and birds, different kinds of wood, perfume essences, and a rubbery substance used in the manufacture of chewing gum.

There's an interesting museum and aquarium featuring local vegetation, a colorful riverside slum district called Belem, and a flock of friendly vultures who hang around the main streets like the cows of Calcutta. The best hotel is the Hotel de Turistas but there are plenty of cheaper places including the Lima, Isabel, and Imperial Amazonas.

Tourist agencies will facilitate your boat trips into the jungle where you can catch glimpses (and sometimes groups waiting to be photographed) of Yagua Indians. Overnight stays can be made at various surprisingly luxurious jungle lodges.

Janet Siskind, an anthropology professor at Rutgers University, wrote an absorbing account of the time she spent among the Sharanahua Indians at Marcos on the Purus river in a remote part of eastern Peru's Amazon jungle.

AN OCCULT GUIDE TO SOUTH AMERICA

She made it clear how worrisome is the period of transition from being self-sufficient in a forest society to the "civilization" of the larger world where "the skills of Sharanahua men are lower class skills in Peruvian society. Getting food directly by hunting, fishing or agriculture are skills held in low esteem, whereas selling, producing, owning and the manipulation of money are respected."

And yet, she said, the Indian who is seduced by the glittering artifacts—the transistor radio, the watch, sunglasses that make life seem brighter, seeks for a way to escape the limits of his own culture without being forced to accept the lower-class role in which Peruvians place the Indian.

But, of course, there are advantages to the nomadic life. "In the Amazon Basin," she writes in **To Hunt in the Morning** (Oxford University Press, 1973), "land and water change as rivers find new channels, pile up silt to form new banks . . . Peruvian towns built as permanent ports find themselves high and dry while Indian villages, moving faster than the changes, are always near a convenient stream or river. The next piece of forest will have the same woods and bamboos for construction, the same game to hunt, fish to catch, land to clear for gardens."

Ms. Siskind writes of the *shori* rituals in which the men of the tribe (rarely the women) communally drink the brew prepared from the hallucinogenic ayahuasca and learn to "call the spirits." The scrolls, snakes, and ropelike images the participants see, she believes, "are symbolic images learned as language is learned, through interaction and communication with those who have them stored as perceptions and triggered by the drunkenness, the singing, the ritual of shori."

At first when the Sharanahua take shori, they are frightened and it is only after months of taking part in the ritual that the snakes they see are transformed into beautiful images. 'This transformation of terror to euphoria is another kind of learning and this learning, I believe, is a significant part of the ritual."

Ms. Siskind says that the shamans of the tribe take shori along with the other men, especially when they want to learn the causes of a sickness. "As they chant the shaman sings a curing song and slowly a vision appears of the image from the sick man's dream, the spirit that is causing his death." In common with other peoples, most Indian tribes set great store by dreams which, they believe, are unconscious expressions of desires or intentions. Wilfred Grubb wrote that among the Paraguayan Lenguas, dreams were regarded "as warnings and guides to conduct" and shamans everywhere look to them for insights. The Lengua and Bolivia's Callawaya, to mention but two tribes, affirm that the astral body leaves the physical one during sleep, transmitting back mentally its experiences which are perceived as dreams.

It was here in the jungle that the mighty Incas were stopped. In other parts of Peru, both the coast and the Andean regions, they were quick to take over and absorb the tribes and cultures they found. But here in the murky Amazonian regions, the fierce jungle tribes practiced a hit-and-run type of warfare that soldiers used to superb advantage that the Incas could not match.

So the Incas left the matter in abeyance for the time being and turned their attention first to Chile in the south, which Tupac marched off to attack, and then to the north. Tupac sent his son, Huayna Capac, to conquer what is now Ecuador and, although Huayna quickly subdued the local Cara Indians, his fateful dalliance with one of them, a Cara princess, led to the eventual collapse of the empire.

The result of this union was an illegitimate son, Atahualpa, whom Huayna eventually came to favor over his legitimate heir, Huascar; this division of the kingdom between them, on his deathbed, started a civil war that was underway when Francisco Pizzaro arrived with a mere 1170 soldiers in 1533. When the Spaniards invaded his kingdom, Atahualpa was in Ecuador with a sizeable Incan army. And it is there we shall go next.

AN OCCULT GUIDE TO SOUTH AMERICA

Chapter 11

Ecuador

Witches and Shrunken Heads

Ecuador's coastal region has proved increasingly attractive to archaeologists and some of their findings about the people who lived here thousands of years ago are beginning to dovetail with long-established folklore.

An ancient legend about a race of giants landing on Ecuador's Santa Elena peninsula is narrated by Cieza de Leon; he says these men, with "eyes as large as small plates" and whose size is such that "from the knee downwards their height was as great as the entire height of an ordinary man," found no water, so they dug wells out of solid rock which they lined with masonry "in such sort that they will endure for many ages."

The giants ate up all the food for miles around, killed many of the native women, sodomized the men, and were universally hated until they were destroyed by an avenging angel as "a punishment in proportion to the enormity of their offence."

Referring to "this cursed sin of sodomy," Cieza de Leon says that he gleaned the details directly from a Jesuit father, Fray Domingo, who described how each temple had a man or two "who go dressed in women's attire from the time they are children."

In his *Historia del Reino de Quito* (Quito, 1841) Juan Velasco also makes reference to a race of giants who, he says, appeared about the beginning of the Christian era, to be followed six or seven centuries later by another group of invaders called the Cara who arrived on large balsa rafts and gradually advanced into the interior. The Cara made their headquarters near Quito and ruled the region until overthrown by the Incas in the fifteenth century.

Excavations around the Santa Elena peninsula from 1906 to 1908 confirmed at least part of the legend in that stonefaced wells of the type described have been found, along with the remains of "a unique aboriginal civilization." Exploring the region forty years later, G. H. S. Bushnell reported (in **Archaeology of the Santa Elena Peninsula**, Cambridge Press, 1951) that the three distinct cultures identified in the area did not seem to be successive and, indeed, that two of them seemed to have come from somewhere else.

This part of the coast is sprinkled with numerous stone seats supported by carved human or animal figures, sometimes bearing images of men or gods. Composite animals, monstrous forms, and what Professor Hartley Alexander refers to as "grotesquely frog-like images of a female goddess" on slabs in bas relief are also numerous and equally enigmatic.

Bushnell suggests, in fact, that the remains of the Manteno culture (the last one before the Conquest) "are so different from those of its predecessors in that area as to make it certain that it was introduced by an immigrant people." It was the only Ecuadorian culture to make extensive use of stone, not only the U-shaped seats but also platform mounds, enclosures, and clusters of houses.

Another curious Manteno relic is the spindle whorl, many of which, along with fragments of textile, were found in ancient graves. It is possibly of ritual significance that the fragments discovered were all woven of threads spun from the left in the so-called S-twist, instead of the more usual righthand or Z-twist used by weavers. John Howland Rowe says that an Incan sorcerer who wanted to bring harm to an enemy would "spin a thread of black and white wool, twisting it to the left (the reverse of the customary direction) and then place a noose of it on a path where the enemy might pass so that it would catch his foot."

The S-twist is called *lloq'e* in the Quecha language, a word that means "left" or "something different." In some areas its use is restricted to the medicine man, in others it is used by anyone who seeks to cast a spell against hexes, certain sicknesses, and bad influences. It is also invoked to assist romance.

Leaving the coast, we turn to Ecuador's capital, Quito, which is away farther inland in the northern part of the country.

AN OCCULT GUIDE TO SOUTH AMERICA

Sprawling across a wide valley and surrounded by dormant volcanoes, Quito (pop. 600,000) has one of the most dramatic settings on the subcontinent. The best overall view of it is from the quaintly named Cerro Panecillo ("bread-roll hill' to the west, at whose foot the winding, cobbled streets spill into deep ravines. Preserved in this section is La Ronda (Calle Morales), an ancient Colonial street sheltering such curiosities as a house with five patios at different levels and a store where elaborate candles are made for Indian processions.

More than half of Quito's population is Indian and although the Indian's status varies widely within his own cultural and economic units, as William Russell wrote in 1949, "he is largely landless, voteless and illiterate. His principal occupation is performing the manual labor that the mestizo and the Ecuadorian scorn.... Ecuador has remained one of the western world's most backward republics by virtue of its isolation. Its precise division into master and subject races, its heritage of suffocating Spanish bureaucracy, and the understandable reluctance of comfortable people anywhere to share and thereby lessen their wealth, ease and power."

Although written nearly thirty years ago, the statement is still largely true today. The Indians who fill the city's streets trudge up and down the hills with heavy burdens and both operate and patronize the many markets, are markedly different from those who run most of the businesses and who deal with guests at the plush Intercontinental hotel at the eastern end of town.

Some of the differences can be seen in the magnificent sixteenth-century San Francisco Church, a mélange of Christian and pagan architecture that has to be seen to be believed. Built on the side of a former Incan palace, the church was designed largely by Indians and it is mainly Indians who worship there today. Baroque altars. gilded pillars and carved pineapples vie for attention 'with the heads of sun gods that peer at the worshippers from all sides.

There are dozens of other churches in Quito, and the city's most prominent landmark is an enormous angel atop Panecillo hill which can be reached either by bus or taxi (40 sucres from town—there's a good restaurant at the summit). But Quito is far from leaving its pagan ways behind. To prove this it's only necessary to take one of the popular trips into the surrounding countryside to attend one of the Indian markets to Santo Domingo de los Colorados, for example, where the witch doctor still practices his Craft and the narcotic drink *nepe* is available for those who seek to keep away evil spirits.

Anthropologist John Murra reported: "Catholic beliefs and ceremonies have not obliterated native notions about the supernatural. The soul of the dead might go to heaven but it does so along the string attached to the roof from the dead man's neck."

Ecuador's Canaris Indians have a myth that they are all descended from quacamayo birds who, dressed as women, visited two brothers who had fled to a high mountain after the flood. The younger bird was trapped by the brothers and lived with them long enough to become the mother of six sons and daughters from which all the Canaris believe themselves to be descended. The tribe still regards the quacamayo bird with reverence, using its feathers in all their celebrations.

Apart from visiting the Indians, the most popular excursion from Quito is to take the Pan American Highway north, skirting Pichincha hill, where Ecuador's national hero Antonio José Sucre won a decisive battle against the Spaniards in 1822. A half hour's drive brings you to the equator.

Ecuador gets its name from the equator, that invisible line that encircles the earth at its widest central point, and the line (latitude $0°$, $0°$, $0°$) is actually marked at a place about 15 kilometers north of the capital, just outside the village (called San Antonio de Pichincha.

Long ago, the Cara Indians of the region discovered a peculiar phenomenon of this spot: twice a year, on the equinoxes (March 21 and September 23) the sun cast no shadow; to mark the occasions they instituted festivals on those days. The harvest festival, still celebrated today, was known as *Inti-raymi*, and the equator itself as *Inti-nan* (road of the sun), both from "Inti," the word for sun.

Marking the equator today, in place of the primitive markers used by the Indians, is an elaborate monument erected in 1936 to commemorate the second centenary of the coming to Ecuador of a French-Spanish mission in 1736. The mission, whose members (Carlos de la Condamine, Pedro Bouguer, and Louis Godin) are memorialized on the monument, spent several years in Ecuador checking measurements (and constantly having their pyramid-shaped markers destroyed by superstitious Indians. One of the permanent results of their research was the establishment of that universal measure of longitude, the meter—"the fundamental base of a new system of weights and measures"—which, for the technically minded, is actually one ten-millionth part of the earth's quadrant (i.e., the distance from the equator to the north pole).

A standard meter was constructed out of platinum to serve as a permanent model, and this historical curiosity has been preserved ever since at the Louvre in Paris.

The trip out to the equatorial monument (which is so large and so prominently surrounded by white U-shaped markers that it can readily be seen from incoming aircraft) usually includes a brief visit to another nearby landmark, the solar museum built by the late Carlos Marin in the nearby village of San Antonio de Pichincha. Oriented to the compass points, and with a minuscule garden containing the flowers and plants of the respective seasons at each side, the museum's shape is similar to one of the ramplike astronomical observatories of ancient India and contains globes and sun symbols from different parts of the world. The Incan terms for the cardinal points (*chincha* =north, *colla* = south, etc.) mark the different sides, and the various names for the equator are listed in a dozen languages.

A larger and infinitely more fascinating museum adjoins the equatorial monument itself. Dominating the entrance hall is a wall-sized map of Ecuador which gives credence to the country's argument that it was "robbed" of millions of square miles of Amazon jungle under a 1944 treaty which ceded the territory to neighboring Peru. Ecuador's argument is that as the upper reaches of the Amazon were first discovered on an expedition that set off from Quito, the territory should still belong to that country. And it does seem clear that the Amazon would form a natural boundary.

The museum is imaginatively laid out and stocked with fascinating displays of feather masks, garments, and headdresses; displays of medicinal herbs from the forest; skins; carved wooden toys; walnut and other jungle woods and a twenty-four-foot boa constrictor, coiled and preserved in a jar. Animals and birds are understandably prominent, not only dried and stuffed insects, birds and snakes, but living varieties such as anteaters, monkeys, parrots, and brightly colored toucans. There are also a brace of turtles from Ecuador's remote Galapagos Islands, 600 miles offshore in the Pacific, which shelters the oldest living animals on earth; some of the turtles on the thirteen islands are four hundred years old. The name "galapagos" means "giant turtles.') When Charles Darwin visited the islands aboard H.M.S. Beagle in 1835, he was quick to see the significance of evolutionary developments in such an isolated place and his resulting theories are still a matter of controversy.

The islands were first discovered by the Spaniards early in the sixteenth century but "were so unpromising in climate and topography," as William Russell wrote in **The Bolivar Countries** (Coward McCann, 1949), that nobody bothered to claim them. The Spaniards and the British pirates who subsequently hid there both gave names to the different islands and both sets are used interchangeably. The volcanic islands, colonized by Ecuador in 1832, support only about two thousand people spread over more than 3,000 square miles of barren, cactus-covered land. The climate and topography are similar to the Peruvian coastal desert and due to the same cause: the cold Humboldt Current offshore which draws off most of the moisture.

Fascinating as the museum's living exhibits—the turtles—are, a series of tableaux around the garden are just as eye-catching. One demonstrates the typical Indian method of agriculture with pairs of hanging corn husks (for fertility), a cactus fence, and a primitive wooden plow. Another display shows an Indian couple in a surprisingly spotless hut with cane mats on the walls and floor, he holding his wooden stave as a symbol of power, she her skein of wool for weaving; in the corner sits a wooden harp and a pile of household pottery that would enhance any suburban kitchen.

More in line with tourists' expectations is a mud-floored communal Jivaro house complete with hammocks, gourds, a trestle for hanging things, and snakeskins on the walls. There is no trace here of the shrunken heads for which the Jivaros have achieved such an ominous reputation over the centuries. "The Jivaros kill by retail but the civilized kill by wholesale," says a sign in the museum. The practice of headshrinking is now prohibited by law, and any shrunken heads that are offered for sale in gift shops are those of animals.

The Jivaros (sometimes spelt Jibaros) are an extremely primitive tribe who live far to the east, deep in the Amazon jungle. "Where the mountain waterfalls give way to the rapids, the country of the Jivaro begins; and where the rapids finally end in placid rivers, so does the Jivaro homeland," explains Michael Hamer. Among anthropologists, the Jivaros are as renowned for their use of hallucinogenic drugs and their pilgrimages to sacred waterfalls as they are for their head-shrinking propensities.

The two customs are related, in fact, because one of the fundamental Jivaro beliefs is that it is enviable to attain *arutam wakani*, a special soul, which' once achieved' makes the possessor invulnerable to physical violence or sorcery; the avenging souls (*muisak*) of dead warriors who have seen visions of *arutam* must be kept captive if they are not to wreak revenge.

In his ***The Jivaro, People of the Sacred Waterfalls*** (Doubleday/Natural History Press, 1972), Michael Hamer explains that a Jivaro boy begins seeking a special soul (*arutam*) when he accompanies his father on a pilgrimage to the highest waterfall in his region. The waterfalls are believed to be "the rendezvous of these souls or spirits, which wander about as breezes, scattering the spray of the long cascade." The vision-seekers, "naked and shivering," pace about between the waterfall and the cliff, chanting and carrying a magical balsa-wood stick specially carved for the occasion, "By night the pilgrims sleep by the falls in a simple lean-to. Here they fast, drink tobacco water and await the appearance of the *arutam*. "

The ritual may continue for as long as five days but at some point, after ingesting a hallucinogenic juice (a derivative of the datura plant which induces vivid dreams), participants experience what is often an animal vision, such as two anacondas or two jaguars fighting each other. When the vision gets close the viewer is supposed to run forward to touch it with hand or stick, causing it to shatter and disappear. In the subsequent dream, says Harner, the soul of the *arutam* in the form of an old Jivaro man comes to the dreamer and promises him a long fife and many kills. After making this promise the old man disappears, his soul entering the body of the dreamer, making him stronger and wiser and creating an urge to kill. This the new Jivaro warrior tries to satisfy as soon as possible to prove himself truly a possessor of the spirit.

To the Jivaro, the true determinants of life and death, adds Horner, "are normally invisible forces which can be seen and utilized only with the aid of hallucinogenic drugs. . . . Thus, within a few days of birth, a baby is given a drug to help it enter the 'real' world, and hopefully to obtain help in surviving the hazards of infancy through seeing an 'ancient spectre.'"

Although the Jivaro's entire life is hemmed in by magical rites and taboos (even during childbirth a Jivaro mother is isolated so as not to contaminate others), it is in his preparation for and participation in war that these become most evident. Once again a hallucinogenic drug plays a major part, this time *cayapi* (better known to us as *yagé*) which is drunk by the shaman who invokes supernatural assistance in the battle to come, while the warriors dance excitedly.

As for the headshrinking, for which the Jivaro are perhaps best known, the only white observer who has reported witnessing it is Fritz Up de Graff, who described the ceremony in his **Head-hunters of the Amazon** (Doubleday, 1923). It is a tedious process which begins with parting the hair, then slitting the skin along the parting down to the skullbone. Cuts are made around the eyes, cars, and nose and then the skin is peeled back from the skull, the flesh and muscle removed and the skin then sewn up with a bamboo needle and palm-leaf fiber. The lips are skewered, the eye holes closed, and the holes of the nose and ears temporarily plugged with cotton.

The purpose of these several operations was to hold the features of the face in position and to seal the openings so that the head could again be expanded to its normal proportions by filling it with hot sand .... The crocks which are used on these occasions have been made with the utmost care by the medicine men in person, far removed from all human eyes and under auspicious lunar conditions; they are brought carefully wrapped in palm leaves to ensure the impossibility of their being touched or seen by an unauthorized person until the moment for the ceremony arrives. . . "

Next, the sand-filled boneless heads were placed in the water-filled pots and the water brought to a boil. It was essential to remove the heads before the water actually boiled; if the operation was performed correctly the heads would have shrunk to about one-third their original size but the flesh would have remained firm and the hair fixed in place.

During the next stage, Up de Graff reported, hot sand was poured into the heads which were then "ironed" with hot stones almost continually for forty-eight hours until the skin was "as tough as tanned leather" and the shrunken heads about the size of a large orange.

"Time and again the cool greasy sand was poured from the half-dried heads, giving out the odor of an evening meal, only to be refilled with a fresh, hot supply. Flat stones were always in the fires, being heated for the constant ironing to which the faces were subjected; they slid easily over the skin, like a flat-iron on linen, due to the natural oil which exuded from the contracting pores."

AN OCCULT GUIDE TO SOUTH AMERICA

In the final stage, "hot, coarse pebbles were substituted for sand, the heads being tilted from side to side to prevent them burning the meat, as dice are shaken in a box. The small amount of oil still exuding on the face was wiped away with fresh cotton as fast as it appeared and the operation continued until all the fat and grease was 'fried out' of the head when it was considered cured or mummified."

When a head had been skillfully prepared, Up de Graff added, it was an exact miniature of the original, even to the facial expression.

As already stated, the preparation of shrunken heads is illegal today and any that are offered for sale are almost certainly fakes (as far back as the 1930s they were bringing $100 apiece), but there has never been anything arbitrary about either their possession or preparation by their Indian owners. The Jivaros have always had a reputation as dedicated warriors—the Incas left them alone when they overran Ecuador in the fifteenth century and, after some severe defeats at their hands a century later, so did the Spaniards—and they have never really been conquered, much less absorbed, right up to current times.

All of this has taken rather a long way from the friendly, civilized museum at the equatorial monument where this diversion first began, and with a final glance at nearby Cotopaxi, the world's highest active volcano, it is perhaps time to retrace our steps to Quito and visit another museum in very different surroundings.

Quito's Archaeological Museum, on the fifth and sixth floors of a modern skyscraper (Central Bank Building, Ave. 10 de Agosto and Briceno, tel: 510-302), must be one of the most elegant in the world. Here there are no creaking floors, no dimly lit corners and dusty fragments of broken stone. Everything is spic and span (if a bit sterile) and, far from looking old, more closely resembles a polished collection from some millionaire's showcase. In a sense this is true, for the collection belongs to the Central Bank of Ecuador which buys the best available items from private owners and puts them on display to all, presumably as a public relations gesture.

It is a good collection, however, and notwithstanding the publicity derived from it—an Inca mask of the sun god appears in the bank's advertising—offers a convenient crash course in Ecuadorian prehistory. The country is particularly rich in ancient archaeological sites with examples of the Valdivia culture (mostly on the Santa Elena peninsula, West of Guayaquil, as we have seen, but some to the east and north) dating back to 3,000 B. C.

A large number of esthetically attractive figurines were found from the Valdivia period which, says Emilio Estrada, "demonstrate the cult of fertility, a classic cult of primitive peoples the world over." The statues had a variety of complicated hair styles.

Indian women have always worn their hair long, in braids, and to be shorn of such tresses is regarded as a disgrace, the mark of a fallen woman or unfaithful wife whose hair was sometimes cut off and attached to the tail of a horse. A story is current at Salto (Uruguay) of an Indian woman who because of illness had to have her hair cut off and, despite her tearful entreaties, it was shorn. Within two days she had died of her misery.

An Indian man also resisted having his locks shorn. Cutting a chief's or warrior's hair was a disgraceful indication to the world of his reduced status and the Spaniards often used to punish recalcitrant Indians in this manner.

The coiffed Valdivian figurines are not clothed except for one which seems to be wearing a crown, and Estrada, the curator of a private museum in Guayaquil, suggests that this is "sometimes an indication of a matriarchal society." Slender clues to an era, four thousand years ago.

Reminding us of the archaeologist's goal of reconstructing "the total cultural patterns of long dead societies" from meager remains, Donald W. Lathrap, a fellow curator, comments that the "bowls, vessels and effigy figures are what give a sense of life and reality to Ecuador's distant past.

Chicago's Field Museum of Natural History staged a comprehensive exhibition of these Ecuadorian ceramics in 1975 and in the accompanying catalog, **Ancient Ecuador**, Lathrap explained how, by studying surviving groups, archaeologists were sometimes able to find a continuity of cultural tradition. He professed to see, for example, an analogy between the drug-taking habits of present-day Amazon tribes and the drug paraphernalia retrieved from the Valdivia and later Machalilla (1500 to 1100 B. C.) and Chorrera (I 100 to 300 B. C.) sites.

"The most common religious practitioner in the Amazon Basin is a shaman, who gets his power through repeated sacramental use of ayahuasca (from the tropical vine *Banisteriopsis*) and/or the snuff ground from seeds of the *Anadenanthera* (a mimosa-like tree). It is believed that while under the influence of these elements the shaman is possessed by or turns into a ferocious animal, most typically a cayman (a kind of South American alligator) or a jaguar.

"Over most of tropical South America east of the Andes," lathrap says, "the symbol of this kind of shaman has for centuries been a wooden stool carved in the shape of a jaguar, a cayman, or sometimes both.

"It is thus of tremendous interest that along with the solid human figurines of Valdivia, which may have served in curing rituals, we find exact miniature replicas of the zoomorphic wooden shaman's stools which are the prerogative of the Tropical Forest curer."

In addition, Ecuador's ancient sites have rendered hollow figurines of the type used when inhaling the hallucinogenic " snuff; ceramic sniffing tubes; and examples of the small containers in which lime was kept preparatory to being mixed with dried coca leaves and chewed in the mouth. The fact that coca-chewing goes back to those early days is confirmed by Valdivia figurines clearly showing the quid of coca in the check.

One of these coca-chewing figurines can be inspected in the Central Bank's Archaeology Museum whose displays are heavily accented towards colorful examples of this kind. The multilingual guides are well aware of the crowd pleasers and never fail to get a response for the musical scale produced by striking a string of volcanic rocks. Other "souvenirs" from the so-called Valley of Volcanoes south of Quito are fragments of black obsidian, that natural volcanic glass which has been used as a mirror since ancient times.

The museum (open every morning, 9:00 A.M. to noon, and 3:00 to 6:00 P.M. Tuesdays through Fridays, closed Monday) is very taken with that favorite theory of archaeologists, diffusion: the belief that the discovery of similar styles in different places is due to the styles spreading through human contact rather than originating independently. In this case, they see and demonstrate with examples similarities between the ceramics of Ecuador and those of both Egypt and Japan's southern island of Kyushu, and back up their theories with maps and charts demonstrating the possible population flow between the different countries.

This theory gained some support with an article in the *Scientific American January 1966*) by Betty J. Meggers and Clifford Evans who refer to "a fragment of a red-slipped and incised vessel with a unique type of rim [which]

. . . rose in a series of castellations," excavated from a Valdivia site in 1961. "This form of rim," the authors maintain, "is rare anywhere in the world except Japan. There it commonly occurs on pottery of the prehistoric Jornon period."

Following up this slender clue, the authors found other similarities between the two widely separate cultures, speculating that a boatload of Kyushu fishermen who set off on a deep-sea trip were swept off course by strong currents, being then caught in a strong northeastern typhoon that finally deposited them on Ecuador's coast, more than 5,000 miles away. As the currents would be too strong for their return, the fishermen "would probably have settled down to await whatever end might be in store for them."

The authors add: "As these New World civilizations have become better known archaeologically, striking parallels have been observed with the architecture, religions, practices, and art styles of Asia."

The most interesting items in the museum's collection are the items that bridge time: the *tupos* or pins used to fasten shawls and the old nose rings worn to stop the incursions of evil spirits. Both these ancient items are still in use among Indians of today.

Quito's best hotel is the InterContinental (Ave. Patri y Amazones, tel: 521-300) predictably luxurious with swimming pool, a mini-zoo, with llamas, and a poetic cloud hanging as an almost constant backdrop to the garden. Singles from around $15, doubles around $30, and quaint eating places called El Pub and La Bistro across the street. Because it's such a long way from the center of town (about 30 sucres by taxi) many visitors prefer the less impressive but considerably more central hotel Humboldt (Calle Espejo 931, tel: 210-070) which has singles from $12, doubles from $15. Both hotels have gambling casinos. A cheap choice is the hotel El Sucre overlooking the San Francisco Church on San Francisco Plaza.

There are various tours to different Indian markets in the vicinity of Quito. The biggest market, at the town of Ambato about 60 miles south, is held only on Mondays but there are also markets at Otavalo (Saturday), Santo Domingo de los Colorados (daily), and such little-known smaller markets as Peguche. Check for details with Turis Mundial (736 Venezuela St, Quito, tel: 216-410).

There are two Saturday morning markets from 6:00 A.M. to noon at Otavalo, where the Indians gather to meet tourists, at the noisy commercial one and to trade among themselves (and be photographed) at the more colorful "silent" one a couple of blocks away. Men wear white shoes and pants, dark ponchos, and brown hats; women are more colorful with gay blouses, long skirts, and red and gold jewelry. Both walk for miles to get to the market. Tours to Otavalo usually leave Quito the day before for the two-and-a-half-hour drive over a lovely mountain road that leads past mango and avocado orchards. The overnight stay is spent at San Antonio or some luxurious accommodations en route. Not far away is Ibarra which invites visits to its new textile factory.

This area is the home base of Atahualpa, the young Incan chief who was born at nearby Carangue and who was tricked and captured by a tiny Spanish invading force, led by Francisco Pizarro, in Cajamarca just across the Peruvian border. He was "ransomed" for two rooms full of silver and gold but, when the gold had been delivered, was strangled by the Spaniards who suspected he was planning to regain control. "Murdered," says John Hemming, despite the fact that he could be accused of no hostile act of any sort." The tragic Atahualpa has become something of a cult figure among certain Latin Americans who regard him as a combination of King Arthur and Robin Hood. Atahualpa was "the ultimate hero, born in Caranqui of our primitive native peoples" writes Silvio Alvear in a paperback book published in Ibarra, **Atahualpa Duchicela**. The book is devoted mostly to the family lineage of Incan royalty.

A glorious temple to the sun once dominated Carangue where Atahualpa's monument stands today, and images of the sun and moon from the facade of that temple line the monument; some of its sculpted stones form part of the apse of the parish church.

In a little hotel at Chorlavi, about three miles from Ibarra, Atahualpa's spirit is supposed to come visiting, returning to the site where he once used to meet his mistresses.

Among the agencies offering excursions to the region is Amazonas Tours (Rio de Janeiro 222, tel. 234-925) whose tours of the city or out to the Equatorial Monument begin at $10; eight-hour tours to the Ambato or Otavalo market ($25); nine-hour tours to visit the Colorados Indians ($40): six hours to Squisili market; ($20). These rates are for one person, with cheaper per person rates for additional people.

For those who want to try an adventurous jungle river trip with (almost) all the conveniences of luxury living, there's a regular tour out of the little town of Coca on a funny-looking four-story barge called the *Flotel Orellana*. It cruises down the river Napo and back for five days, during which passengers are briefed on the local flora and fauna, with occasional side trips into the rain forest, and aboard paddle dugouts into tiny lagoons. First-class accommodations aboard the *Flotel Orellana* (including all meals, guide service, tours, and flight to and from Quito) range from about $300 per person, and reservations can be made by writing to Metropolitan's Unseen Amazon (P.O.B. 2542, Quito, tel- 524-400).

In common with most South American countries Ecuador has its own version of the El Dorado legend but it's a waste of time going in search of it, either independently or on a tour, because legendarily it can he seen only on Good Friday. It's called the City of the Caesars, adjoins a sacred lake somewhere in the Andes, and when seen from afar appears to be all silver and gold. Reputedly it still has its original inhabitants who neither get older nor die, and the city will be revealed to everybody only at the end of the world.

The name probably stems from Francisco César, dispatched on an expedition in search of El Dorado in the 1520s by Sebastian Cabot who had himself conducted an unsuccessful expedition up the Parana and Paraguay rivers in a fruitless quest for the mythical city.

Cuenca, Ecuador's third largest city, was originally called Santa Ana of the Four Rivers of Cuenca. The four rivers—Tomebamba, Yanuncay, Machangara, and Tarqui—encircle the town providing interesting views in every direction. The local Spanish guidebook refers to the Tarqui as "pastoral and gentle, that resembles a sweet song licking the marvel of the fields," and says the Tomebamba "has caprices of a child, playing hide and seek among the mints and herbs."

There are both old and new cathedrals in the city as well as two museums. The new cathedral incorporates Italian marble floors, Ecuadorian marble pillars, hand-carved chairs from jungle wood, stained glass windows from Belgium and Germany, and a golden altar.

The Municipal Museum is housed in an old Colonial house and the Museum Padre Crespi, full of Indian artifacts, in a former school. Many of the preserved Colonial houses (the town was founded by the Spaniards in 1557) are located on the main street named after Simon Bolivar. Another hero honored here with a statue is Abdon Calderon, the Ecuadorian patriot who died on the slopes of Pichincha in 1822.

One of the streets in Cuenca (pop. 80,000) is named after Huayna Capac, the Incan ruler who extended the empire as far as Ecuador's present border with Colombia. He was resting near here, possibly at Ingapirca, when word arrived of the landing of Pizarro's men at Tumbes on the Peruvian coast to the south.

The best time to visit Cuenca is during the Cruz del Vado festival at the beginning of May when there are folklore celebrations and dancing in the streets. The best hotel is the cozy El Dorado (Gran Colombia and Luis Cordero) with a simple cafe and television in the balconied rooms. ("Mary Hartman, Mary Hartman" was showing daily on my last visit.) Rates are about 360 soles for a single, 460 soles for a double. The hotel Cuenca (Calle Borrero 841) costs about half that.

On Sundays there's an interesting straw market at nearby Gualaceo which stages a peach festival every March.

Taxis charge 600 soles to Ingapirca and back, a trip that takes about two and one-half hours each way. There are also thermal baths near town.

Three airlines connect Cuenca with Quito and each (Tame, San, and Saeta) has daily flights costing about $15 each way and taking about one and one-half hours. There are also buses.

The best-known ruins in Ecuador are those of Ingapirca, an Inca fortress in a tranquil valley about 60 miles to the north of Cuenca. There are occasional tours from Cuenca but usually it's necessary to rent a car or take a taxi for the two-hour drive which is through gentle, beautiful countryside. Cactus plants line the road for part of the way and at one point we pass through cloudshrouded mountains before descending again to countryside filled with white-painted houses with roofs of thatch or soft red tiles.

A few kilometers before the town of Canar we turn off the Pan American Highway onto an unpaved road to the right (marked Ingapirca) and thread our way all around the edge of an immense valley where there is little sign of life except for the dogs which see the car coming for miles and race across the hillside to meet it. Finally, the road dead-ends in a dusty square and the Incan ruins are but a few yards' walk, past a grove of purplish eucalyptus trees.

AN OCCULT GUIDE TO SOUTH AMERICA

"If these mysterious rocks and fallen temples lay within the borders of the United States," wrote William Russell (**The Bolivar Countries**, Coward McCann, 1949), "there would be a four-lane highway lined with hot dog stands three deep sweeping right up to the hills on which they stand. But as they are in Ecuador it is necessary to go to Canar, from there ride for two days on horseback and walk the rest of the way. "

The Pan American Highway, of course, has made Ingapirca much more accessible since Russell's book was published, but the site is still relatively hard to get to and certainly not very touristy.

Ingapirca, built by Huayna Capac around 1489, was intended to serve as a stopping-off point for Incan chieftains on their visits to the most northerly part of their empire. The stonework is characteristic of all such Incan construction with the blocks fitted tightly together, without the aid of mortar. It is fortified, although probably was never defended in battle, and faces west, conceivably as if expecting an attack from the coast but possibly because of being oriented to the setting sun.

It was the Incan custom to incorporate sun temples into their fortresses and it was to this defensive position that the natives of the surrounding area went with their weapons in time of attack.

Like many a race before (and since) them, the Incas felt they were doing a favor by introducing their beliefs and philosophy to any race they conquered. Calling themselves "Children of the Sun," they had a complete rationale for their colonial expansion, sending messengers ahead to their enemies "requiring them to submit and obey the child of the Sun, abandoning their own vain and evil sacrifices and bestial customs.'"

There are, of course, many historical precedents, from the Roman emperor Julian's paean ("I am a votary of the Sun. ... Are you alone ignorant that summer and winter are produced by Him and that all things are alone vivified, and alone germinate from Him?) to the veneration of the Egyptians whose worship of the solar cult took place as many years before Christ as the Incas were afterwards.

"Hail to thee, beautiful god of every day," reads an inscription by Amenhotep's architects. "When thou sailest across the sky all men behold thee though thy going is hidden from their sight. When thou showest thyself at morning every day ... under thy majesty, though the day be brief, thou traverseth a journey of leagues, even millions and hundred thousands of time. Every day is under thee."

If you fly to Cuenca you might find yourself making a stop at Ecuador's major port of Guayaquil, which among other things is the world's biggest banana exporter. A famous monument here called La Rotonda commemorates the 1822 meeting of South America's two liberators, Simon Bolivar and José de San Martin, as a result of which the city became part of Bolivar's La Gran Colombia. San Martin had already managed to free Argentina and Chile from Spanish rule and Venezuelan-born Bolivar had liberated his native land, followed by Bolivia and Peru. It was assumed by commentators afterwards that, at the meeting, San Martin tried to persuade Bolivar to join forces, and that the latter refused and went on to free Ecuador on his own.

A curiosity about the monument is that, due to some architectural trick, two people whispering on different sides of it can hear each other perfectly.

The other major sights of Guayaquil are the Colonial-style street, Calle Pompilio Liona y Malecon, known as Barrios las Penas; the hill known as El Mirador de la Ciudad with its excellent overall view of the city; the Moorish-style clocktower at Ave. Diez de Agosto y Malecon (the riverside walk which is at its most interesting at night); the general cemetery at Calles Julian Coronel and Quito, a sea of white marble; and the city's two main museums, both closed between noon and 3:00 P.M., as well as on weekends. The Municipal Museum, in addition to examples of different Ecuadorian cultures and Colonial art, has a rare collection of *tzantzas* (shrunken heads), and the Museum of the Ecuadorian House of Culture has a fascinating collection of ceremonial Indian artifacts, as well as dozens of ancient gold ornaments.

Guayaquil is the usual takeoff point for trips to the volcanic Galapagos Islands which can be reached either by air or the numerous cruises aboard the yacht *Delfin* or the 900-ton *Iguana*. Five or eight-day excursions are organized by Metropolitan Touring (in Quito, call 524-400). Other agencies also arrange tours, among them Turis Mundial whose Guayaquil office is at 9 de Octubre Ave. 125, tel: 522-222. 201

For the tourist with plenty of time, the 280 miles between Quito and Guayaquil is best covered via train, the railroad track passing through an incredibly varied region of jungle, banana plantations, volcanoes, and rivers, at one point reaching 11,800 feet in the Urbina Pass near to Ecuador's highest mountain, the snow-capped Chimborazo.

AN OCCULT GUIDE TO SOUTH AMERICA

There are still plenty of witches in Ecuador, oddly enough located more in the cities than the rural areas. Guayaquil, for example, is full of "consultaries" where, says Dario Guevara, fortunetellers carry on their profession as if it were the most natural thing in the world. Their offices are always full of people representing every social class and condition. For any problem that is posed, there is an appropriate ceremony to solve it.

In the cities the fortunetellers are mostly women who "know the secret of giving luck, glimpsing the future and exorcising spells," but in the rural areas of Otavalo, Santa Domingo, and the Colorados, the witches and soothsayers are male.

"Fortunetelling by cards is an open business," writes Guevara in **Un Mundo Magico-Mitico en la Mitad del Mundo**) (Imprenta Municipal, Quito, 1972). "It is allowed by the same authorities who pursue witch doctors (in defense of medicine) and witches (in defense of civilization) and in various parts of the capital, particularly Ave. 24 de Mayo, a subject can be seen distributing cards to clients and a woman, inside a box with only her head showing, giving the answers to those interested.

Healing practices are still pretty much the same among the Indians today as they have always been. Only the *brujo* or witch doctor can drive away the evil spirits which are causing sickness, the Indian believes, and as the best *brujos* live in the tropical jungle of the Amazon or in Santo Domingo de los Colorados, that is where the patient goes.

Carrying matches, candles, cigarettes, red roses, eggs, medicinal herbs, and a bottle of liquor, the sick man arrives at the house of the *brujo* who begins his treatment by laying out the everyday objects, now transformed into magic amulets on a straw mat in front of him.

"The *brujo* lights the candles and a small quantity of liquor that has been placed in the cup. All three, the *brujo*, the helper and the patient, then light up cigarettes. The *brujo* blows smoke from his cigarette in big gulps, one after the other, producing a noise like a strong wind and involving the blessings of the [local] *brujos*, the power of the mountains and of the waterfalls. Then he takes a mouthful of liquor and blows it in a fine spray at the candles. The vapor flames as it passes over the lighted candles. The room seems filled with blue fire. . . . Suddenly the *brujo* leans forward, seizes two of the eggs and rubs them over the back and chest of the sick man. The illness is absorbed into the eggs . . . ."

AN OCCULT GUIDE TO SOUTH AMERICA

The description is from *The Awakening Valley* by John Collier and Anibal Buitron, a beautiful picture book published in Ecuador by the Otavalenian, Institute of Anthropology (P.O. Box 1478, Quito) in what its authors describe as "an attempt to combine the method and accuracy of a social scientist with the warmth of an artist-observer."

Now we are ready to leave Ecuador and fly north to the final country of our tour: Colombia.

AN OCCULT GUIDE TO SOUTH AMERICA

AN OCCULT GUIDE TO SOUTH AMERICA

Chapter 12

Columbia

The Land of Eldorado

The fourth largest South American country, with both a Pacific and an Atlantic coastline, Colombia, has always been of interest to archaeologists because of the clues it might offer to migration patterns between the two halves of the American continent.

Bisected from west to east by the equator and dominated by the Andes, Colombia offers a grab bag of climates and temperatures to suit everybody. In the tropical lowlands it is always summer; in the intermediate Andean valleys perpetual springtime; and higher still,, fall. The highest mountains are snow-covered year-round.

When the Spaniards first discovered Colombia in the sixteenth century, they were lured further and further inland, despite constant setbacks and occasional defeats by marauding Indians, in search of gold. The legend of El Dorado originated here and the prospect of finding this celebrated stockpile of riches proved a potent goad to exploration. The tantalizing promises however were never to be satisfied.

Among the early searchers for El Dorado was a German knight, one Amros von Alfinger, who set off from Venezuela with a group of slaves who were linked together with rings around their necks. As each slave died of fatigue, he had only to cut off their heads to detach them from the chain. Wounded in the neck by a well-deserved native arrow, he died of the injury before finding any gold.

The origin of the legend about the treasure was a mountain lake in the main territory of the Chibcha tribes where two contending rulers, the Zipa

201

of Bogota, and the Zaque of Tunja (the North" and the "South') were vying for supremacy of the main Chibcha territory when the Spaniards arrived. It was mainly because of their feuding that the invaders were able to triumph so easily. (A similar situation later prevailed among the Incas.)

Every year the Zaque of Tunja, at the head of a procession of gorgeously costumed men dressed as animals, made an annual pilgrimage to Lake Guatavita. There, his body covered in sticky resin, he rolled himself in powdered gold and, after being rowed on a raft to the center of the lake, plunged in. The ceremony was an offering to the mysterious snake god Bochica, who was believed to dwell in the lake.

Lake Guatavita is reached from the village of Sesquile, about 28 miles north of Bogota. The highway peters out six kilometers beyond the village from which point the ascent to the conical summit of the nameless peak where the lake sits at 10,500 feet—"is set like a cup to catch the rays of the sun" — must be made on horseback or on foot.

In her book, **Land of the Condor** (Aeditora Editores, Bogota, 1963), Edwina Tooley - Martin retells the ancient legend of the wife of an ancient Guatavita chieftain who jumped into the lake with her child, after her lover had been put to death for committing adultery with her, and how the chief sent his magician into the lake to (unsuccessfully) seek her return.

Every year after that, she wrote, the chief declared that his subjects must gather around the lake as he performed a ritual sacrifice to his dead love. Covered in gold dust and emeralds, he was rowed to the center of the lake and submerged in the frigid water shedding his gold and jewels at the same time the Indians threw in their golden gods.

"The story had a strange effect on the people which was not a passing delusion but lasted, and the resort to the lake grew in importance," Sir Clements Markham wrote in **The Conquest of New Granada** (Smith, Elder & Co., London, 1912). "'The offerings continued to increase and came from many of the principal chiefs. Rumors of El Dorado spread all over Europe. The Spaniards sought for him in the basin of the Amazons, the English on the Orinoco, the Germans in the Venezuelan forest; while all the time he was a hero of a local ceremony in a town of the Chibcha mountains."

Henry Lionel Williams suggests in **Fantastic South America** (Horizon Press, 1958) that the whole story might have been a hoax concocted by the Indians, "some of whom have a far greater sense of humor than is generally suspected."

Many attempts were made to drain Lake Guatavita, the first of which was financed by the Spanish Crown in 1560. A fifty-foot trench, still visible today, drained off some of the water revealing a handful of emeralds, but the work was too expensive and had to be abandoned. Other unproductive attempts were made over the years, the last one by an English company earlier in this century.

Other Chibcha lakes were also sacred, among them Cuasca, Ubaque, and Teusaca. One Chibcha religious ceremony consisted of a 50-mile run around an area in which these likes were situated, calling at the places of worship situated on each shore and sacrificing gold and precious stones by throwing them into the water.

To the Chibcha, a god named Chibehacun was the protector of their race and the personification of the forces of nature who could release the elements. Once, out of vengeance, Chibehacun caused the Tibito and Sopo rivers to overflow, flooding the surrounding plain, according to folk legend. But the people prayed to Bochica, who answered their pleas and, striking the rocks with his golden scepter, caused the Tequendama Falls; these drained the water from the land and allowed it to again become fertile.

The majority of historians regard Bochica as the deification of the civilizer who, coming from the cast, was among the Chibchas to teach them art and morality," writes Dario Rozo who notes, in his *Mitologia y Escritura de los Chibchas* (Imprenta Municipal, Bogota, 1938), that there are many similarities between Bochica and the Aztec god Quetzalcoatl.

"The worship of mountains, serpents and lakes was implied in many of the Chibcha rites," says Professor Hartley Alexander. "Slaves were sacrificed and their bodies were buried on hilltops; children, who were the particular offering to the Sun, were sometimes taken to mountaintops to be slain, their bodies being supposed to be consumed by the Sun; and an interesting case of the surrogate for human victim was the practice of sacrificing parrots which had been taught to speak."

In an annual ceremony at Tunja, abode of the chieftain known as the Zaque, twelve men in red, presumed to represent the moons of the year, danced around a blue man who was meant to be the sky god.

The Chibchas regarded the rainbow as being a sign of peace between heaven and earth and at Chibcha festivals it was customary for two men to carry a net, a symbol of death, to remind the living of life's uncertainty.

Chibcha priests enjoyed high prestige and authority, and religious neophytes, selected from among the nobility, trained for twelve years, during which time they lived in special buildings, remained chaste, and ate little but maize mush. "Their inauguration," says Alfred Métraux, "was celebrated with great feats. At this time their ears and nose were pierced and the chief gave them a calabash of coca, symbolic of their office."

Once invested, the priests lived in or near the temple, fasted frequently, and did almost perpetual penance. In times of drought they conducted a primitive rainmaking ceremony from the top of some nearby peak by throwing ashes into the clouds.

The Chibcha were cruel victors and commonly blinded or otherwise tortured their prisoners during victory feasts. Cutting off prisoners' heads and displaying them as trophies was widespread among tribes in the fertile Cauca valley to the southwest, and the Spaniards found rows of heads hanging from homes or temple walls and piles more on sacrificial platforms in the village plazas. Cieza de Leon reported in 1554 seeing on a platform in Cali, "corpses which had been opened and flayed with a flint knife and eaten. The skins were then stuffed with ashes, the faces remodeled with wax; they were set up in a lifelike position."

Julian H. Steward explains that warfare was essential to the class system of most tribes in western Colombia, for cannibalism and the display of human trophies were means of gaining prestige, and captives constituted a slave group. Female warriors supplemented the fighting ranks and even female chieftains were not unknown. There is a report of an eighteen year-old girl killing eight Spaniards with her arrows. East of the Cauca river, prisoners were fattened before being killed and eaten, and the Caramanta ate not only their own prisoners but slaves bought from other tribes to add to their larder. Prisoners were also used as sacrificial victims. The Caramanta believed that cutting out a victim's heart helped to control the weather.

The Patangoro was a tropical forest tribe that practiced cannibalism and to this end honed their war-making skills, taking as many prisoners as possible who were "'killed at once, either being cooked or else cremated then ground and mixed with chicha—an Amazonian trait," wrote Steward. Deities were celestial, including one which sent thunder and lightning. These tribes practised earth burial and believed in an afterworld that was so pleasant that people sometimes committed suicide."

West of the Cauca river lived the Quimbaya who sacrificed a captive daily to their god named Nabsacadas and one of whose customs, when a chief died, was to bury his wives and slaves alive with him. About their neighbors, the Arma, Juan Lopez de Velasco wrote in 1916., "Brother eats sister, husband eats wife and father eats son; they fatten prisoners and have festivities and dances when they consume the living, limb by limb." Reporting this, the Colombia etymologist Gregorio Hernandez de Alba says cannibalism was definitely practiced but that claims like this were probably "extravagant and indiscriminate."

But, he added, these tribes displayed trophies of their sacrificial victims. The Picara, Paucura and Pozo placed trophy skulls on the tops of bamboo posts in front of their houses. The Pozo also kept skulls and bones inside their houses and placed corpses on large poles to face the rising sun...

Despite their tendency to human sacrifices and other bloodthirsty customs—children fattened up like chickens in the temples to be killed at special festivals—the Chibchas were well on the way to becoming a nation rather than a disparate group of nomadic tribes by the time the Spaniards arrived. Wendell Bennett wrote that the Chibchas were generally considered to represent "one of the New World's major centers of higher civilization."

Their capital was situated where Bogota is today, at an elevation of 8,600 feet on an Andean plateau that stretches for 40 miles. The best view of the city is from the 10,000-foot peak of Monserrate to the east. This can be reached by cable and funicular railways. From the convent there you'll look down on a city that is a mix of modern and Colonial architecture. The mixture is reflected in the streets, too, with rich and poor alike demonstrating how much of Colombia's population is composed of the numerous indigenous tribes that existed here before the outsiders arrived bent on conquest and exploitation.

In the city's Gold Museum (Parque Santander, 9:00 A.M. to 5:00 P.M. closed Mondays), you can inspect the product of some of these Indian cultures. It displays what is probably the world's largest collection of pre-Colombian gold work—more than 10,000 pieces.

Much of the gold in the museum is actually tumbaga, a Colombian alloy of gold, copper, and a little silver which made the metal easier to work

AN OCCULT GUIDE TO SOUTH AMERICA

and gave it a distinctive shade. The most splendid objects, reports H. D. Disselhoff in *The Art of Ancient America* (Crown, 1961), came from shaft graves along the Cauca river. These objects include heavy helmets, hollow figures, masks, and jars. There are gold disks and breastplates with eagles in relief, not unlike the gold figures from Costa Rica, as well as solid and hollow nose ornaments with granulation and filigree—so exquisite that one is inclined to forget the barbaric nature of this kind of ornament."

See also the National Museum (Carrera 7, Calles 28 and 29, open Tuesday to Saturday, 10:00 A.M. to 5:00 P.M., closed Mondays and Sunday afternoons) with four rooms devoted to Indian cultures in what was once a prison; the Museum of Popular Arts and Handicrafts in a restored monastery; the former Mint (Calle 11, No. 9-77); the lavishly decorated Colon Theatre; the seventeenth-century building housing the Colonial Museum on Calle 10, where the Palace of San Carlos in which Simon Bolivar once lived is also located. Both are near Plaza Bolivar, the heart of the city, dominated by a statue of Bolivar himself.

On your way to Monserrate visit Quinta de Bolivar (open 10:00 A.M. to 5:00 P.M., closed Mondays), Bolivar's former home, at the foot of Monserrate.

Out of town at Zipaquira, about an hour's drive away, is an amazing salt mine which is so large that you can drive (or walk) through it. It's been worked for hundreds of years—the Chibchas traded salt to the Mayans and the Aztecs in return for gold—and has enough salt left to last another hundred years. It's open daily 8:30 A.M. to 4:30 P.M., including Sundays when masses are held in an enormous cathedral and free concerts demonstrate the striking acoustics.

There are great views from the rooftop bar of the Hilton hotel, which is also one of the best places to stay, albeit expensive. Ditto for the famous Tequendama hotel, a famous local institution. Cheaper are the Cordillera (Carrera 8, 1685), the Continental (Ave. Jimenz, 4-16) and the out-of-the-way Commendador (Carrera 18, No. 384).

Between Bogota and Girardot, to the southwest, are the great falls of Tequendama where the water of the Funza river drops 400 feet into a gorge, believed to have been a creation of the Snake (or Sun) God Bochica, who bore an odd resemblance to both the Aztecs' Quetzalcoatl and the Incas' Viracocha. Both of these were invariably described as being an old white sage who came from somewhere in the east.

206

AN OCCULT GUIDE TO SOUTH AMERICA

One of Colombia's major tourist sites is San Agustin. There are Chibcha-speaking tribes (Paniquita, Paez, Pantagora, Pijao, and Andaki) around San Agustin, in the forest-covered mountains where the rivers Cauca and Magdalena rise.

Here, in the Valley of the Statues near Pitalito, are more than three hundred carved statues, bas-reliefs, and scratchings on rocks that have intrigued archaeologists for at least a century. The culture had disappeared long before the Spaniards arrived, and little is known about its people. It has been suggested that there are parallels between this style and that of Chavin and Recuay in Peru; some have even detected traces of the Tiahuanacu style from the Bolivian plains.

The German ethnologist Horst Nachtigall suggests that some of the monoliths were representations of human figures and only a few were gods, but these latter must certainly include ones with the fangs of beasts similar to those found at Chavin.

When Leo Miller of New York's Museum of Natural History visited the San Agustin region in 1915, most of the interesting statues were not neatly laid out for inspection as they are today but rather hidden in the forest. Here he found what he presumed to be a huge sacrificial altar, "on four richly carved stone columns six feet high," and carvings of the sun and moon in an underground cave.

Theorizing on the sudden end to the San Agustin culture, Miller mused: "Whether the reigning classes who withheld their knowledge from the common people for selfish purposes were annihilated by an uprising of the servile hordes, or by an outside invasion, or whether some great cataclysm of nature extinguished the progress of ages at a stroke, may forever remain a secret."

Some of the carved stone figures serve as grave markers or tomb covers but among the most interesting carvings are those to be found in the beds of streams, which may have been adapted as baths for ritual purposes. In the Lavapatas stream, ducts distribute the water into pools which have snakes, lizards, and tadpoles carved on the sides, as well as a monkey in the shape of a seat.

Statues were found in stone tombs, some as large as ten feet by fifteen feet roofed with a single large slab. The hardpacked mud floors slope down to the center where the statues were found and geometric designs were found on the walls. More temples are covered with large earth mounds. A considerable number of sculptors' tools were found in the tombs.

Jaguar teeth are a feature of a few of the "human" statues and this characteristic has led some investigators to make connections with the Olmec culture of Veracruz whose representations of this motif go back two thousand years or more. The jaguar obviously expresses some deep-seated religious idea, possibly connected to the magical belief among Central and South American tribes that under certain conditions the shaman can turn into a jaguar.

"The jaguar is a helper who lends his exterior form and powers to the shaman," declares Gerardo Reichel-Dolmatoff. "At death, the shaman is said to return to life in the form of a jaguar."

In his book, *San Agustin: A Culture of Colombia* (Praeger, 1972), Reichel-Dolmatoff says that among the Kogi Indians of the Sierra Nevada is a legend about their ancestors, the Jaguar People, who were the fruit of a union between a ferocious jaguar and the Universal Mother. The same myth is shared by other aboriginal tribes, notably the Paez Indians of Tierradentro, who believe that at the beginning of time a young Indian woman was raped by a jaguar, resulting in the birth of Thunder Jaguar who disappeared into a lagoon in the mountain when he grew up.

Thunder is a central theme of all Paez myths, says Reichel-Dolmatoff, and is closely associated with the concepts of fertility, the jaguar spirit and shamanism. In his apprenticeship, a shaman has a hallucinatory experience, induced by one of many plant drugs, and calls upon the thunder to receive him into his supernatural office.

Not far from San Agustin is another ancient site, Tierradentro, characterized by subterranean chambers with walls carved in relief and painted with geometric shapes in black, red, and white. Although the stone carvings seem simpler than at San Agustin and lack variety, archaeologists feel that when more thoroughly investigated there will prove to be links between the two places.

Horst Nachtigall dates the end of Tierradentro to the eighth century A.D., and other historians have agreed that the culture postdated San Agustin, whose statues bear faces that seem more expressive, if less human, in appearance.

AN OCCULT GUIDE TO SOUTH AMERICA

Neither the Andaqui Indians of the San Agustin region nor the Paez who were at Tierradentro at the time of the Conquest, were aware of these archaeological remains in their own territory when queried by the archaeologists who discovered them.

Apart from the ruins at San Agustin, most visitors to Colombia are anxious to visit the coastal resorts. The Pacific coast of Colombia, dominated by a range of mountains called the Serannia de Baudo covered in tropical rain forest, is one of the wettest areas on the continent, producing a general environment very similar to that of the Amazon. The Choco Indians in the north and the Colorado, Cayapa, and Barbacoa Indians in the south have a lifestyle similar to that of the Amazon tribes.

Santa Marta (pop. 70,000) on the Caribbean coast is earning a reputation for being the sort of unspoiled resort that so many semiprimitive Caribbean places were before the high rises and the high prices. It's the country's most popular seaside spot.

Founded in 1525 by one of the Conquistadores, Santa Marta claims to be the oldest city on South American soil and it was here that Simon Bolivar, South America's famous liberator, came to spend his last days in 1830. The site, a hacienda called San Pedro Alejandrino just outside the city, is marked with a plaque.

The now-extinct Tairona culture was centered around Santa Marta and in the precipitous mountains (with peaks of up to 20,000 feet) behind, There are more than forty different sites containing remains of houses, burial mounds, and terraced platforms. Many ceramic and stone artifacts were found in the tombs.

"The stone objects are both utilitarian and ceremonial," Dr. Wendell Bennett reports. "The ceremonial objects are well-made polished axes, batons with geometric incised designs, broadwinged pendants, animal amulets, small carved tables with four legs and beads of many kinds."

Santa Marta offers plenty of choice between deep water bays, jungle, the Foothills of the Sierra Nevada with its lush banana plantations, El Rodadero beach, fishing villages, coastal walks, and the attractive La Guajira Peninsula with its virgin beaches, four hours away to the northeast on the new Trans-Caribbean Highway.

If you want to stay at the beach, choose one of the places at El Rodadero just outside town: the thirty- four-room La Sierra or Motel El Rodadero are both about $10 for a double. The Santamar (with swimming pool) and Tarnaca Inn (with casino) are classier and cost about $15 for a double.

The four-lane Trans-Caribbean Highway will take you to Barranquilla on the Magdalena River (about an hour and a half drive) or to Cartagena (about three hours) going west. Rental cars cost about $7 a day plus mileage.

Caribe Tours or Sportour arrange local excursions which include fishing trips, inspection of coffee plantations, or even a search for the pygmy-like Kogui tribe who live up in the mountains.

Planes land at Santa Marta airport from Barranquilla, Bogota, and most other Colombian cities, and the city is also connected to Bogota by a daily train (twenty-two hours).

The ancient city of Cartagena was once one of Spain's major ports in the New World, for it was the place from which the riches of the continent were funneled back to Europe. Founded in 1533, it was made into a fortress later in that century by order of the Spanish king Felipe II. But the fortifications were insecure and after Sir Francis Drake sailed in and sacked the city in 1586, a more elaborate system of defenses was worked out. By 1798 when this was completed, Spain had spent a total of 59 million ounces of gold on the fortifications whose only use today is as a tourist attraction.

In the city's Palace of the Inquisition, now a museum, is the receipt for 10 million pesos that Drake gave the city for agreeing not to burn it down when he had captured it.

Take a boat ride to Boca Chica from the dock opposite the Clock Tower; visit San Fernando fortress and the nearby fishing village of La Boquilla; inspect Dr. Vidal's preColombian art collection (Calle 41, No. 1-56) and more of the same at the Galeria Cano (Edificio Antillas); take an afternoon harbor trip (at the dock beside the Hotel del Caribe) and a $6 parachute ride (pulled by boat) around the bay (call 44400 for information).

Graturismo (tel: 42727) organizes half-day city tours; Caribe Tours (tel: 41221) arranges boat trips to private beaches. Outside the Hotel del Caribe you can book a ride in a horse-drawn carriage around the old town. The best hotel is Las Velas, with swimming pool, beside Boca Grande beach (about $20 and up for a double) but nearby, also at Boca Grande, is the hotel

AN OCCULT GUIDE TO SOUTH AMERICA

Flamingo for about half the price.

The Spanish adventurer Rodrigo de Bastidas touched down on Colombia's Cartagena coast for the first time in 1501 and the conquerors who followed kept up an unceasing search for gold. Sometimes they killed the Indians for their jewelry (some tribes, for example, covered their genitals with fringes of fine gold tubes), more often they robbed the graves. But the Indians' resistance and the rough terrain delayed the conquerors for a while and it wasn't until 1536 that Spanish soldiers, advancing both south from the coast and northwards from Peru, had pacified the area. The decimation of the Indians came swiftly after that and by the end of the century many of the tribes had been wiped out.

The tiny horseshoe-shaped island of San Andrés, only 150 miles off the coast of Nicaragua, actually belongs to Colombia, 500 miles to the southeast. It's a free port with stable year-round temperatures and is popular with vacationers who seek a change from slick, modern resorts. Even the Colombian tourist office brochure undersells it, commenting that "Tap water is undrinkable; hot water is simply not available; guests must shower with brackish water, and there are frequent breakdowns or rationing to save precious electricity." How can you find fault with honesty like that?

To some visitors, the brochure adds, "these hardships seem to be part of the fun and they feel that San Andrés, still unspoiled and underdeveloped is just the place to get away from it all at prices substantially lower than those in the rest of the Caribbean."

Originally settled by British pilgrims, the island changed to Spanish rule in 1681, but served as a base for pirates of many nationalities. The Welsh-born privateer Henry Morgan hid a treasure of gold bullion here back in the sixteenth century, it's said. It has never been found and there have been plenty of searchers.

Go fishing, cruising, treasure-hunting, shopping, drive around the island or just lie on the beach. The forty-two room hotel Isleno (about $18 for a double) is good, but there are lots of other choices including the cheap hotel Morgan (about $8 for a double).

Avianca has daily jet service to San Andrés from many Colombia cities; Aero Condor, SAM, and TAO also have flights.

AN OCCULT GUIDE TO SOUTH AMERICA

AN OCCULT GUIDE TO SOUTH AMERICA

Bibliography

Authorities cited in this book include numerous books by Colonial-era authors in modern translation. Among these are:

Relation of the Discovery and Conquest of the Kingdoms of Peru by Pedro Pizarro (1571), trans. by Philip Means (Cortez Society, New York, 1921).

The Travels of Pedro Cieza de Leon (1553), trans. by Harriet de Onis, edited by Victor Wolfgang von Hagen (University of Oklahoma Press, 1959).

Primera Parte de los Comentarios Reales by Garcilaso de la Vega (1609), trans. by Harold V. Livermore (University of Texas Press, 1966.

Among the works translated by Sir Clements Markham and published by the Hayklut Society, London, during the nineteenth century were:

An Account of the Fables & Rites of the Incas, written by Cristobal de Molina between 1570 and 1584; *Report by Polo do Ondeganio* written in the 1550s; *An Account of the Antiquities of Peru* by Juan de Santa Cruz Oachacuti, written circa 1620; and *A Narrative by Francoco de Avila*, written in 1608.

There are numerous quotations from:

The Handbook of South American Indians, Julian H. Steward, ed., prepared by the Smithsonian Museum (six volumes and index), published by Cooper Square Publishers, 59 Fourth Avenue, New York City.

Authors quoted include: Junius B. Bird (American Museum of Natural History, New York); John M. Cooper (Professor of Anthropology, Catholic University of America, Washington, D.C.); Alfred Métraux (Smithsonian Institute); Curt Nimuendaju (Museu Paraense Emilio Goeldi. Belem, Brazil); Wendell C. Bennett (Professior of Anthropology, Yale University); Gregorio Hernandez de Alba (Director del Museo Arqueologico, Bogota, Colombia); Weston LaBarre (Rutgers University, New Brunswick, N.J.); Rafael Larco Hoyle

AN OCCULT GUIDE TO SOUTH AMERICA

(Director del Museo de Arqueologia "Rafael Larco Herrera", Trujillo, Peru); Samuel K. Lothrop (Peabody Museum, Harvard University); John Howland Rowe (Peabody Museum); Harry Tschopik, Jr., (Peabody Museum); Luis E Valcarcel (Director del Museo Nacional, Lima, Peru); Claude Levi-Strauss (New School for Social Research, New York); Erwin H. Ackerknecht (American Museum of Natural History, New York); Lila M. O'Neale (Dept. of Anthropology, University of California, Berkeley). Charles Wagley (Department of Anthropology, Columbia University, New York).

Sources by individual country include:

BRAZIL

Candomblé da Bahia by Edison Carneiro (Edicoes de Ouro, Salvador).

Candomblé no Brasil by Jose Ribeiro (Editora Espiritualista, Rio, 1972).

Orizas da Bahia by E. G. de Magalhaes (Salvador, 1974).

Curaciones Fspirituales en el Brasil.

Brazil, Land of Contrast by Roger Rastide.

Negroes in Brazil by Donald Pierson (Southern Illinois Univ. Press, 1942).

Los Negros Brujos by Fernando Ortiz Madrid, 1904).

O Animismo Fetichista dos Negroes Bahianos by Nina Rodriques.

Contemporary Review. Dec. 1974, article by Frances Rust on "The Spirit Possession Cults."

The Moon & Two Mountains by Pedro McGregor (Souvenir Press, London, 1966).

The Book of Spirits by Allan Kardec (Lake, Sao Paulo, 1876).
The Negro in Brazil by Arthur Ramos, trans. by Richard Pattee (Asso-

214

ciated Publishers, Washington, 1939).

The Masters & the Slaves by Gilberto Freyre, trans. by Samuel Putnam (Alfred A. Knopf, New York, 1946).

Guia de Salvador, ed. by Victor Civita (Quatro Rodas, Sao Paulo).

Indians of Brazil in the 20th Century (Inst. for Cross Cultural Research, Washington, 1967).

Naturalist on the River Amazons by Henry Walter Bates (John Murray, London, 1876, reprinted by Dover Books, N.Y.).

Mundurucu Religion by Robert Murphy (Univ. of California, 1958.

Among Wild Tribes of the Amazon by Chas. Domville-Fife (J. P. Lippincott Co., 1925).

Exploration of the Valley of the Amazon by William Herndon (Washington, 1853).

Brazil, The Amazons and the Coast by Herbert J. Smith (Sampson Low, London,1879).

An Introduction to Brazil by Chas. Wagley (Columbia University Press, 1963).

Brazil by T. Lynn Smith (Louisiana Univ. Press, 1972).

The Northwest Amazons by Thomas Whiffen (Duffied & Co., N.Y., 1915).

The Green Continent, article by José Vasconcelos in anthropology (Alfred Knopf, N.Y., 1944).

Studies in the Religion of the South American Indians East of the Andes by Rafael Karsten (Finska Vetenshaps Societen Comm., 1964).
Pre-Columbian American Religions by Walter Krucheberg

AN OCCULT GUIDE TO SOUTH AMERICA

(Weldenfeld, 1968).

Panorama de Alimentacao Indigena by Nunes Pereira (Livreria, Sao Jose, 1974).

Larousse's Encyclopedia of Mythology.

International Encyclopedia of the Social Sciences (MacMillan, 1968).

The Amazon by Tom Sterling (Time-Life Books).

Visiting the Amazon by Carlos Binda (EVC, Manaus).

ARGENTINA

Superstitions of the Rio de la Plato by Daniel Granada (Kraft, Buenos Aires, 1947).

La Difunta Correa by Augustin Pardella (Editorial Plus Ultra, 1975).

Argentina: Past and Present by W. H. Kocbel (Kegan Paul, London, 1910).

South America by Clarence F. Jones (Henry Holt, N.Y., 1930).

Mythology of All Races by H. B. Alexander (MacMillan Co., 1948).

Latin America by William R. Shepard (Henry Holt, N.Y., 1914).

Esqueme del Folklore by Augusto Cortazar (Editorial Columbia, B.A., 1965).

CHILE

Through the Heart of Patagonia by Hesketh Prichard (D. Appleton Co., N.Y., 1902).

Encyclopedia of Philosophy & Religion.

AN OCCULT GUIDE TO SOUTH AMERICA

Magia, Hechiceria y Medicina Popular Boliviana by Enriques Poblete (Fdiciones Isla, 1971).

Isla de Pascua by Jorge D'Amato (Fdiciones Manutara, Buenos Aires, 1970).

Easter Island: Island of Enigmas by)ohn Dos Passos (Doubleday, 1971).

Aku Aku by lThor Heyerdahl (Rand McNally, 1958)

Island at the Centre of the World by Sebastian Englert (Chas. Scribners' Sons, New York, 1970).

Archaeology of Easter Island by Thor Heyerdahl and Edwin Ferdon.

Native Peoples of South America by Julian H. Steward and Louis C. Faron (McGraw Hill, 1959).

BOLIVIA

American Hero Myths by Daniel G. Brinton (H. C. Watts Co., Philadelphia, 1882).

Comentarios Reales de los Incas by Garselaso de la Vega.

Relacion de las Fabulas y Rilos de los Incas by Cristobal de Molina, 1553).

Brujerias, Tradicionas y Leyendas by Antonio P. Candia (Difusion Ltda. La Paz, 1969).

Historia del Nuevo Mondo, by Father Bernabé Cobo (Madrid. 1653).

South American Mythology by Harold Osborn (Paul Hamlyn, London, 1968).

Tiahuanacu by Arthur Posnansky (republished by J. J. Augustin, N.Y.,

1945).

Tiahuanaco by Simone Waisbard (Editorial Diana, Mexico, 1971).

Mirador Indio by Luis E. Valcarel. (Lima, 1935).

Peru Before the Incas by Edward P. Lanning (Prentice Hall, 1967).

The Secret of the Andes by Brother Phillip (Nevile Spearman, London, 1961).

Bolivia, A Profile by William Carter (Praeger, 1971).

In the Wilds of South America by Leo E. Miller (Charles Scribner's Sons, New York, 1918).

ECUADOR

The Bolivar Countries by William Russell (Coward McCann, 1949).

The Jivaro. People of the Sacred Waterfalls by Michael Harner (Doubleday, 1972).

Head-hunters of the Amazon by Fritz Up de Graff (Doubleday, 1923).

Indians of South America by Paul Rondin (reprinted, Creenwood Press, 1969).

OOLUMBIA

San Agustin: A Culture of Columbia by Gerardo Reichel-Dolmatoff (Praeger, 1972).

The South American Handbook edited by John Brooks (Trade & Travel Pub'ns, Bath, England, 1974).

Die Amerikanichen Megalith-kulturen by Horst Nachtigall (Berlin

1958.

The Pre-Columbian Mind by F. Guerra (Academic Press, 1972).

The Impossible Adventure by Alain Gheerbrandt (Victor Gollancz, 1953).

The Art of Ancient America by H. D. Disselhoff and S. Linne (Crown, 1961.

Land of the Condor by Edwina Tooley -Martin (Aedita Editores Ltda, Bogota, 1963)

AN OCCULT GUIDE TO SOUTH AMERICA

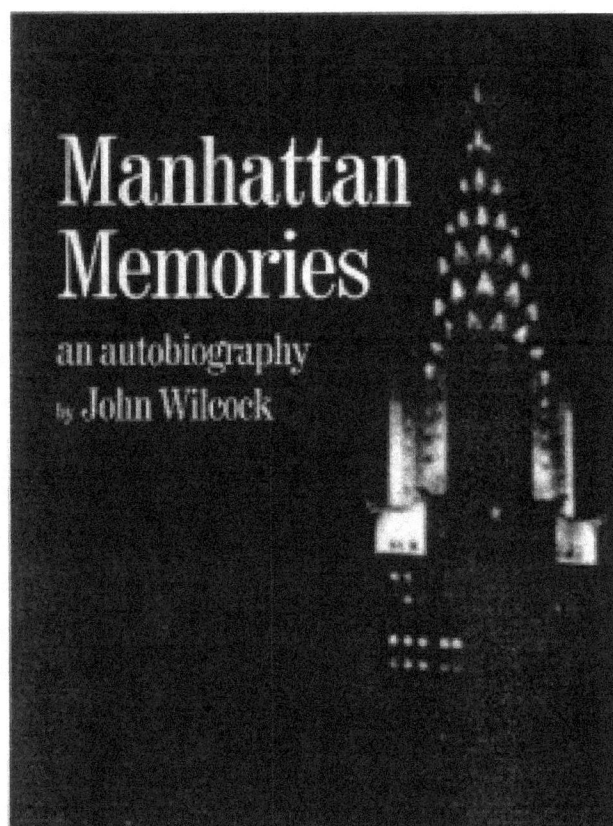

John Wilcock
Manhattan Memories: An Autobiography

"**A GOOD WAY** to describe John Wilcock is to say that he is a talented bohemian counter-culture journalist who once played a major role in the emergence of America's underground press. Born 1927 in Sheffield, England, he left school aged 16 to work on various newspapers in England, and on Toronto periodicals before moving to New York City. There in 1955 he became one of the five founders of the Village Voice in which he and co-founder Norman Mailer wrote weekly columns. Wilcock called his column "The Village Square", an intended pun. He and young Mailer were not quite friends, although Wilcock was at times annoyed, but always amused, by Mailer's monstrous ego."

-*From the preface of Manhattan Memories, by Martin Gardner*

Manhattan Memories is available from lulu.com and is also available for download on Kindle.

There is also a DVD available in color, accompanied by samples of the hundreds of JW's travel shows. To order the DVD, go to www.ojaiorange.com/manhattanmemories/order_dvd.php

AN OCCULT GUIDE TO SOUTH AMERICA

Timothy Green Beckley brings back the lost revelations of Brother Philip's mysteries and studies of the South American Andes. Expanded edition includes material from Timothy Beckley, Brent Raynes, Harold T. Wilkins, Joshua Shapiro, John J. Robinson, and Charles A. Silva.

When most of us think of the Peruvian Andes we think of Indiana Jones, Shirley McClain, Machu Picchu and the Nazca Lines. We usually don't associate this lofty land with images of the lost continents of Atlantis and MU, or giants carrying a huge sun disc relic in a covered canapé across the vast mountain ranges.

Yet all these things are part and parcel of a wondrous land that too many of us seems so far removed from our everyday lives. But yet, there is all this and a lot more than meets the inner eye, as we shall see as we "invade" the realm of South American magic. Brother Philips - known to American followers as George Hunt Williamson -- went in search of a mystical kingdom few outsiders know about, only to return eventually to a distant, uncivilized, world full of greed, crime and corruption. His spiritual exploits and the knowledge he gained has had a lasting impact since his story was told.

Now with the release of this expanded edition filled with adventures such as those of Brent Raynes and Harold T. Wilkins, we have added yet more evidence that Peru and the Andes Mountains play home to many great mysteries from UFOs to the existence of underground realms and cosmic voyages. It is a reality that is impossible to escape - nor should we want to!

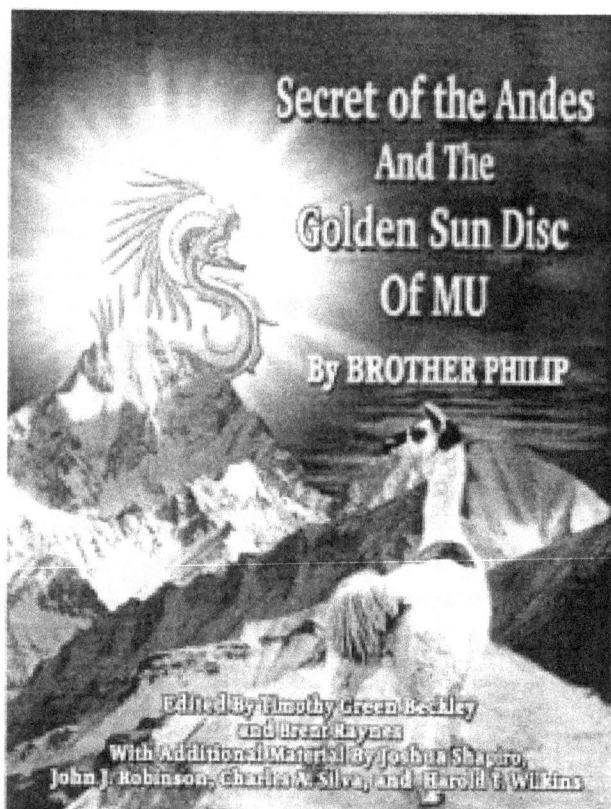

WAS HOUDINI'S FANATICAL DEBUNKING OF PSYCHICS AND MEDIUMS A SUBTERFUGE TO CONCEAL HIS OWN REMARKABLE PARANORMAL ABILITIES?

At his burial some curious and suggestive words were used by the presiding rabbi:

"HOUDINI POSSESSED A WONDROUS POWER THAT HE NEVER UNDERSTOOD AND WHICH HE NEVER REVEALED TO ANYONE IN LIFE!"

The creator of Sherlock Holmes, Sir Arthur Conan Doyle, and Harry Houdini were strange bedfellows. Doyle was a contemporary of the world's greatest magician and escape artist, who continually battled his friend over the legitimacy of life after death and the reality of spiritualism. Doyle was a "true believer," while Houdini made it his "mission" to denounce just about all things preternatural.

Doyle was convinced – from what he personally witnessed and what others confided in him – that Houdini could read minds, dematerialize, possessed supernatural strength, and was guided by angelic forces which shielded him from harm even during the most dangerous of escape performances which likely would have caused death to others.

Doyle stated that Houdini had once remarked, "There are some of my feats which my own wife does not know the secret of." And a famous Chinese conjurer who had seen Houdini perform added, "This is not a trick, it is a gift." Sadly, many of Houdini's feats died with him, even though they would have been an invaluable asset. "What can cover all these facts," states Doyle, "save that there was some element in his power which was peculiar to himself, that could only point to a psychic element – in a word, that he was a medium."

Here is both sides of the story – in the actual words of the famed Sherlock Holmes originator and Houdini himself, who went out of his way to create the impression that fakes and phonies were afoot everywhere in the "shady world" of table tapping, levitating trumpets, spirit photography, slate writing, as well as the materialization of ectoplasmic forms in the darkening shadows of the séance room.

Revealing the Bizarre Powers of Harry Houdini;
$29.95 +$6.00 Shipping & Handling

Global Communications, Box 753, New Brunswick, NJ 08903
Credit Card Orders 732 602-3407   MRUFO8@hotmail.com

AN OCCULT GUIDE TO SOUTH AMERICA

224

AN OCCULT GUIDE TO SOUTH AMERICA

AN OCCULT GUIDE TO SOUTH AMERICA

www.ingramcontent.com/pod-product-compliance
Lightning Source LLC
Chambersburg PA
CBHW081148090426

42736CB00017B/3225